Conceptual Modelling

Series editors: Tony Hoare and Richard Bird

Series listing continued at back of b

Conceptual Modelling

Magnus Boman
Janis A. Bubenko, Jr
Paul Johannesson
Benkt Wangler

University of Stockholm

Prentice Hall

London   New York   Toronto   Sydney   Tokyo   Singapore
Madrid   Mexico City   Munich   Paris

ADG_8799

First published 1997 by
Prentice Hall Europe
Campus 400, Maylands Avenue
Hemel Hempstead
Hertfordshire, HP2 7EZ
A division of
Simon & Schuster International Group

© Prentice Hall 1997

Printed and bound in Great Britain by Biddles Ltd,
Guildford and King's Lynn

Library of Congress Cataloging-in-Publication Data

Conceptual modelling/Magnus Boman.
      p.   cm. – (Prentice Hall series in computer
science)
   ISBN 0-13-514879-0
   1. System design. 2. Mathematical models.
3. Computer simulation. I. Boman, Magnus.
II. Series.
QA76.9.S88C664   1997
658.4'0352–dc21   96-39963
                             CIP

British Library Cataloguing in Publication Data

A catalogue record for this book is available from
the British Library

ISBN 0-13-514879-0

---

1 2 3 4 5   01 00 99 98 97

Contents

Preface

Background

Information systems belong to the most complex artefacts built in today's society. Developing and maintaining an information system raises a large number of difficult problems, ranging from the purely technical to organisational and social ones. Many of these problems are ill-structured, meaning that there are no algorithms or mechanical methods for solving them, or that they cannot even be precisely formulated. The problems are ill-structured mainly because the development of an information system involves many kinds of stakeholders with different and conflicting needs and views. These differences and conflicts must be sorted out and negotiated. This is a difficult task as information systems are notoriously hard to illustrate and describe in terms which are easily understandable to non-experts. Communication problems are rather the rule than the exception. There is no panacea for these problems, but there are aids by which the problems can be described more clearly, in a more structured way, and sometimes even be formally represented so that formal techniques can be applied. These aids consist of solid conceptual frameworks and clear notations to be used when describing systems at the conceptualisation and problem formulation level. It is our experience that adequate concepts and good notations significantly improve the dialogue and co-operation between stakeholders in the development of information systems. This book is about a framework, called *conceptual modelling,* for representing enterprises and systems at the conceptual level.

Describing a system by means of conceptual modelling means viewing the world as consisting of objects. These objects belong to different classes, have distinct properties, and are associated with each other in various ways. They are born at certain points in time; during their lifetime they are affected by events; they acquire properties and lose them; they connect and disconnect in relationships with other objects; and eventually they die. This way of viewing the world provides a powerful tool for representing systems in a structured and more easily understandable way. Conceptual modelling has therefore been put to use in many different contexts. It has been used for enterprise engineering, e.g. for clarifying and developing the mission and goals of an enterprise. It has been used for building requirements specifications for information systems. It has been used for reverse modelling of existing systems as a step in legacy systems migration. And there are many other applications of conceptual modelling, ranging from product data models to natural language systems.

We believe that conceptual modelling will play an essential role in the development of enterprises and information systems of the future. Conceptual modelling will therefore be an important subject for students as well as practitioners in the areas of computer science, information systems, or business administration. In this book we give an introduction to the subject by combining a solid theoretical foundation with practical methodological principles.

Purpose of this Book

The main purposes of this book are:

- To provide a thorough and systematic treatment of conceptual modelling.
- To base this treatment on a solid foundation in logic and linguistics.
- To show the role of conceptual modelling in the larger contexts of requirements and enterprise engineering.
- To provide methodological principles for carrying out conceptual modelling in practice.
- To show how logic programming can be used for creating executable conceptual models.
- To serve as the basis of a large collection of study material that includes case studies, graphical editors, and computerised quizzes, all available through the World Wide Web.

Audience

This book is useful for two different audiences:

1. Students in computer science and information systems, who need a rigorous treatment of conceptual modelling.
2. Practitioners (business analysts, systems analysts, consultants, programmers) who need a better understanding of the use of conceptual modelling in information systems design and enterprise engineering.

The book is self-contained, but the reader will benefit from some background in information systems design. Furthermore, to appreciate fully Chapters 4, 5, and 9, a basic knowledge of logic is required.

Outline of the Contents

Chapter 1 discusses the nature of problems that are encountered in the design of information systems and argues that they are typically ill-defined. Such ill-defined problems can often be effectively addressed by means of conceptual modelling, and the chapter outlines the use of conceptual models in this context.

Chapter 2 provides a background to conceptual modelling by introducing a number of basic notions from linguistics, logic, and the philosophy of language. In particular, the division of language into syntactics, semantics, and pragmatics is explained in detail.

The chapter also includes an introduction to the issues of classification, abstraction, and definition.

Chapter 3 introduces the basic building blocks in conceptual modelling, including objects, attributes, inheritance, events, and rules. The chapter also discusses the architecture of information systems by viewing an information system as consisting of a conceptual schema, an information base, and an information processor.

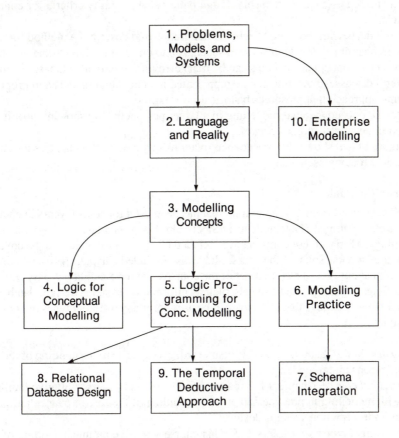

Precedence relationships among the chapters

Chapter 4 investigates the logical foundations of conceptual modelling. In particular, the foundations of logic programming are presented, and special attention is given to the limitations of both formal and non-formal approaches. Together with Chapter 2 and Appendices 4 and 5, the chapter gives a concise overview of the promises and the problems of the formal aspects of conceptual modelling.

Chapter 5 explains how logic programming can be used for creating executable conceptual models, and it shows how modelling constructs can be represented in the logic programming language Prolog.

While Chapters 2–5 describe the fundamental, theoretical ideas of conceptual modelling, Chapter 6 takes a more practical stance by advising how a conceptual model of good quality is to be constructed. The chapter discusses techniques for declarative rule elicitation and representation, reusable design patterns, and quality criteria for conceptual models.

Chapter 7 deals with the topic of schema integration and describes a method for integrating a number of separately developed schemas into one single global schema. Chapter 8 shows how conceptual schemas can be translated into relational database schemas.

Chapter 9 discusses how time can be represented in conceptual models and proposes a modelling approach that preserves historical information.

Chapter 10 puts conceptual modelling in a larger perspective by showing how it can be utilised in enterprise engineering.

The figure above shows the precedence relationships among the chapters and indicates possible reading sequences.

How to Use the Book

This book originated from a compendium that has been used for several years in courses given to a total of almost 3,000 students at Stockholm University and the Royal Institute of Technology. Most of these courses have included Chapters 2–5, which can be covered in two to three weeks. Some of the courses have also included Chapters 6–10, which can be covered in about two weeks. In most of the courses, we have taught not only conceptual modelling, but also related subjects such as information systems design, databases, and even logic. We believe that the book can be used for many different types of courses. For example:

- *A crash course.* Chapters 1–3. This course will give a basic understanding of the notions in conceptual modelling.
- *A practical course.* Chapters 1–3, parts of 6, and 10. This course will give familiarity with modelling in practice and an understanding of the role of conceptual modelling in information systems design.
- *A theoretical course.* Chapters 1–5. This course will give an understanding of the theoretical underpinnings of conceptual modelling.
- *A full course.* Chapters 1–6, 10, and parts of Chapters 7–9 as time permits. This course will give practical modelling experience as well as a theoretical understanding.

We realise that conceptual modelling cannot be learnt only by studying a book – much practical exercise is also needed. Over the years, we have therefore developed a large collection of complementary study material which is now available, free of charge, at our Web site, http://www.dsv.su.se/~mab/CM.html. This material includes large case studies, computerised quizzes, software for a graphical editor, a meta interpreter in Prolog, and much more. The material will evolve continually, and we want to invite you as a reader to add your comments and contributions to our Web site. Just visit the site and you will find instructions on how to contribute.

Acknowledgements

The authors would like to thank Guy Davies for his extensive proof-reading with respect to language, Kristiina Kalliomaa for the artwork, and Petia Wohed for her help with preparing the camera-ready copy. Further thanks to Love Ekenberg for extensive comments and for sharing his experiences of using earlier versions of this book as a course textbook, and to Torkel Franzén for many suggestions and clarifications. Thanks also to the students and staff at the various DSV courses on conceptual modelling and information systems. The authors are also grateful to Jackie Harbor, acquisitions editor at Prentice Hall, for many editorial suggestions.

Regarding the responsibilities of the authors for the various chapters,
PJ has contributed to Chapters 1, 2, 3, 5, 6, 7, 8, and the appendices.
MB has contributed to Chapters 2, 4, and the appendices.
JB has contributed to Chapters 1, 9, and 10.
BW has contributed to Chapter 6.
Additionally, every author has made minor contributions to virtually every chapter.

CHAPTER 1

Problems, Models, and Systems

This book is about a technique, called conceptual modelling, for representing systems. The technique is based on a view that certain relevant aspects of systems can be represented by objects, their attributes, and their relationships, which are from time to time changing owing to influences from events. We believe that a good representation technique offers considerable help in solving different kinds of problems. In this chapter we first examine the notion of problem and discuss what is meant by solving a problem. Next we examine typical kinds of issues and problems in developing information systems for enterprises. A simple case is used to illustrate our main notions. The chapter is concluded by discussing the applicability of conceptual modelling.

1.1 Problems and Solutions

Developing an information system is to a large extent a problem-solving process. A typical, simplified view of problem-solving is depicted in Figure 1.1. It is assumed that the existing problem is first formulated precisely, and then a design process is applied to the formulated problem, leading to some sort of solution.

Figure 1.1 is in a crude way right, but it conceals that there are many different kinds of problems, and, consequently, many different ways in which solutions can be sought. The simplest way of categorising problems is to partition them into *well-structured problems,* which can be formally defined, and ill-structured, *wicked problems*, where a formal representation does not exist.

Examples of well-structured problems are: "Solve this set of linear equations", "Find the shortest driving path between these two addresses in this city", or "Calculate the losses in transferring energy in this network from point X to point Y". The first problem is a purely mathematical problem. There is no question about it approximating some reality or not. The correctness of the solution of the second problem depends on how good our model is of the streets of the city, and whether the model contains information about one-way streets and other constraints. The correctness of the solution of the third problem depends on how good our model is in representing the electrical network, and how correct our method is for calculating losses.

1

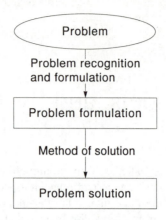

Figure 1.1 *A simple view of problem solving*

The latter two problems are typical engineering problems. In engineering disciplines, well-proven models and calculation methods for different kinds of problems have been developed and practically tested for many decades. These models and methods are typically mathematical. Some look for optimal solutions, where a well-defined function, to be optimised, is given in advance. The correctness of a solution is sometimes dependent on how much computing power one is willing to apply to a problem. In some cases a solution correct to three decimal places is acceptable, while in other cases this may not be sufficient. In engineering disciplines it is often simpler to recognise typical problems, where models and methods (and nowadays also special software tools) are available.

Wicked problems lack all these nice features. In the case of a wicked problem people often cannot even agree upon what the problem is really about. This is generally due to the fact that wicked problems often cannot be formulated at any desirable level of accuracy. Consequently, it is practically impossible to prove that the problem formulation indeed corresponds to the perceived problem in reality. Furthermore, it is almost impossible to prove that an alleged solution of a wicked problem is indeed a solution, albeit the optimal solution.

It may be tempting to conclude that wicked problems are so fuzzy that they cannot be addressed by means of models and methods from science and engineering. Such a conclusion would be sad indeed, as an overwhelming number of the problems we face in technology, business administration, and management, and in most areas of our society, are wicked. However, we do believe that scientific and engineering methods can be used to address wicked problems; even if it is not possible to construct mechanical methods of solving such problems, we can tackle them in such a way that they may be partially tamed. This means that wicked problems can often be described more clearly, in a more structured way, and that parts of them can even be formally represented so that formal techniques can be applied.

The problem-solving picture of Figure 1.1 should be expanded to reflect these issues; this is done in Figure 1.2. In this figure, validation means to make sure that the problem formulation corresponds to the real problem. Verification means to ensure that an alleged solution indeed solves the formulated problem.

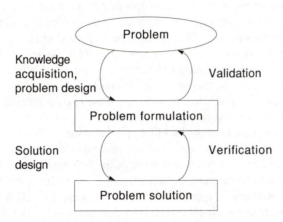

Figure 1.2 *A problem solution requires validation as well as verification*

We will now discuss some examples of wicked problems. A first example might be: "To design a beautiful, functional building for the Ministry of Informatics". Clearly, in discussing the requirements for such a building, different views, needs, and requirements will pop up. Many parties – we may call them *stakeholders* – are involved in this process. In this case the stakeholders may include the Government, the Parliament, the minister of informatics, the staff of the ministry, the labour unions, etc. Most certainly there will be different views, perhaps even conflicts, between different departments, and between different employees about space, form, and functionality of rooms, illumination, choice of colours, and design of access ways, to name a few. Some of these conflicts may turn out to depend on pure misunderstandings of what certain drawings or descriptions mean, or what certain directives mean. Several constraints – economic, environmental, cultural and social – will come from outside the ministry. For instance, the maximum cost of the building is dictated by the Parliament. Environmental laws may add the requirement to preserve the park and lake nearby. Social laws may add requirements about the minimum size of office rooms, the existence of a window in each office, the existence of a rest-room for every 20 persons, etc.

What we have shown by this example is that the formulation of the problem is far from easy. It is in the first place a complex social process. Abstractly speaking, the product to be developed will be part of a social infrastructure to act as a "climate modifier, a behaviour modifier, a cultural modifier, and a resource modifier" [Hillier72], and consequently, include humans as essential components. In the formulation of wicked problems, many parties and views are most often involved. There is no single, totally accepted formulation of the problem. It is also difficult to show, or prove, that the designed building indeed corresponds to the requirements stated. In fact, it is not even certain that all relevant requirements have been observed and documented. And how do we balance requirements against the maximum available cost or time to complete the building?

It is obvious that an architect who has only learnt how to draw is not a suitable person to manage this wicked situation. The person who will be able to manage the situation must possess a number of other skills and knowledge of how to deal with complex social situations. On the other hand, if during the requirements analysis phase the architect is also able to observe, represent, and articulate different needs, ideas, and problem designs in an illustrative way, and is able to communicate these to colleagues as well as to stakeholders, then there is a good possibility of success.

Unfortunately, the success of the building process, if any, will most often not be possible to measure in quantitative terms. One reason for this is that measurable criteria for a successful project are most often not stated at the beginning. Consequently, failures will also not be possible to measure. The architect will collect his or her fee and then continue with other jobs, if any. The employees of the new ministry will move in. Some will be happy, some will complain about their rooms, non-functioning elevators, the beautiful ceramic tiles falling down from the external walls, or the increased distance they now have to travel. Some employees will quit. Most will stay. The perimeter of the building will be strung with nets so the beautiful falling tiles will not hurt the occupants. After a while the debate will cease, and the current employees will, until the ministry is reorganised (another wicked problem), find the situation (probably) acceptable.

Other examples of wicked problems are "To reduce crime in society", "To develop the Öresund bridge" (connecting Sweden and Denmark), or "To re-engineer the business processes of company X". Note that the bridge problem is not even defined here as a problem. It is not untypical that problems often have their roots in other problems. So, the bridge problem may have other, more basic problems as roots, such as "To improve transport and communication between Sweden and the rest of the European Union", and/ or "To stimulate business and industry, especially in the southern region of Sweden". There may be other causes for the final decision to build the bridge, but they will perhaps never become publicly known. Even this is typical for wicked problems, where politics, economics, technology, and other cultural and social forces are involved.

What has all this to do with conceptual modelling and information systems? We believe there are many similarities between developing an information system and the kind of wicked problems we have described above. Like a bridge, a house, or a superhighway, an information system is to be considered as an infrastructure component in an organisation or in society. In the process of developing an information system we experience most of the kinds of wicked problems we have discussed above. Many kinds of stakeholders exist. Requirements are unclear and conflicting. Different needs and views exist. In addition, information systems are notoriously difficult to illustrate and describe in terms which are easily understandable to non-specialists. Communication problems are more the rule than the exception.

However, in the same way as good illustration skills in architecture facilitate communication between the architect and the stakeholders, it has been found that adequate concepts and a clear notation are essential in information systems development. A good notation, when describing information systems at the conceptualisation and problem formulation level, can significantly improve the dialogue and co-operation between stakeholders and, in this case, systems analysts and designers. Conceptual modelling is such a technique. This has been experienced in a number of system development projects in Sweden. On the other hand, it must be realised that conceptual modelling, as any other technique, needs to be carefully introduced to its users. But first we will turn our attention to the concept of an information system.

1.2 Information Systems and Enterprises

Computer-based systems can be found in all kinds of places from the most mundane to the most exotic, from washing machines to space-craft. They augment our intellectual capacity through the use of pocket calculators, electronic encyclopaedias, but also in such specialised areas as medical diagnosis. Powerful computer-based systems are used to pay our salaries, to co-ordinate the activities of multinational companies, and to link the world together with global networks.

One of the most widespread types of computer-based systems are the information systems. The purpose of an information system is to support the use of information in an organisation. The system must provide accurate and up-to-date information that satisfies the information needs of an enterprise and thereby supports routine operations of the enterprise and improves its decision making. Some examples of information systems are:

- An airline reservation system.
- A system for the management of bank accounts.
- A system used by geologists to help search for mineral deposits.
- An interactive system used by senior managers to monitor the operation of their organisation.

In order to make clear how an information system can support an enterprise, we may distinguish between three different types of information systems: data-processing systems, management information systems, and decision support systems.

Data-processing systems are information systems that process and store large amounts of data from routine business transactions, such as payrolls, billing, and stocktaking. They support the day-to-day (operative) activities of a business by relieving people of the tedious and time-consuming aspects of manually performing necessary operational transactions. A data-processing system runs programs on an automatic basis, interactively with users or at regular intervals. Data-processing systems have become more and more integrated in and mission critical for enterprises and their operations at all levels. This can be exemplified by airline reservation systems or bank account management systems. When these systems break down, the operations of airlines or banks are more or less halted, resulting in large losses economically as well as losses with respect to the image of the enterprise.

A *management information system* (MIS) is seen as an extension of a data-processing system. Its purpose is not only to process routine transactions but also to provide managers and decision makers with information about the activities of their organisation. These are often presented in an accumulated and more abstract form. Whereas a data-processing system for a payroll sees to the payment of salaries, the corresponding MIS will provide statistical information about average salaries, levels of education, turnover rates, career development, etc. An MIS should help management in spotting business opportunities, detecting long-term trends, and noticing deviations from measurable business goals. Strategic decisions at senior management level have, however, always depended more on information about the environment of the enterprise, e.g. competitors, stock market, and political decisions, than on its internal information and operations. MIS-type systems have, therefore, during recent years focused increasingly on how to support management with such external information; this activity is often called *business intelligence.* New possibilities have emerged here owing to the existence of generally available databases and international networks, e.g. the *World Wide Web (WWW).*

A *decision support system* (DSS) is often used to extend a management information system. It introduces more advanced tools for analysis and decision making. For example, a DSS may contain components for optimisation, such as linear programming. A DSS may include functions which perform data mining on the databases of the enterprise in order to discover new knowledge of, for instance, the company's customers. This new knowledge may give the enterprise hints about how to move into a more competitive position. It should be emphasised, however, that although a DSS supports decision making, the decisions themselves still remain, in most cases, the exclusive province of the decision makers.

A common feature of all the types of information systems above is that they primarily handle structured and formalised information. However, most of the information in an organisation is informal and is communicated by, for instance, face-to-face meetings, telephone, fax, letters, blackboards, and electronic mail. Recently, computer-based tools for supporting this type of informal communication have appeared, e.g. conference systems and work-flow systems. These tools are also being integrated with information systems for structured information.

A computer-based information system is always a part of a larger *enterprise system*, see Figure 1.3. An enterprise system is a complex combination of enterprise objectives, strategic plans, business language and concepts, business processes, work practices, people and actors, and external relations and constraints. The computer-based information system basically consists of an information base, a set of information processes, and information technology. All these components should be organised to support the organisation in achieving its goals. In the following, we discuss the above concepts further.

In every organisation, there exists a more or less generally accepted way of expressing and denoting things. In order to communicate within the enterprise, the adopted *business language and concepts* must be understood and used. By *external relations and constraints,* we mean the environment of the enterprise, for instance customers, vendors, competitors, government regulations, and international agreements. Here we may also include relations with external information systems and inter-organisational systems. By *people and actors* we denote which performers exist in the enterprise and how they are organised, e.g. who is responsible for what and who reports to whom.

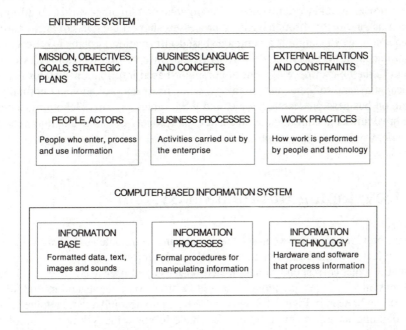

ENTERPRISE SYSTEM

| MISSION, OBJECTIVES, GOALS, STRATEGIC PLANS | BUSINESS LANGUAGE AND CONCEPTS | EXTERNAL RELATIONS AND CONSTRAINTS |

PEOPLE, ACTORS — People who enter, process and use information

BUSINESS PROCESSES — Activities carried out by the enterprise

WORK PRACTICES — How work is performed by people and technology

COMPUTER-BASED INFORMATION SYSTEM

INFORMATION BASE — Formatted data, text, images and sounds

INFORMATION PROCESSES — Formal procedures for manipulating information

INFORMATION TECHNOLOGY — Hardware and software that process information

Figure 1.3 *The computer-based information system as a part of an enterprise system*

Business processes are activities carried out when an organisation produces products and performs services. More precisely, a business process is a series of activities that add value to a product (or service), i.e. make it more valuable to a customer. When designing business processes, it is vital to ensure that they effectively and efficiently contribute to the goals of the enterprise. The relationships between business processes and the supporting computer-based information system are, consequently, of special interest when developing information systems.

Work practices are the methods used by people to carry out work. They not only include rule-based procedures prescribed by operation manuals, but include also general ways in which people communicate, make decisions, co-ordinate work, and perform other tasks in an enterprise. When people perform their work tasks they may need information that can be provided by a computer-based information system. The *information base* of such a system may take many different forms, such as formatted data, text, images, or sound. An important part of most work practices are *information processes,* i.e. tasks such as capturing, transmitting, storing, retrieving, manipulating, or displaying information. These information processes are supported by *information technology,* which consists of hardware and software: for example, personal computers, workstations, mainframes, bar code scanners, transaction processing software, and word processors.

A computer-based information system is useful only to the extent that it supports the business processes and work practices of an organisation. In other words, an information system must, indirectly through business processes, support the goals of an organisation. Consequently, when building a computer-based information system, it is necessary to take into account all the aspects above as well as information technology. A common problem in the field of development of computer-based information systems is that the technical staff tend to focus on technology, while users and stakeholders normally concentrate on business processes, people, and work practices. This dichotomy can easily create breakdowns in communication between developers and users and may even result in complete system development failures.

1.3 Developing Information Systems

From the previous section we can see that developing a computer-based information system is, in fact, a wicked and complex task. No useful information system can be built in isolation. It must correspond to anticipated business and user needs and requirements, and it must always be adopted to a context of existing components and information systems. As can be seen in Figure 1.3, we have to take into account a large number of issues when building an information system. We have to solve many kinds of problems of which only a few can be formally defined. We have to deal with many kinds of people with different attitudes, knowledge, needs, and requirements. An additional problem here is the difficulty of evaluating the benefits of a solution, as information systems are organisational infrastructure components.

In a crude way, we may distinguish the following kinds of tasks in the upper stages of systems development; that is, those stages that precede the implementation of a system:

- **Business engineering:** Business engineering typically aims at examining an organisation, its objectives, processes, products, external relations, people, and actors with a particular regard to the effectiveness of the organisation or its competitive ability. It may result in more or less radical changes in all these components, i.e. changed objectives, re-engineered business processes, changed relations to customers or to vendors, etc. Most often business engineering leads to changed as well as new requirements regarding information support.
- **Requirements engineering:** Requirements engineering denotes the activity of

defining requirements for a computer-based information system. Requirements are classified as functional or non-functional. Simply speaking, functional requirements specify what a system shall do; they are expressed by the conceptual schema of an information system (as will be discussed further in this book). Non-functional requirements, on the other hand, concern issues like ease of use, robustness, or security. Naturally, requirements determination must be based on business needs. Typically, these needs are determined and formulated as an extension of the task of business engineering.

- **Information systems engineering:** Information systems engineering is concerned with the functional and non-functional requirements of an information system, how these requirements are specified, verified, and how they can best be used to design an operational information system including humans as well as technological components. The designer has to consider the availability of standard software components, cope with problems of legacy, i.e. old systems, choice of and use of new software and communication technology. The result of the information systems engineering task is normally a system design specification, to be used as a basis for the development of software as well as of human procedures.

Information systems development is, thus, concerned with problems in all the areas above. Furthermore, it includes software development and implementation, user training, system installation, system operation, and system maintenance. In these phases of information systems development, methods and techniques from the area of software engineering can be employed. This book is, however, mainly concerned with a technique for describing functional requirements for information systems. At the end of the book, we show how this technique can be extended to a method for dealing with enterprise modelling in the area of business engineering.

The result of requirements engineering is a requirements specification, which plays several roles in the process of information systems development. First, it is the basis for and part of a contract between requirements holders and systems developers. Secondly, it is an architectural, implementation-independent drawing of the future system to be built. Thirdly, it provides an explicit basis for reasoning with the clients about various qualities of the system to be built. Later on, after delivery of the system, it is the only (*sic!*) instrument that can be used to check whether the implemented system corresponds to what has been ordered or not. When the enterprise and, consequently, the requirements on the information system change, the role of the requirements specification also changes; it becomes a basis for remodelling the enterprise and discussing how the information system should be adjusted.

Requirements engineering is, typically, characterised by:

- co-operative work, where co-ordination is vital,
- complex user–analyst dialogue and problems of (mutual) understanding of enterprise goals, concepts, processes, and other issues,
- often ill-defined and unclear problem situations,
- the need for reuse of existing systems and/or knowledge of existing systems,

- the need to resolve conflicting user/client views and requirements,
- the need to consider many situational factors, such as user skills, attitudes, experience, and leadership, in order to take the most adequate approach,
- the problem that users often either do not know requirements or do not utter their requirements, assuming that the systems developer knows them better.

These characteristics must be considered when developing adequate methods and support environments for requirements engineering. The problems above indicate also the need for a special professional who assists and carefully guides the requirements acquisition work. It can be understood that the process of developing an information system is not a linear, sequential one, where one step is fully completed before the next one begins. It is rather a complex, iterative design process (Figure 1.4), where the starting point ideally is the enterprise and its mission, but not necessarily so. The process can be seen as a spiral, where one gradually approaches the solution by stepwise refinement, focusing, and trying out different alternatives. Information systems development can be anything between the extreme cases (1) where users have a vague business problem they do not know how to articulate, and (2) where the information technology experts have a technical solution, but they are not sure for what problem. In the first case a solution must be sought by proceeding towards a better problem definition. In the second case the question is in what way the technical solution supports business goals and requirements. These two cases are often called *application pull* and *technology push,* respectively.

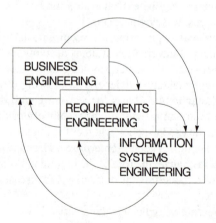

Figure 1.4   *The iterative process of systems development*

1.4 An Example of an Information System

We illustrate the notion of an information system by describing some properties of a simplified system. The system is intended to support an enterprise which in this case is "the management of the submitted papers and program of a scientific conference". The purpose of a scientific conference is to bring together scientists so that they can discuss and disseminate the latest results within a particular field of research. Below we present a fairly typical, and traditional, way of running a scientific conference today.

The talks given at a conference can be divided into two categories: tutorials and paper presentations. A tutorial is a lecture that surveys a specific research topic and is usually given by a senior and renowned scientist. A paper presentation is a short talk, typically 30 to 45 minutes long, in which a scientist presents his or her most recent findings. Paper presentations are usually grouped into sessions with each session containing between two and four presentations.

Organising a scientific conference requires extensive preparations. This work is usually divided between two committees: the programme committee, and the organising committee. It is the task of the programme committee to compile a good programme for the conference, consisting of tutorials, paper presentations, exhibitions, social events, etc. Experienced researchers are invited to suggest tutorials, and a call for papers is placed in scientific journals, announced on the WWW and in various newsgroups, as well as mailed directly to potential authors. In response to the call for papers, researchers submit their papers to the conference. Each paper is then carefully judged by several reviewers. The papers are judged from several different aspects such as originality, technical quality, and relevance. The final decision as to which papers are accepted for presentation at the conference is taken by the programme committee based on the judgements of the reviewers, and a discussion at the programme committee meeting. From the set of tutorial suggestions, the programme committee also selects a number of tutorials to be invited and presented.

The organising committee takes care of financial matters and local arrangements such as hotel accommodation and conference premises. An information system for managing scientific conferences should support the work activities of both the programme committee and the organising committee.

The following is a sample list of activities which typically should be supported:

- Prepare a list of persons to invite for tutorials.
- Register submitted papers and send letters of acknowledgement.
- Evaluate and select papers to be accepted for presentation.
- Inform paper authors about the selection result.
- Send call for attendance to journals and selected persons.
- Provide venue, hotel, and travel information to all interested parties.
- Generate a list of attendees.

Most of the work practices to be supported are fairly routine, and the information system should therefore mainly be a data-processing system. However, some of the activities are more complex, notably the evaluation and selection of papers for inclusion in the conference programme. The emergence of high-speed networking facilities is gradually changing the way papers are submitted and the way they are evaluated. It is not uncommon nowadays that papers are submitted in electronic form, e.g. as Postscript files, and that the evaluation process utilises support from WWW facilities. Programme committee members access papers on the network, make their assessments, and supply their evaluation directly in appropriate WWW pages on the computer of the organising site. There also seems to be a tendency to organise the review reports in such a way that they supply a better basis for decisions by the programme committee. While this may imply more work for the reviewers, it may reduce the need for programme committee members to attend meetings. Several conferences have, lately, consequently dropped these physical meetings altogether. This saves time as well as travel expenses.

In the following section we will discuss how an organisation, or an enterprise, can be viewed and analysed from different perspectives. These perspectives will then be illustrated using the simple conference case above.

1.5 Goals, Processes, Actors, and Objects

It can be understood from Section 1.2 that when designing an information system for an enterprise, it is necessary to view this enterprise from different perspectives. The most essential perspectives seem to be: the goal perspective, the process perspective, the object perspective, and the actor perspective (see also Figure 1.5).

Investigating an organisation from the goal perspective involves asking questions like: Why does the organisation exist? What are its goals? What are actors in the organisation trying to achieve? What warrants the pursuit of these activities? In this way we try to find out what the organisation's mission and goals are. We also try to discover potentially conflicting goals, and circumstances that could prevent goals from being fulfilled, as well as opportunities that may assist in fulfilling them. Some of the high-level goals in the example of the preceding section could be: "To stimulate dissemination of high quality research results and practical experiences", "To make a surplus for the organisers", "To stimulate a high participation from industry and business". Some goals at a lower level might be: "A sufficient number of speakers should be invited", "Only the best papers submitted should be accepted", and "The conference should be attended by at least one hundred participants". We can see also that most of these goals are rather vague and need further elaboration.

Investigating an organisation from the process perspective involves asking questions like: What processes are performed in the enterprise? Do all processes contribute to the goals of the enterprise? Does this process create value for the customer? Are the processes performed efficiently? Can the set of processes be re-engineered to meet the objectives better? In the above example we have listed a number of processes for tasks to be carried out by the programme and the organising committees. Some of the processes are: "Send invitations to the selected speakers" and "Send notifications of acceptance to all authors, even those not accepted". This, however, reflects the current situation of how conferences are run. A question to be asked here could, therefore, also be: Is this the best way to achieve the overall goal "To stimulate dissemination of high quality research results and practical experiences"? A question like this may trigger a redesign activity where the traditional organisational structure of conferences, the committees, as well as the way submissions are made and evaluated are radically changed. It may also radically change the way papers are collected, presented, and published.

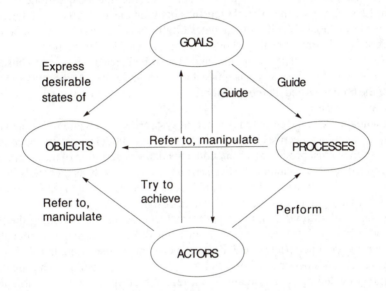

Figure 1.5 *Perspectives of an enterprise*

The actor perspective is concerned with people, roles, and business units, the actions they perform, and the goals that guide their performance. The main aim here is to identify the actors of the organisation, their relationships to enterprise goals and to the activities being carried out, and the structure of responsibility. Analysis of actor–process–goal structures may also reveal interesting dependency relations between actors, e.g. "In order to achieve a goal, this actor is dependent on a large number of other actors", which may indicate that this actor's chances of achieving the goal are not high. A careful examination of the actor perspective, may, together with other perspectives, lead to radical changes of the structure of actors for a conference.

Investigating an organisation from the object perspective involves asking questions like: What phenomena, objects, and concepts exist in the organisation and in its environment? What properties do objects have? How are objects related to each other? How do they come into existence, how do they change, and how do they cease to exist? Which events influence objects? We look for objects in the enterprise, their properties and inter-relationships, as well as for their behaviour over time. We also try to identify rules that constrain the possible states and behaviour of objects. Continuing with the conference example, we can, assuming a traditional conference, identify object types such as: Persons, Papers, Sessions, Reviewers, Authors, Speakers, etc. The object perspective also includes business rules. Two examples of rules are: "Papers that arrive late will not be reviewed" and "Papers must not be reviewed by anybody in the same organisation as the author". On the other hand, a more radical analysis of this enterprise may perceive the conference in a different way. Even the concept of a paper may be questioned.

Figure 1.5 summarises the interrelationships between the goal, process, actor, and object perspectives. Goals specify which states of affairs are desirable, i.e. which objects should exist, which properties they should possess, and how they should be interrelated. Processes influence the states of affairs, and should be carried out so as to ensure that goals are satisfied. In this way, goals guide and direct processes. Actors perform the activities of the processes and thereby manipulate the objects. Actors also try to achieve the goals of the enterprise.

An essential task in developing information systems is the creation of models of the enterprise from all perspectives introduced above. These models must fulfil two requirements. First, they must provide an easily understandable description of the enterprise that can be used for communication between users and systems analysts. Secondly, the models must be sufficiently detailed and unambiguous to be used as a basis for subsequent steps in systems development, such as database design.

There are many different, more or less formal techniques for modelling the process perspective, e.g. data flow diagrams (of various kinds), Petri nets, and state transition diagrams. For the goal perspective and the actor perspective, the situation is different. So far there are only rudimentary techniques for goal and actor modelling. This area, denoted enterprise modelling, is still mainly in a research stage; we return to this topic in Chapter 10.

In order to model the object perspective of an organisation, a large number of techniques exist. One of the earliest modelling approaches for the object perspective was the Entity–Relationship (ER) approach. A limitation of the ER approach is that models created within this framework can only show a static structure for the objects and a few simple rules. To overcome this problem, so called object-oriented approaches have been proposed, which also address the dynamic aspects of objects, i.e. their behaviour over time. In this book, we shall use the term *conceptual model* to denote a model of an enterprise as seen from the object perspective, including static structural aspects as well as dynamics and rules. In one sense, the conceptual model of an enterprise is the most fundamental one. To be able to construct precise models from the goal, process, and actor perspectives, we must know which objects and concepts are relevant, i.e. we need a conceptual model as a basis. The conceptual model provides a common language and terminology for expressing goals and processes, and it thus serves as a foundation for tying together models from all perspectives.

1.6 The Use of Conceptual Modelling

Conceptual models can be used for many different purposes, in information systems development, in requirements determination, as well as in enterprise development. Conceptual models are also used in areas such as computer integrated manufacturing (CIM), or in the construction industry, for the description of products and product structures. Different purposes may require different levels of detail and precision of a conceptual model. For instance, initial conceptual models in enterprise modelling will typically be incomplete and contain only the most important concepts and relationships, while models for developing a software product must be complete and precise.

Typical activities in enterprise development are redesigning the business processes in an organisation, identifying new business areas, and articulating attitudes and values of employees. In the context of enterprise development, it is important that every participant should hold a common view of the enterprise and use a common language in order to facilitate communication. Conceptual modelling can make it easier for the actors of an organisation to arrive at consensus on a common "world view", to use the same language, and to agree on rules that should prevail in the organisation. Conceptual modelling can also help people to focus on the most important parts of the enterprise and to question old and ingrained notions and assumptions. The help conceptual modelling provides is a clear definition of concepts, their properties and relationships, as well as clear definitions of the dynamics of such systems. Clear definitions help to detect disagreements and to arrive at consensus.

In the early phases of information systems development, conceptual modelling is used in the same way as in enterprise development. A common view and language should be built in order to facilitate making decisions on such matters as whether to maintain an old system, develop a new one, or purchase a standard system. In the later phases of information systems development, a conceptual model must be constructed to serve as the basis of the design and implementation of a computer system. In particular, the model should be used in designing the database. However, in contrast to so-called data models, a conceptual model should not focus solely on the data to be stored in the database; it should also specify the rules and constraints pertaining to the objects and describe the events that govern their behaviour. Making rules and events explicit in a conceptual model is a valuable aid in acquiring a clear and complete understanding of the functionality of an information system. This degree of understanding cannot readily be obtained by inspecting the finished implementation of an information system. This is because the rules and events are encoded in the programs that manipulate the data, and consequently they are hard to identify and understand.

In this introduction we have presented a brief overview of the notions of problem-solving and information systems development. When developing information systems, some of the biggest road-blocks to improved productivity are the designer's lack of understanding of the application domain, and poor communication between participants in development projects. One way to improve substantially user participation and domain expert communication is the application of modelling techniques. One of the basic aims of good conceptual specifications is to promote understanding of the problems at hand. Furthermore, results from the emerging field of *computer supported co-operative work* (CSCW) may be adapted to and incorporated in requirements engineering environments. This technology can be used in order to facilitate co-operation between teams of analysts, users, and domain experts, located in different sites, by means of tele-working using high-speed communication networks.

One of the fundamental aims of conceptual modelling is to create a language that can be used to reason about an enterprise and its information systems. Chapter 2, therefore, begins with a brief survey of some basic ideas in linguistics and the philosophy of language. It discusses syntactics, semantics, and pragmatics, and shows how language is used in classification and abstraction.

1.7 Some Relevant Literature and Conferences

The notions of well-structured and wicked problems are discussed in [Rittel84] and [Simon84]. The history of conceptual modelling, in the sense described in this book, started at the end of the 1950s. One of the earliest modelling approaches for the object perspective was the binary model developed at the beginning of the 1970s by Michael Senko [Senko73]. Later, in 1975, the Entity–Relationship (ER) approach was presented at VLDB'75 and published in 1976 [Chen76]. The NIAM approach [Nijssen77] appeared at the same time.

The importance and utility of considering the dynamic, temporal aspects of information in systems modelling was recognised by Young and Kent [Young58] in 1958. They presented an abstract modelling formalism where it was possible to relate information to time, and to reason about the information system in an extended time perspective. Later, during the 1960s, Langefors [Langefors67] introduced the "elementary message", considered to be the smallest meaningful element of information. The elementary message included a reference to the point in time when the information was valid.

During the 1980s, a number of approaches (e.g. [Greenspan86; Furtado88; Hagelstein88; Kung83; Kung88]) extended the modelling framework to deal formally with dynamic (state transition) aspects of information systems. At this time research was also started on temporal databases (for a comprehensive textbook see [Tansel93]). Temporal databases typically follow the relational model. The distinguishing characteristic of such databases is that tuples or attribute values are time stamped. The validity of a tuple or an attribute value is given by a time interval expressed as start time and stop time.

A purely deductive temporal approach to conceptual modelling was published in 1977 [Bubenko77]. It was followed by the CIAM method [Bubenko80; Gustafsson1982] and work by Olivé's group in Barcelona (e.g. [Olivé86; Olivé89]), particularly concerning the problem of efficient implementation (the temporal deductive approach is presented in Chapter 9 of this book).

After having completed this book, the reader who wants to know more about conceptual modelling should consult the research literature. There are several journals that publish material on conceptual modelling, e.g. *Information Systems, Data and Knowledge Engineering, IEEE Transactions on Knowledge and Data Engineering, VLDB Journal, ACM Transactions on Information Systems, Information Systems Journal, The International Journal of Intelligent and Cooperative Information Systems*, and *Requirements Engineering*. There are also several relevant conferences and workshops that take place regularly: the *ER conference* series, the *Very Large Data Bases* (VLDB) *conference* series, the *Conference on Advanced Information Systems Engineering* (CAiSE) series, the *ACM SIGMOD* conferences, the *EDBT* (Extending Data Base Technology) series, and the *European–Japanese Seminars on Information Modelling and Knowledge Bases*. International symposia or workshops on requirements engineering is another source, e.g. the IEEE annual symposia on requirements engineering. An efficient way to get more information about current research on information systems is to consult the World Wide Web. A good site to visit is IS World, http://www.isworld.org/isworld.html, which provides information on research and teaching on information systems. Another interesting site, with many links, is SYSLAB, http://www.dsv.su.se/research/syslab/syslab.html, which is the research laboratory of the authors of this book.

CHAPTER 2

Language and Reality

One of the major aims of conceptual modelling is to construct a language that can be used to reason about some part of reality. Theories about language are therefore important foundations for conceptual modelling. The structure of language, the relationship between reality and language, and the actual use of language as a means of communication between people are particularly important. This chapter discusses a few basic concepts of language that are relevant to conceptual modelling, drawing on results from linguistics and the philosophy of language. The first section compares language to other forms of symbol systems and distinguishes between natural and artificial languages. This is followed by a brief survey of the three major areas of linguistics: syntactics, semantics, and pragmatics. We then go on to discuss formalisations of language, followed by an explanation of how language can be used for classification and abstraction. We admit to treating very hastily in this chapter many open questions within the philosophy of language. The reason for this is that we only discuss aspects of language that are relevant to conceptual modelling. And as a matter of fact, in conceptual modelling many theories about language can be successfully applied, even some that are problematic from a philosophical point of view.

2.1 Natural Languages and Artificial Languages

A *language* is a symbol system used by individuals in a group to communicate. In human communication, many other symbol systems besides language are used. Such systems are evident in maps and blueprints, in road signs, and in the conventions of representational art, such as the golden haloes crowning saints. Musical notation and dance notation are symbolic systems, where pitch in music or movement in formalised styles of dancing is designated by graphical symbols. Symbols also occur in the communication systems of animals, such as bird calls intended to ward off predators. The most advanced animal communication system known so far is the bee dance, through which one bee can convey to others the strength of nectar and the location of its source, by carrying out various systematic movements in the hive. Common to all these systems is their use of *symbols*; that is, objects which can refer to other objects. Human language also makes use of symbols, commonly called words, but differs from most other symbol systems in several important respects. Below, we list some salient features of language, which help to explain its expressive power and versatility:

- *Arbitrariness*. In general there is no intrinsic connection between a linguistic symbol and what it denotes. In English, for example, the word "human" is used to denote featherless bipeds, while other languages use different words, such as "Mensch" or "människa". In Figure 2.1, the arbitrariness of language is illustrated by a classic example from [Carroll1872].
- *Abstractness*. A sentence may abstract from many details of a situation, and focus on just one aspect. For example, the sentence "Clyde weighs 400 kg" tells us nothing about Clyde, except his weight. Symbols in many other systems cannot be equally abstract; a picture of Clyde would reveal many of his properties, such as his being an elephant.
- *Productivity*. We do not learn a language sentence by sentence. Instead, we learn the elements of sentences, and words, as well as the principles of how to combine them to make complete sentences. We are therefore perfectly able to understand even unusual sentences like "The elephant climbed up the telegraph pole and played the pizzicato polka on the wires". In this way, it becomes possible to construct and understand an infinite number of sentences, with knowledge of only a finite number of words and rules.
- *Power*. In contrast to the communication systems of animals, human language is unrestricted in what it can represent. We humans can talk about a vast range of topics: "tables, people, molecules, light rays, retinas, air waves, prime numbers, infinite classes, joy and sorrow, good and evil" ([Quine66]), quite a contrast to the monomania of the bee dance.

"...-and that shows that there are three hundred and sixty-four days when you might get un-birthday presents-"
"Certainly," said Alice.
"And only one for birthday presents you know. There's 'glory' for you!"
"I don't know what you mean by 'glory'," Alice said.
Humpty Dumpty smiled contemptuously. "Of course you don't know - till I tell you. I meant 'there's a nice knock-down argument for you!'"
"But 'glory' doesn't mean 'a nice knock-down argument'," Alice objected.
"When I use a word," Humpty Dumpty said, in rather a scornful tone, "it means just what I choose it to mean - neither more nor less."
"The question is", said Alice, "whether you can make words mean so many different things."
"The question is," said Humpty Dumpty, "which is to be master - that's all."

Figure 2.1 *Humpty Dumpty on the arbitrariness of language*

A *natural language* is an ordinary hereditary language, spoken by a group of individuals as their native tongue. An example of a natural language is English. Natural languages are mainly studied by linguists, even though philosophers and computer scientists also study language through the philosophy of language and through computational linguistics. The above definition excludes Esperanto from the set of natural languages, as well as all present or future computer languages. These languages are called *artificial languages*. A subclass of the artificial languages is that of *machine languages* which, as the name implies, are used by a machine to code letters, numbers, instructions, and storage locations in such a way that a computer does not require any translation in order to function according to its coded instructions. Pascal, C++, and Prolog are examples of machine languages. Formal languages are also artificial languages. A *formal language*, put simply, is a set of symbols that is accompanied by rules for concatenating the symbols into sequences. The special notation used in describing a game of chess is an example of a formal language, as are languages used to calculate in logic or mathematics. In computer science the ability of various formal languages to reflect the subtleties in descriptions of natural language is carefully studied, especially within the fields of conceptual modelling, database theory, and software engineering. Interest here lies mainly in the expressive power of languages. Other factors such as correctness, soundness, and completeness are discussed later in Chapter 4. The ideal language for any one given purpose is the smallest, yet that which allows everything required of it to be expressed with the greatest of ease. With such a language at our disposal the representation of a message could be made more abstract and manageable than would have been possible in the original natural language. Yet this could be achieved without losing content in the process. In Figure 2.2, a simple classification of languages is presented.

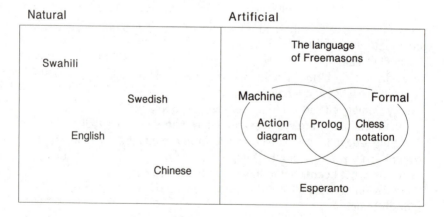

Figure 2.2 *The relation among four different classes of languages, with examples*

2.2 Semiotics

The study of communication between all kinds of agents—be they humans, animals, or computers—through language and other symbol systems is sometimes called *semiotics*. Certain aspects of conceptual modelling can be considered semiotic because of the pre-occupation with signs and symbols. Semiotics is a fairly recently developed discipline. It is similar to cognitive science in that it is interdisciplinary in nature, resting mainly within philosophy and linguistics. Semiotics is divided into three areas: syntactics, semantics, and pragmatics. Rather than discussing semiotics *per se*, we take a brief individual look at each of these areas.

2.2.1 Syntactics

Syntactics, or syntax, is concerned with the way sentences are constructed from smaller parts, such as words and phrases. Two steps can be distinguished in the study of syntactics. The first step is to identify different types of units in the stream of speech and writing. In natural languages, such units include sentences, phrases, and words. In artificial languages, lexemes, tokens, and formulae are usually found among the basic units. The second step is to analyse how these units build up larger patterns, and in particular to find general rules that govern the construction of sentences.

The smallest building blocks of languages are signs. A finite non-empty set of signs is called an *alphabet*. For instance, the English alphabet is the set of letters from *a* to *z* together with parentheses and punctuation symbols, where each of the elements is a *sign*. The binary alphabet consists of the set {0,1}. From any given alphabet we can form *strings* by concatenating a finite number of its elements. The same element may be chosen more than once or no elements at all may be chosen. We call the latter case the empty string and represent it with ε. Examples of the former case are `king`, `kngi`, and `kingking` from the English alphabet, and `010` from the binary alphabet. Thus, a string is an ordered sequence of elements from a certain alphabet, where the position of each element in a string is significant. This means that `inter` and `inert`, `rentsite` and `interest` are different strings. Names can be introduced for alphabets as well. For instance, E might denote the English alphabet, and B the binary alphabet. The set of all strings that can be built from an alphabet is called its *closure*. A convenient way to denote the closure of an alphabet is with the *Kleene star*, named after the logician Stephen Cole Kleene. The closure of the binary alphabet would thus be denoted B^* and is an infinite set; $B^* = \{\varepsilon,0,1,00,01,10,11,000,...\}$.

A language, defined over an alphabet X, is a set of strings that can be constructed from X. Thus, every language is a subset of X^*. English is a proper subset of E^*, for instance. Similarly the language used to express binary numbers is a proper subset of B^*, since B^* contains strings, such as `000`, that do not belong to the language. The alphabets on which different natural languages are based usually vary slightly, even though two different languages may be based on the same alphabet. As a basis for formal languages, B is a fairly common alphabet, as is $\{0,1,2,3,4,5,6,7,8,9,+,\cdot\}$, a simple arithmetical alphabet. Since languages are sets, all the usual set operators can be applied to languages. For instance, the word ombudsman lies in the intersection of English and Swedish. In Example 2.1, this and other examples are written in the notation of set theory. The Swedish alphabet is denoted by S.

Example 2.1   The use of set-theoretical ideas applied to languages.
   The string ombudsman can be built from the closure of the English alphabet:

   ombudsman $\in E^*$

as well as from the closure of the Swedish alphabet:

   ombudsman $\in S^*$

and it can therefore also be built from their intersection:

   ombudsman $\in (E^* \cap S^*)$.

In fact, the stronger condition:

   ombudsman $\in$ (English $\cap$ Swedish) holds good too.[1]

The string horse is an English, not a Swedish, word, and so it belongs to the difference between English and Swedish:

   horse $\in$ (English $-$ Swedish)

whereas the reverse difference is true of häst:

   häst $\in$ (Swedish $-$ English).

The English language is a strict subset of the closure of the English alphabet:

   English $\subset E^*$.

The Swedish language is not a (strict) subset of the closure of the English alphabet since the Swedish alphabet contains the signs å, ä, ö, which are alien to E, as exemplified by the string häst:

   Swedish $\not\subset E^*$.

The following three signs that all look similar to the letter E, say that the empty string is an element of the closure of the English alphabet. In fact, it is an element of the closure of every alphabet:

   $\varepsilon \in E^*$.

One well-known technique for analysing and displaying the structure of sentences is *immediate constituent analysis*. This technique divides a sentence into its constituents in a series of steps. At each step, a construction is divided into its major constituents, and the process continues until no more divisions can be made. For example, if we are to analyse the sentence The man joins the club, we carry out the following three steps. First,

---

1) Stronger as opposed to weaker in this context means that a strong definition is more restrictive than a weaker one.

we identify the two major constituents, i.e. `the man` and `joins the club`. Secondly, we divide the next-biggest constituent into two, i.e. `joins the club` into `joins` and `the club`. Thirdly, we divide these constituents until we cannot continue, which means that `the man` is divided into `the` and `man`, and `the club` is divided into `the` and `club`. A nice way of representing this constituent structure is by means of a tree diagram as shown in Figure 2.3.

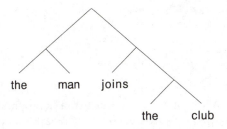

Figure 2.3 *An immediate constituent diagram*

This type of tree diagram clearly displays the constituents of a sentence, but it does not provide any deeper understanding of the structure of the sentence. In particular, a tree diagram does not inform us about the type or function of the sentence constituents displayed in the diagram. In order to provide such information, we could label the nodes in the diagram.

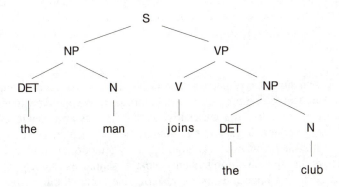

Figure 2.4 *A syntactical tree structure*

For the example sentence (S) above, the first division gives rise to a noun phrase (NP), `the man`, and a verb phrase (VP), `joins the club`. The second division produces a verb (V), `joins`, and another noun phrase, `the club`. Finally, the third step divides each noun phrase into a determiner (DET) and a noun (N), the + man and the + club. The resulting tree diagram is shown in Figure 2.4.

Analysing single sentences, as in the example above, may have a certain merit in itself. A more ambitious project, however, is to construct general rules that govern the structure of the sentences in a language. Such rules should be able to generate tree structures of the type above. An example of a set of rules that are capable of generating the tree in Figure 2.4 is:

```
S   → NP   VP
VP  → V    NP
NP  → DET  N
V   → joins
DET → the
N   → man | club
```

The first rule states that a sentence can consist of a noun phrase followed by a verb phrase; the second that a verb phrase can consist of a verb and a noun phrase; the third that a noun phrase can consist of a determiner and a following noun. Finally, each of the abstract categories V, DET, and N is associated with a number of words. A set of rules of the form above, together with the alphabet used and an identification of the start symbol S, is called a *grammar*. The purpose of a grammar for a natural language is to tell us how to generate grammatically correct sentences in a language, i.e. sentences that are grammatically acceptable to the native speakers of the language. The simple grammar above allows us to generate the sentence The man joins the club if we choose the man for the first NP and the club for the second NP. If we make the choice the other way round, we arrive at the sentence The club joins the man, which is also grammatically correct. By adding more words to the abstract categories V, DET, and N we can generate a large number of sentences, such as the following:

```
V   → joins | likes | elects
DET → the | a
N   → man | club | president
```

Some example sentences that can be generated from this extended grammar are The man likes the club, and The club elects a president. We could try to generate even more sentences by including the intransitive verb walks as an element of V. But this would result in the grammar generating "ungrammatical" sentences such as The man walks the club. When constructing a grammar for a (fraction of a) natural language it is important to ensure that no intuitively unacceptable sentences can be generated, while at the same time the grammar must be capable of generating all the grammatically correct sentences of the language. Constructing a complete grammar for a natural language, such as English, is obviously an overwhelming task. However, it has been argued that in principle it would be possible to write down the complete grammar for English and present it as a definitive document. Unfortunately, its absolute authority as to which concatenations are grammatically correct sentences in English would probably not last very long.

In contrast to natural languages, it is often easy to specify a grammar for a formal language. In fact, a formal language can be defined as a language for which there is a grammar that generates all its sentences. As an example of a formal language, we specify the alphabet and the grammar for the language of *propositional logic* in Figure 2.5. Here, sentences are called *propositions*. In fact, the formal language in Figure 2.5 is only one of many possible propositional logics. For instance, a different propositional logic might use the same syntactics except for two place connectives where it might use only ∧. An important set of connectives is {¬, ∧, ∨}, used for clausal form logic (discussed in Chapter 4). This set is complete with respect to truth functions in that any proposition involving any other connectives can be rewritten as a proposition using connectives from this set only. There are many other connectives than the five mentioned here that are popular, including *absurdity*, *nor*, *nand*, and *xor*. For convenience, one might also want to choose a larger set of proposition letters. The three symbols used here are to be thought of as the leftmost letter (l) of any name, the rightmost (r), and the letters in between (zero or more qs). Hence the names used in this calculus include lr and $lqqqr$, which are not very mnemonic. The advantage is that one may easily define the *atomic formulae* of the calculus as all formulae of the form $lq^n r$, for $n \geq 0$. A simpler naming convention is used for predicate logic below (see Figure 2.9).

ALPHABET:
    One-place connective ¬
    Two-place connectives ∧, ∨, →, ↔
    Parentheses (,)
    Proposition letters l, q, r

GRAMMAR: Given the auxiliary symbols S and N, we have the following grammar.
    $N \texttt{-->} \varepsilon$
    $N \texttt{-->} Nq$
    $S \texttt{-->} lNr$
    $S \texttt{-->} (S \wedge S)$
    $S \texttt{-->} (S \vee S)$
    $S \texttt{-->} (S \rightarrow S)$
    $S \texttt{-->} (S \leftrightarrow S)$
    $S \texttt{-->} \neg S$

Figure 2.5 *A syntactic description of a propositional logic*

2.2.2 Semantics

Semantics is the study of meaning in language, i.e. the study of the relationship between linguistic expressions and reality. This should be compared with syntactics, which is only concerned with the form of expressions in a language. The difference between the syntactic and semantic properties of language is illustrated in the following example. Consider the sentence: "Colourless green ideas sleep furiously". From a syntactic point of view, this sentence is perfectly correct. It contains the subject "Colourless green ideas" and the predicate "sleep furiously". Semantically, however, the sentence is quite absurd since it does not describe any conceivable state of affairs. The adjective "colourless" indicates the property "without colour", but it is combined with the adjective "green", which bestows the property "green in colour". This is unreasonable since something cannot be both green and without colour at the same time. Several other semantic violations also occur in the sentence, making it an example of a syntactically correct but meaningless sentence. It is instructive to compare the sentence with a syntactically incorrect sentence such as "Sleep colourless furiously green ideas". This sentence contains the same words as the previous one but in an order that makes it syntactically incorrect. It lacks sufficient structure to make it possible to say what is wrong with it.

In linguistics and philosophy, there are a large number of approaches to semantics. Common to many of these is the idea that the meaning of a sentence is completely determined by the meanings of its constituents. This idea is commonly called *the principle of compositionality*. The principle states that the meaning of any phrase can be obtained by some operation on the meanings of its parts. So, given a sentence, it should be possible to work out its meaning by first finding the meaning of the individual words, then combining these to understand the meaning of small phrases, then combining these to understand larger phrases, and so on. This process is repeated until the meaning of the whole sentence becomes clear. The principle of compositionality could be regarded as the semantical justification for the syntactical study of constituents. It may seem self-evident at first sight, but there are many situations where applying the principle is inadequate, see Figure 2.6.

The sentence "Man is a wolf" can be interpreted in at least four different ways:
1. Man is subject only to the laws of the jungle.
2. Man wears sheep's clothing.
3. Men can change into werewolves at full moon.
4. The first men were reared by wolves.

If we encounter the sentence "Man is a wolf" in a text, we would probably not have much difficulty in deciding which of these interpretations, if any, was appropriate. So, the meaning of a sentence is to a large extent determined by the context in which it appears. The social context in which the sentence occurs also influences its meaning. This is exemplified above, where the interpretations are derived from a poem by Kipling, a Greek fable, and legends about werewolves and wolf children, respectively. The point of this example is that not only the constituents of a sentence, but also its context, determine its meaning. Consequently, in certain situations, the principle of compositionality is inappropriate for analysing the meaning of sentences.

Figure 2.6 *A problem with the principle of compositionality*

To understand the meaning of individual words and expressions, it is often helpful to distinguish between their *extension* and their *intension*. The extension of an expression means the object or the set of objects in the real world to which the expression refers. The extension of the word "dog" is the set of all dogs, and the extension of the expression "President of the United States in 1996" is Bill Clinton. Different expressions may have the same extension. For example, the expression "The Morning Star" refers to the planet Venus, and so does the expression "The Evening Star". However, it was not until the latter half of the nineteenth century that astronomers discovered that "The Morning Star" and "The Evening Star" actually denoted the same planet. For centuries, people had used the expressions to mean two completely different things: "The Morning Star" referred to a certain star that could be seen in the morning, and "The Evening Star" referred to a star seen in the evening. So, there is more to the meaning of an expression than its extension.

The *intension* of an expression means its sense: that which a person normally understands by the expression. For example, the intension of the word "dog" might be something like "hairy mammal with four legs and tail, often kept as a pet". Returning to the example above, we would say that the expressions "The Morning Star" and "The Evening Star" have the same extension, but different intensions. However, two expressions with the same intension must have the same extension. Admittedly, the concept of intension is not very clear, but it is often indispensable in situations where an extensional analysis is insufficient. The relationships between linguistic expressions and their extensions and intensions can be depicted graphically in a figure called *Ogden's triangle*, see Figure 2.7. The figure illustrates that the term "dog" has the concept of dog as its intension, and the set of all dogs as its extension.

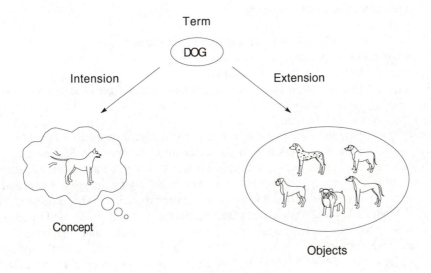

Figure 2.7 *Ogden's triangle*

Sometimes the truth value of a sentence only depends on the extensional meaning of its components. Consider the sentence "The king of Sweden is having dinner". If we substitute "The king of Sweden" with the expression "Carl XVI Gustaf", the truth value of the sentence would not change.[2] In fact, we could replace "The king of Sweden" with any expression denoting the king, without changing the truth value of the sentence. A sentence is called *extensional* if its truth value remains unaffected by replacing any of its constituents with a constituent that has the same extension. So, "The king of Sweden is having dinner" is an extensional sentence. Note that this is in keeping with the principle of compositionality. Now, suppose that the following sentence is true: "Mary believes that the king of Sweden is having dinner". If Mary is unaware that "The king of Sweden" and "Carl XVI Gustaf" refer to the same person, we cannot assume that the following sentence is true: "Mary believes that Carl XVI Gustaf is having dinner". The sentence is therefore *intensional*.

We will now consider how to give meaning to phrases and complete sentences, not only to individual words. We will begin by studying the propositional calculus, the syntax of which has already been given in Figure 2.5. The atomic components of this language are the propositional letters, which are meant to stand for propositions, such as "The cat is on the mat", "Socrates is mortal", or "John loves Mary". The atomic propositional letters can be combined into molecular propositions by means of the propositional connectives. For example, the proposition $(A \land B) \to (A \lor B)$ should be read as "if A and B, then A or B". In propositional logic, we give meaning to a proposition by specifying its truth conditions, i.e. by specifying when the proposition is true and when it is false. For the propositional letters we simply assign a truth value, true or false, to each one of them. For propositions that contain one or more connectives, we compute their truth values using the following rules:

1. $A \land B$ is true iff (if and only if) A is true and B is true
2. $A \lor B$ is true iff A is true or B is true
3. $A \to B$ is true iff A is false or B is true
4. $A \leftrightarrow B$ is true iff both A and B are true, or both A and B are false
5. $\neg A$ is true iff A is false

In order to compute the truth value of a given proposition, it is useful to start by constructing its tree diagram according to the techniques introduced in Section 2.2.1. To each leaf of the tree, i.e. to each propositional letter, we assign a truth value. We also assign a truth value to each interior node of the tree by following the rules above, and by doing so we finally arrive at a truth value for the entire proposition. This process is illustrated in Figure 2.8, which shows a tree diagram where each node is labelled by its associated truth value. The propositional letter A is assigned the truth value true, while B gets the value false; therefore $A \land B$ becomes false, while $A \lor B$ becomes true. So, the entire sentence $(A \land B) \to (A \lor B)$ is true. It should be noted that this way of giving a seman-

---

2) Carl XVI Gustaf will not reign for ever, but, for now, we ignore the temporal dimension.

tics, in this case the so-called *Tarski semantics*, to a language is exactly what the principle of compositionality prescribes. First, a meaning (a truth value) is given to the smallest components (the propositional letters) of a proposition. Based on the meanings of these components, the meanings of larger components are computed according to a few simple rules, and by repeating this process the meaning of the entire proposition is determined. Gottlob Frege, who observed more than one hundred years ago that this held true for the language of propositional logic, dubbed it the *principle of extensionality* since it is only the extension of a proposition that constitutes its meaning.

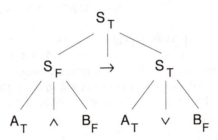

Figure 2.8 *A syntactical tree diagram augmented by semantic values*

In the language of propositional logic, it is possible to give only a very coarse analysis of sentences—a sentence can be broken down only if it contains a connective. A more detailed and finer analysis can be given in the language of predicate logic, also called first-order logic (FOL). The predicate calculus provides language constructs for denoting individual objects, properties of objects, and relationships between objects. The syntax used for this purpose is shown in Figure 2.9. What is added to the propositional syntax presented in Figure 2.5 are quantifiers and names for variables, predicates, functions, and constants, none of which are part of any propositional logic. We have chosen not to present the predicate logic syntax as a grammar (cf. Exercise 2.13), since such a description becomes very cluttered. Predicates and functions have arity, indicated in Figure 2.9 by a superscript digit. A predicate of arity 1 is called a *monadic* predicate, while a predicate of arity 2 is called *dyadic*, or more often *binary*. For the purpose of this book, we do not have to consider predicates of higher arities, since there are formal means of translating such predicates to predicates of arity 1 and 2. For the beginning logic student, the understanding of functions usually poses a great difficulty. Happily enough, we have only a limited need for functions in this book. We will return to this issue in Section 4.5 below. It suffices here to note that functions of arity 0 are called *constants*. Informally, names for constants and variables are used to denote objects, while names for predicates denote properties and relationships.

Furthermore, it is possible to construct universal and existential statements by means of the universal quantifier $\forall$, to be read "for all", and the existential quantifier $\exists$, to be read "there are". Only one of the quantifiers is needed as a primitive, but it is convenient to use both. Thus, one of the two quantifiers is used merely for allowing formulae to become shorter or clearer. As an example, the following formula in the predicate calculus expresses the natural language sentence "Every cat chases Jerry":

$\forall$x(Cat(x) $\rightarrow$ Chases(x, Jerry))

This is true also for the following formula:

$\neg\exists$x(Cat(x) $\wedge\neg$Chases(x, Jerry))

In these sentences, Cat and Chases are (names for) predicates, x is a variable, and Jerry is a constant, i.e., a zero-place function. The formulae could be read as "for all x, if x is a cat, then x chases Jerry" and "there is no x such that x is a cat and x does not chase Jerry", respectively.

To allow for formulae such as the two just mentioned to be expressed in our predicate logic we would have either to augment the lists of names in Figure 2.9 to include, for example, the Cat predicate name, or to find a mapping between our unimaginative names and whatever mnemonic names we would like to use in our formulae. The latter way is the standard way, since the former method works only for a static language. We will return to this issue in Chapter 4.

SYMBOLS:
   One-place connective $\neg$
   Two-place connectives $\wedge$, $\vee$, $\rightarrow$, $\leftrightarrow$
   Quantifiers $\exists$, $\forall$
   Parentheses (,)
   Variable names x_1, x_2, x_3, ...
   Predicate names $P^1{}_1$, $P^1{}_2$, $P^1{}_3$, ..., $P^2{}_1$, $P^2{}_2$, $P^2{}_3$, ..., $P^n{}_1$, $P^n{}_2$, $P^n{}_3$, ...
   Function names $f^0{}_1$, $f^0{}_2$, $f^0{}_3$, ..., $f^1{}_1$, $f^1{}_2$, $f^1{}_3$, ..., $f^m{}_1$, $f^m{}_2$, $f^m{}_3$, ...

BASIC DEFINITIONS:
   Term (inductive definition):
   (i) Every variable is a term,
   (ii) If f is an m-place function and t_1, ..., t_m are terms, then $f(t_1, ..., t_m)$ is a term.
   Atomic formula:
   If P is an n-place predicate and t_1, ..., t_n are terms,
   then $P(t_1, ..., t_n)$ is an atomic formula.
   (Well-formed) formula (inductive definition):
   1. Every atomic formula is a formula.
   2. If F is a formula, then $\neg F$ is a formula.
   3. If F and G are formulae, then $(F \wedge G)$, $(F \vee G)$, $(F \rightarrow G)$, and $(F \leftrightarrow G)$ are formulae.
   4. If F is a formula and x is a variable, then $\exists xF$ and $\forall xF$ are formulae.
   5. There are no other formulae than those generated by 1–4 above.

Figure 2.9 *A syntactic description of a predicate logic*

To provide a semantics for a (predicate calculus) language means to map the language constructs into some "reality". The first task in constructing a semantics is therefore to choose such a reality, commonly called a *universe of discourse (UoD)*. A UoD is defined as a set of objects—these objects could be people, buildings, numbers, or anything whatsoever. In the example of Figure 2.10, we depict a small UoD containing two cats and three mice.

Figure 2.10 *A universe of discourse*

The next step in providing a semantics is to give meanings to the constants and the predicate symbols of the language. The constants are mapped to objects in the UoD, while the predicate symbols are mapped to sets or relations in the UoD. The idea is that constants stand for individuals in the real world, while the predicate symbols represent properties of the individuals or relationships among them. In Figure 2.11, the constants Garfield and Tom denote cat objects, while Jerry, Gus, and Pete denote mouse objects. The predicate symbol Cat is mapped to a set of objects—the cats. Similarly, the predicate symbol Mouse is mapped to another set of objects—the mice. The predicate symbols Chases and Likes are mapped to different relations over the UoD, which are represented by arrows. In fact, we have now completely specified a semantics for the small predicate calculus language in Figure 2.11, because the meaning of all other expressions in the language can be computed by means of a small set of rules. These rules include rules 1 through 5 above that specify how to compute the truth values of sentences including connectives. In addition to these, we need a rule that states when atomic sentences are true. An atomic sentence consists of a predicate symbol followed by one or more constants (or variables) and is true if and only if the tuple of objects denoted by the constants (or variables) is an element of the set or relation that is the meaning of the predicate symbol. So, in our example, chases(Tom, Jerry) is true, whereas chases(Jerry, Tom) is false. Finally, we need rules that govern the quantifiers:

6. $\forall x F$ is true iff F is true for every assignment of an object in the UoD to x.
7. $\exists x F$ is true iff F is true for some assignment of an object in the UoD to x.

We will now illustrate how to find the meaning of a sentence in predicate calculus, using the following example:

$\forall x (\text{Cat}(x) \rightarrow (\text{Chases}(x, \text{Jerry}) \lor \text{Likes}(x, \text{Jerry})))$

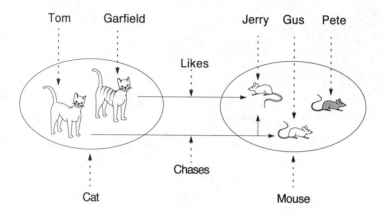

Figure 2.11 *Giving meaning to a language*

This sentence states that every cat chases or likes Jerry. In order to find the truth value of the sentence, we apply rule 6 above, which means that we must determine whether the sentence `Cat(x)` → (`Chases(x, Jerry)` ∨ `Likes(x, Jerry)`) is true for any assignment of an object in the UoD to x. We start by constructing the tree diagram for the sentence, see Figure 2.12. We then determine if this diagram yields a true sentence irrespective of which object we assign to x. As there are five objects in the UoD, we have to consider five versions of the tree diagram; these diagrams are shown in Figure 2.13. In each diagram, an object (a cat or a mouse) has been assigned to the variable x—this is shown with a dotted arrow. For each node in the diagrams, we have indicated its truth value. Note that all these truth values are computed using the rules introduced above. It turns out that the original sentence is true, as each diagram yields a true sentence.

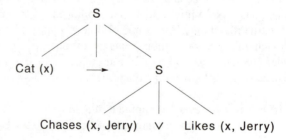

Figure 2.12 *A syntactical tree diagram*

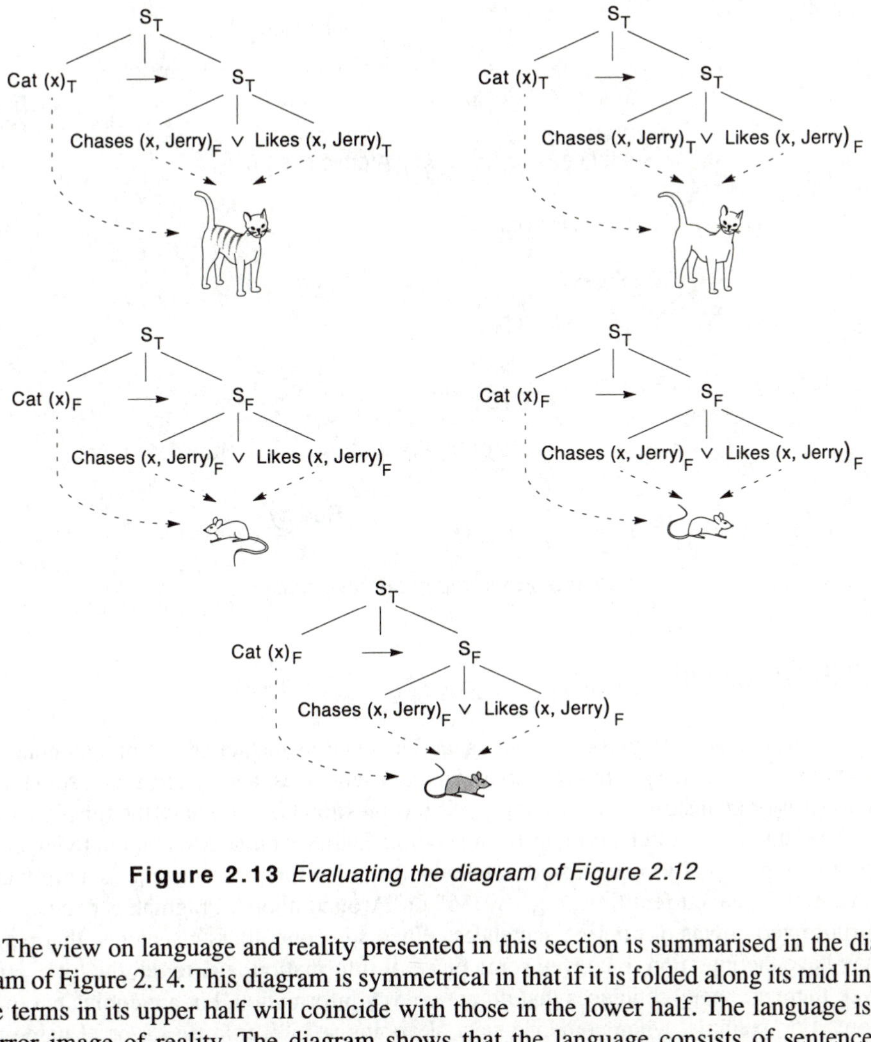

Figure 2.13 *Evaluating the diagram of Figure 2.12*

The view on language and reality presented in this section is summarised in the diagram of Figure 2.14. This diagram is symmetrical in that if it is folded along its mid line; the terms in its upper half will coincide with those in the lower half. The language is a mirror image of reality. The diagram shows that the language consists of sentences, where each sentence can be analysed into atomic sentences, and the meaning of a sentence can be derived from the meanings of its atomic sentences. The atomic sentences are built up by combinations of names (constants in the predicate calculus), which correspond to objects in the real world. The atomic sentences are images of facts, which are combinations of objects. The facts are combined into states of affairs, which together make up the reality.

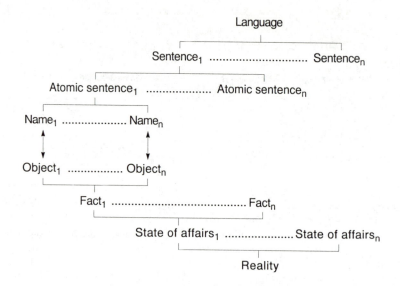

Figure 2.14 *Language and reality*

2.2.3   Pragmatics

Pragmatics is the third part of semiotics, and it concerns the actual use of a language by its speakers and listeners. In order to understand sentences, a syntactical and semantical analysis is often insufficient. An example is the question "Do you have the time, please?" A "Yes" answer would be correct from a syntactical as well as a semantical viewpoint, but not pragmatically correct, since we know that what the person wants as a reply is an indication of the current time, e.g. "11:56" or "Around noon". Pragmatics concerns the purpose and effects of uttering sentences. When someone utters a sentence that person may have the intention to convey some piece of information, e.g. to tell the time. However, there are many sentences that do not convey information, but are equivalent to actions. For example, when someone says "I apologise", "I promise...", or "I name this ship...", the utterance immediately conveys a new psychological or social reality. The utterance changes the world. An apology takes place only when someone admits to having been at fault, and a ship is named only when the act of naming is complete. In such cases, to speak is to perform. Statements such as those above are called *performatives,* or *speech acts*, and differ in many respects from statements that convey information, particularly in that performatives are neither true nor false. For example, if someone said "I name this ship...", it would be unreasonable to comment "That is not true".

In the analysis of speech acts, the effect of utterances on the behaviour of the speaker and listener is studied using a threefold distinction. First, we recognise the bare fact that a communicative act has taken place: the *locutionary* act. Secondly, we consider the act performed as a result of the speaker making an utterance: the *illocutionary* act, e.g. betting, welcoming, promising, or warning. Thirdly, we look at the particular effect the utterance has on the listener, who may feel amused, persuaded, or warned as a consequence. Inducing such effects is a *perlocutionary* act. Note that the illocutionary act of an utterance and its perlocutionary effect may not coincide. If someone is warned against a particular course of action, he or she may or may not heed the warning.

Speech acts can be divided into five different categories: assertives, commissives, directives, declaratives, and expressives. An *assertive* is a speech act, the purpose of which is to convey information about some state of affairs of the world from one agent, the speaker, to another, the hearer. Examples of assertives are "It is raining" and "The cat is on the mat". A *commissive* is a speech act, the purpose of which is to commit the speaker to carry out some action or to bring about some state of affairs. Examples of commissives are "I promise to be at home before nine o'clock" and "I swear to bring it back". A *directive* is a speech act, where the speaker requests the hearer to carry out some action or to bring about some state of affairs. Examples of directives are "Please bring me the salt" and "I order you to leave the room". A *declarative* is a speech act, where the speaker brings about some state of affairs by the mere performance of the speech act. Examples of declaratives are "I hereby pronounce you man and wife" and "I hereby baptise you Samuel". An *expressive* is a speech act, the purpose of which is to express the speaker's attitude about some state of affairs. An example of an expressive is "I do not like coffee".

Some speech acts like apologising, promising, and thanking can be performed by anyone, whereas others like baptising, arresting, and declaring war bear important restrictions, allowing only qualified people to perform them under suitable circumstances. Nowadays, even computer systems can be allowed to perform speech acts, e.g. granting parking permits, issuing passports, etc.

2.3 The Project of Formalisation

In addition to serving communicative purposes, language can also be used to support our faculties for reasoning. Whenever we think about a certain topic, language is one of the most effective vehicles for making our line of thought clear. Through the judicious use of language we can make an argument precise and explicit and check whether it is valid or not. Consider the following two examples of valid arguments:

Lucy will buy the house only if John likes it.
However, John does not like the house.
So, Lucy will not buy it.

The union will stop the strike only if the company starts to negotiate.
But the company will not start to negotiate.
So, the union will not stop the strike.

Note that the arguments above are valid by virtue of their form or pattern. To convince ourselves that the arguments are valid, we only need to study their forms; we do not need to make any empirical observations of John, Lucy, or unions. This means that we can determine whether the arguments are valid without understanding the meaning of the sentences. To see this clearly, consider the following example:

The clapyhedra will defect only if it can vrenculate.
But the clapyhedra cannot vrenculate.
So, the clapyhedra will not defect.

Although we cannot understand the sentences in this argument, we willingly accept it solely because of its form. All the arguments above have the following common form:

A only if B.
It is not the case that B.
So, it is not the case that A.

This is an example of an *argument-form*. It is the argument-form used in the arguments above, since these will result from replacing A and B with suitable phrases. Another example of an argument-form is

All F are G.
All G are H.
So, all F are H.

An instance of this argument-form is

All dogs are mammals.
All mammals are animals.
So, all dogs are animals.

In practice, when investigating the role of language in reasoning, especially the structure of valid arguments, researchers have proceeded by turning away from natural languages. They have chosen to construct and study artificial languages, like propositional logic or predicate logic. The reason for preferring artificial languages is that the sentences of natural languages like English do not adequately reflect the logical properties of the ideas they wish to express. A simple correspondence between the physical make-up of a sentence and the logical features of the idea it expresses would be the ideal situation, but natural languages seldom provide such a correspondence. In the rest of this section, we discuss ways in which natural language can obscure the logical features of arguments.

A salient feature of natural languages is the presence of *lexical ambiguity*. The same linguistic symbol can have many different meanings. Just check the entries of any dictionary, where there are several explanations for almost every word. This entails that the same sentence can be given different interpretations, as shown by the following example:

Waste fruit spoils.

This can be interpreted in the following ways: a statement meaning left over fruit goes bad; an incitement to throw away stolen fruit; a reference to a trophy for fruit grown in the desert; a statement meaning that fruit from the desert does not stay fresh very long; a statement meaning surplus produce goes bad; a number of combinations of these and other interpretations.

Lexical ambiguity can invalidate an argument which may seem valid if only its form is taken into consideration. An example of this is

A pencil is an article.
An article is a report.
So, a pencil is a report.

Some sentences are ambiguous, yet the ambiguity cannot be attributed to individual words in the sentences. In such cases, we say that the ambiguity is *structural,* not lexical. Here are some examples of structurally ambiguous sentences, taken from [Sainsbury91], with alternative interpretations given in brackets.

Harry is a dirty window cleaner.
[(a) Harry is a dirty cleaner of windows;
(b) Harry is a cleaner of dirty windows]

John and Mary are visiting friends.
[(a) John and Mary are visiting some people, and they are friends with these people;
(b) John and Mary are friends with one another, and they are visiting somewhere;
(c) John and Mary are visiting some people, and these people are friends with one another]

Bernard has written a book about everything.
[(a) Bernard has written a book, and it treats every subject;
(b) for every subject, Bernard has devoted at least one book to it]

The following example shows how structural ambiguity can make it impossible to decide if an argument is valid or not.

Logic, epistemology, and metaphysics are all the philosophical subjects there are. Bernard has written a book about logic. Bernard has written a book about epistemology. Bernard has written a book about metaphysics. Therefore, Bernard has written a book about every philosophical subject.

There is no simple answer to the question of whether this argument is valid or not. Its validity depends on how we interpret the conclusion, which is structurally ambiguous as explained in the previous example.

Another problem with natural languages is the presence of lexical and structural *redundancy.* Lexical redundancy occurs when different words denote the same object or idea; that is, when words are synonymous. The following example illustrates how lexical redundancy makes it more difficult to check the validity of an argument.

All boys are children.
Some lads are hungry.
So, some children are hungry.

Intuitively, we consider the argument above as valid, but we cannot decide its validity only by studying the form of the argument; we also need to know that the words "boys" and "lads" are synonymous.

Structural redundancy occurs when the same idea can be expressed by different sentences, even though they contain the same words. The following is an example of structural redundancy.

John gave the book to Mary.
The book was given to Mary by John.

Yet another problem with natural languages is that expressions of the same form can contribute in very different ways to the meanings of the sentences in which they occur. We would intuitively accept the following argument as valid.

Human beings are mortal.
Socrates is a human being.
So, Socrates is mortal.

We would also accept that the argument is valid by virtue of its form. It is an instance of the argument-form

F are G.
α is an F.
So, α is G.

It is tempting to believe that all instances of this argument-form are valid. However, this is not the case. The following example, also from [Sainsbury91], shows another instance of this argument-form.

Human beings are evenly distributed over the earth's surface.
Socrates is a human being.
So, Socrates is evenly distributed over the earth's surface.

The above examples illustrate how natural languages are inadequate for bringing out the logical properties of arguments, and why this makes them unsuitable for many tasks that involve logical reasoning. Natural language is particularly inappropriate for mechanical reasoning. If a machine is to test the validity of an argument, every logically relevant feature of that argument must be correlated with some property that is intrinsic to the physical appearance of the sentences in the argument. Since a correlation of this kind does not occur in natural languages, we must resort to artificial languages. Constructing artificial languages that explicitly represent the logical structure of reasoning has inspired a philosophical tradition called *philosophical logic*. The main thesis of this tradition is that the inherent structure of natural language, and of our thought, can only be adequately represented by an artificial language, such as predicate logic. The problem with this approach is how the results obtained for artificial languages can be applied to natural language and to our everyday thoughts. This question gives rise to a new task, the task of formalisation. The aim of formalisation is to reveal the logical form of natural sentences by pairing them with artificial ones. By pairing sentences, the validity obtained for the artificial language can be imposed on the natural one.

The following chapters introduce an artificial language and show how it can be used to create specifications for information systems. The main problem in using this language is not mastering its technical machinery, which is really quite simple, but transforming blurred and informal ideas into precise and formal sentences in the artificial language.

2.4 Classification and Abstraction

In perceiving the world, people constantly try to structure and organise their perceptions. There seem to be three basic ways in which people do this. First, reality is seen as consisting of distinct objects, such as stones and trees. These objects possess various properties, such as size and colour, and they may stand in different relationships to each other, such as one object being above or beneath another. Secondly, certain objects are seen to be composed of other objects, just as a tree may consist of roots, trunk, branches, leaves, and so on. Thirdly, objects that display sufficient similarities are grouped into classes. Often these classes are organised into hierarchies of subclasses and superclasses: for example, the class of mammals is a superclass of the class of dogs, but a subclass of the class of animals.

These modes of reasoning so pervade our manner of thought that making them explicit may seem trivial. It is therefore enlightening to realise that even in areas where reality cannot be naturally differentiated into separate objects and classes, people still try to impose such a structure upon it. An example of this is the colour spectrum. The spectrum is a continuous band, lacking any clear physical boundaries. In spite of this, we have divided it into distinct colours (blue, red, green, etc.), which we see as objects and to which we attribute properties, such as warm, cold, dark, and light. A more elaborate example of our inclination to structure the world and conceptualise it through objects is given in Example 2.2.

Example 2.2   A musical chord, e.g. $c \sim e \sim g$, is an acoustic phenomenon that is a uniform whole and is not composed of any constituents. However, for someone with a trained ear, it is virtually impossible to listen to a chord $c \sim e \sim g$ without conceiving the parts $c, e,$ and g. The sole reason for thinking of a chord in this way is its kinship with innumerable other chords already known to us. The chord $c \sim e \sim g$ is akin to all chords that can be produced by striking the key c and two other keys on a piano. Because of this kinship, we can also talk about chords being related to each other and classify them accordingly.

However, a person not acquainted with the musical tradition of the Western world cannot possibly comprehend the relationship between the theoretical structure and the physical experience of hearing a chord. The Eskimo scale has only five notes and they correspond only approximately to *f*, *g*, *b* flat, *d* flat, and *e* flat. To play Eskimo music properly on Western instruments is impossible.

How concepts of objects and classes are formed is a profound philosophical question, which has not received a satisfactory solution in spite of over two thousand years of enquiry. But these philosophical difficulties do not stop people from classifying; in fact, the ease with which people classify objects is remarkable. For example, a child forms the concept of dog having been exposed only to a few specimens of dog. Loosely speaking, classes seem to be formed by focusing on certain aspects of objects and disregarding others. For example, we can form the classes Englishman, Frenchman, Swede, ... by focusing solely on the nationality of people.

In scientific classification schemes, the boundaries of classes are usually clear cut; it is always apparent whether a given object belongs to a certain class or not. On the other hand, in natural language, we use words like "cup" and "glass", "hill" and "mountain", "stream" and "river", fairly indiscriminately without any clear boundaries. When does a stream become a river, or a hill a mountain? Similar problems surface with the design of information systems when a conceptual model is to be created. A blurred and enigmatic reality must be structured using the Procrustean concepts of objects, properties, and classes.

Language often strongly influences how we perceive reality and relate to it. To clarify this, let us compare how different languages impose structure on the same reality, as in Example 2.3.

Example 2.3   In the "real" world, fathers and mothers may have brothers and sisters. In English, there are no single words that express "mother's brother", "father's brother", "mother's sister", or "father's sister", so we have to use a circumlocution to make the distinction. In other languages, however, single words do make this distinction. In Swedish, for example: *farbror* means "father's brother"; *morbror*, "mother's brother"; *faster*, "father's sister"; and *moster*, "mother's sister". In the Australian language Pitjanjatjara: *mama* means "father's brother"; *kamuru*, "mother's brother"; *kurntili*, "father's sister"; and *ngunytju*, "mother's sister". There is also a complication (to the English way of thinking) in that *mama* also means "father", and *ngunytju* also means "mother". In Figure 2.15, the terminology of these three languages is summarised. We see that Swedish is the most precise, providing a separate word for each relationship. On the other hand, Swedish is the least economic language since it requires six words to describe the relationships, whereas the other languages make do with four. The choice between precision and economy is a frequently occurring dilemma when choosing a language for conceptual modelling.

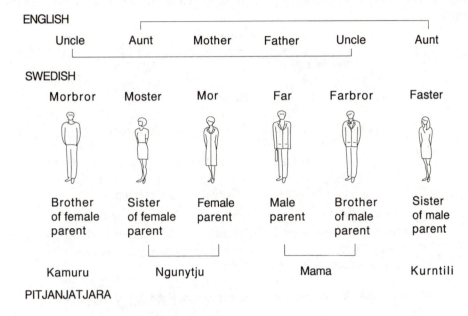

Figure 2.15 *Languages for kinship relations*

2.4.1   Abstraction Hierarchies

New concepts can be created by abstracting from existing ones. This means disregarding certain aspects of a concept in favour of others. Starting with the concept dog, we can disregard certain properties of dogs and arrive at the more abstract concept mammal, which in turn can be abstracted to animal, etc. Abstraction is often useful when given a large number of concepts with the aim of finding out what they have in common. To achieve this a new, more general concept than the previously given ones is constructed. For example, the concepts triangle, square, rectangle, pentagon, and hexagon can be abstracted to polygon. The more general concept is called a *generalisation* of the more specific one. Conversely, the more specific concept is called a *specialisation* of the more general one. So, mammal is a generalisation of dog and a specialisation of animal. Note that every property that can be attributed to a concept can also be attributed to a specialisation of it, but the opposite does not hold true. For instance, the properties weight, colour, and brain volume, which are relevant to mammals, are also relevant to dogs, but the property tail length which is relevant to dogs is not generally applicable to mammals.

A convenient way to describe a set of concepts and the relationships between them is to use an *abstraction hierarchy*. An abstraction hierarchy is a tree, in which the nodes are concepts and the branches describe generalisation relationships: the parent of a concept is a generalisation of that concept. This means that the root of an abstraction hierarchy represents the most abstract concept, and the leaves represent the most concrete, see Figure 2.16.

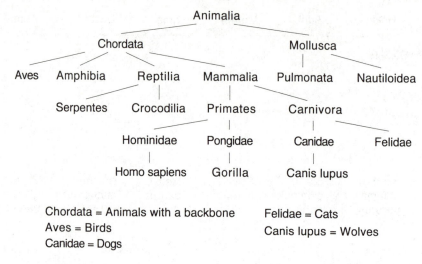

Chordata = Animals with a backbone   Felidae = Cats
Aves = Birds   Canis lupus = Wolves
Canidae = Dogs

Figure 2.16 *A small part of the classification of the Animal Kingdom*

In modelling, it is always possible to use different concepts and different classifications to describe the same piece of reality, and it therefore often becomes necessary to choose between classifications. It would be useful, when making such a choice, to have access to some general criteria for judging the quality of a classification. Regrettably, it seems impossible to find such criteria, even though, in certain cases, people easily agree as to whether a proposed classification is unnatural. See Figure 2.17 for a classical example of an entangled classification. For abstraction hierarchies, however, there is at least one generally accepted quality criterion: if we think of the nodes in an abstraction hierarchy as sets (cf. extension of expressions, above), it is required that the children of a given node should constitute a partition of it, i.e. the children should be mutually disjoint and jointly exhaustive.

In his essay "The Analytical Language of John Wilkins", Jorge Luis Borges mentions a Chinese encyclopedia, the *Celestial Emporium of Benevolent Knowledge:* "On these remote pages it is written that animals are divided into (a) those that belong to the Emperor, (b) embalmed ones, (c) those that are trained, (d) suckling pigs, (e) mermaids, (f) fabulous ones, (g) stray dogs, (h) those that are included in this classification, (i) those that tremble as if they were mad, (j) innumerable ones, (k) those drawn with a very fine camel's hair brush, (l) others, (m) those that have just broken a flower vase, (n) those that resemble flies from a distance."

Figure 2.17 *Another classification of the Animal Kingdom*

A common problem in practical modelling situations is that natural language does not always contain words for concepts at the appropriate level of abstraction. Often there are words for only very concrete concepts. A realistic illustration of this is the following.

Example 2.4   An industrial enterprise was planning the manufacture of its latest product: a new type of ventilation equipment, capable of performing many different functions. The equipment was expected to filter, dry, moisten, warm, and cool air. In an early phase of the modelling process, the project team agreed that the equipment consisted of three parts: a steel cover, an electrical component, and one or more components for performing the desired functions (filtering, drying, etc.). After this insight, however, the discussion ground to a halt. The problem was that no appropriate abstract term could be decided upon for the most important part of the product: the part performing the actual functions. The team could talk about filters, dryers, or coolers, but not about a more general concept. When they tried to explain what the general purpose of this part of the product was, they said things like "...a component for processing air...". This provided the clue for the term they sought: "Air Processing Component", abbreviated APC. Before long, people confidently used this new term and soon arrived at a consensus on the product structure.

2.4.2   Definitions

In order to communicate the meaning of symbols, people use definitions. A *definition* is a process, whether verbal or otherwise, by which one individual informs another individual about the meaning of a symbol. By the meaning of a symbol is meant its extension and/or intension. Thus, a definition states which concept and/or which objects a symbol refers to. Note that a definition always defines a symbol; it is not meaningful to talk about the definition of a concept or an object.

Definitions can be classified into two types, based on their purpose. First, there are *descriptive definitions* whose purpose is to explain the way in which some symbols have been or are used by some actual people. A descriptive definition is a form of history as it refers to the actual past. It tells what certain people meant by a certain symbol at a certain specified time and place. This means that a descriptive definition always involves three persons: first the definer who is explaining the meaning of the symbol, secondly the hearer to whom the meaning is defined, and thirdly the people who have used the symbol and thereby given it its meaning. This third person must always be there because the meaning of a symbol is what it means to some person or persons. So, when asking for a descriptive definition, one should not ask "What does this symbol mean?" but rather "What do (or did) certain persons use this symbol to mean?"

The second type of definitions consists of the *stipulative definitions* whose purpose is to set up, or legislate, the meaning of a symbol. People use stipulative definitions when they want to introduce a new symbol that has never been used before, or when they want to change temporarily the meaning of an established symbol. When someone makes a stipulative definition, that person chooses the meaning of the symbol and does not record its previous use. A stipulative definition, therefore, involves only two persons: the definer who assigns a meaning to the symbol and the hearer to whom the meaning is defined. There is no third person involved as in a descriptive definition. So, when asking for a stipulative definition, the correct question is neither "What does this symbol mean?" nor "What do these people mean by this symbol?" but "What have you decided this symbol to mean?"

Definitions can be classified not only according to their purpose but also according to their method. By the method of a definition is meant the means by which it achieves its purpose. A simple method of definition is the *synonyms method*, which consists in giving the learner a synonym with which he or she is already familiar; that is to say, in telling the learner that the symbol being defined means the same as some familiar symbol. For example, "chat" means cat. Another method of definition is the *method of analysis* (also known as Aristotle's method of defining by genus and differentia), which defines the thing meant by a symbol by giving an analysis of it. For example, the word "rectangle" means a polygon with four sides. To specify what object (or concept) a symbol means, one names a bigger class within which the object falls, and then names something that distinguishes it from the rest of that class. For example, if man falls within the bigger class of animal, and is distinguished from all other animals by rationality, then the word "man" can be defined as meaning the rational animal. Still another method of definition is the *synthetic method*, which defines a symbol by indicating the relation of the thing it means to other things. An example of the synthetic method is: the word "feuillemorte" means the colour of withered leaves in the autumn. A particular colour is defined here by mentioning where it can be found; no synonym is given, nor is the colour analysed. The thing meant is assigned to its place in a system of relations, synthesised into a whole with other things. Whereas the analytic method indicates the thing meant by showing it as a whole consisting of parts, the synthetic method does so by showing the thing as a part of a whole.

All the methods of definition in the preceding paragraph have the common feature that they define a word in terms of other words; they are therefore named *verbal methods*. They presuppose that the learner already knows some other words and, thus, they are useless to someone who does not know these words; in particular they are useless to a small child who has not learnt any words at all. There must therefore be another method of definition, which can dispense with words altogether. This method is called the *ostensive method*, and it consists in presenting a concrete example to the learner. For example, the word "rose" can be defined by pointing to a rose and saying "that is a rose".

We also need to explain *inductive* and *recursive* definitions. An inductive definition often defines infinite sets, as in Figure 2.5. In short, given a basic case and a case n, an inductive step (a kind of generalisation) is taken to the case $n + 1$, which is proved using the case n, and so the definition holds for any n. A recursive definition begins by giving an object belonging to the class to be defined, and then specifies a procedure for generating the rest of the elements in the class. Given that the set of positive integers has been ordered in an ascending sequence, we can use recursion to determine whether an integer x is higher than another integer y in the sequence: $x > y$ if (i) x is the integer immediately following y in the sequence, or (ii) x is higher than the successor of y. For example, the integer 4 is higher than 3, since case (i) applies, and 5 is also higher than 3, since 5 is higher than the successor of 3, i.e. 4, matching case (ii), and 5 is the successor of 4.

2.5 Some Relevant Literature

A general textbook on linguistics is [Fromkin83]. A more easy-going, yet thorough, introduction to language is given in the comprehensive encyclopaedia [Crystal88]. A very readable introduction to modern linguistics is [Pinker94]. A lucid introduction to the philosophy of language can be found in [Devitt87]. [Linsky70] is a collection of a number of classical papers on the philosophy of language. Much of the theoretical basis of conceptual modelling stems from modern analytical philosophy; the classical work here is [Wittgenstein61], another influential text is [Carnap67], and a collection of important papers on logical positivism is [Hanfling81]. The works of Frege and many of his contemporaries are beautifully explained in [vanHeijenoort67], while a large collection of Tarski's writings can be found in the volume [Tarski93]. Two recent textbooks on philosophical logic with a special eye on linguistics are [Sainsbury91] and [Gamut91]. A comprehensive overview of the area of philospohical logic is given in [Gabbay84]. The basic philosophical and linguistic assumptions put forth in this chapter have not gone unchallenged; a strongly argued critique of these assumptions is given in [Winograd87]. Most of the definitions in this chapter are standard ones from philosophy or linguistics, and so they can be found in numerous dictionaries, e.g. [Speake79]. A good mathematical textbook on formal languages is [Lewis81].

2.6 Exercises

2.1   Give an example of two different expressions, both of which have the empty set as their extension, but have different intensions.

2.2   In the novel *Crome Yellow*, Aldous Huxley's character Old Rowley says: "Look at them, sir, rightly are they called 'pigs'", pointing to some swine wallowing in the mud. Explain why Old Rowley has not understood anything about the arbitrariness of language.

2.3   Analyse the proverb "Forbidden fruit is the tastiest" by comparing illocutionary and perlocutionary effect in the context of prohibitions.

2.4   One suggested criterion of a declarative speech act is whether you can begin it with "I hereby". If you say sentence a) aloud, it sounds like a genuine apology, but sentence

b) sounds funny because you cannot perform an act of knowing.
  a) I hereby apologise to you.
  b) I hereby know you.
Test the following sentences to see if they are declaratives by inserting hereby. Those that sound "right" are declaratives.
  c) I testify that she met the agent.
  d) I know that she met the agent.
  e) I suppose the Yankees will win.
  f) I dismiss the class.
  g) I teach the class.
  h) I swore I didn't do it.
  i) I swear I didn't do it.

2.5   For each of the following sentences, determine whether it is extensional:
  a) Walter Scott is the author of *Ivanhoe*.
  b) I do not know whether Walter Scott is the author of *Ivanhoe*.
  c) Long John is called so because of his length.

2.6   Suppose a couple are sitting in a car. The man keeps complaining that it is too cold in the car. The woman replies.
  a) The heater are on.
  b) The steering wheel is old.
  c) The mat has eaten the cat.
Which of the following faults are true of the woman's three replies?
  1. syntactically incorrect,
  2. semantically incorrect,
  3. pragmatically incorrect.

2.7   Let *L* be a language. Suppose that each word in *L* is defined by a verbal definition, constructed with words from *L*. Explain why at least one of the definitions must be circular.

2.8   Construct an abstraction hierarchy, with a least one path that contains four arcs. It should contain the following concepts: apple, penguin, rose, book, carrot.

2.9   Is it possible for an ambiguous word to occur in an unambiguous sentence?

2.10   If any of the following is ambiguous, provide unambiguous paraphrases of the alternative interpretations:
  a) Every man loves a woman.
  b) Time flies like an arrow.
  c) In the whole wide world, Don Camino was the only person who knew where he was.

2.11 The example below is taken from the television comedy series *Benson*. The following conversation takes place when Benson, a black man, attends an otherwise all-white gathering. He is addressed by the hostess:

> Hostess: "How do you like your coffee, black?"
> Benson: "Us niggers do have names, ma'am."

Explain why this joke illustrates a shortcoming of the compositionality principle. Discuss what types of knowledge are needed to understand the joke.

2.12 Consider the next two sentences:

  a) The headmaster said "Unless those convoys of lorries are stopped, a child is going to get killed".
  b) The terrorists said "Unless those convoys of lorries are stopped, a child is going to get killed".

These two sentences have an identical syntactical structure. In spite of this, the speech acts performed by the headmaster and the terrorists are very different. Explain the different senses of "is going to get killed" and discuss what types of knowledge are needed in order to remove ambiguity from these sentences, changing the verb phrase accordingly.

2.13 Describe a simple predicate logic with only three symbols, each representing the variables, constants, unary functions, monadic predicates, and binary predicates, as a grammar. Use the adequate set of connectives $\{\neg, \rightarrow\}$ and both quantifiers.

2.14 In propositional logic, it is possible to define all connectives in terms of only two of them, e.g. $\neg$ and $\rightarrow$. In the first years of the twentieth century, it was shown that even a single connective could do the job. One that will do is *Sheffer's stroke*, or *nand*, written $|$, as in $A|B$, and read "not both A and B are true". Working with propositional logic, one is free to choose a (so-called adequate) set of connectives, like $\{\neg, \rightarrow\}$ or $\{\neg, \wedge\}$, using which all propositional sentences can be expressed. Explain why $\{|\}$ is an extremely unpopular adequate set, in spite of its simplicity.

CHAPTER 3

Modelling Concepts

An effective approach to analysing and understanding a complex phenomenon is to create a model of it. By a *model* is meant a simple and familiar structure or mechanism that can be used to interpret some part of reality. Typical examples of models are maps, sets of differential equations, and miniature replicas. The purpose of a model is to make it possible to learn things about reality by analysing the model instead of observing reality directly. Using a map, we can find the distance between two cities instead of measuring along the Earth's surface. A model is always easier to study than the phenomenon it models, because it captures just a few of the aspects of the phenomenon. A map of the world, for instance, may focus on either the political or the topographical properties of the Earth. In this chapter, we shall study modelling concepts that are useful in constructing models for information systems.

When creating a model, it is essential to clarify what part of reality is to be described. Knowing exactly what to model is seldom obvious at the beginning of the modelling process. A conscious effort must therefore be made to decide what parts and what aspects of the real world to describe. Which aspects of reality to focus on is determined by the anticipated use of the model. We shall refer to that part of reality for which a model is to be created by the term *object system*. A synonym for "object system" is UoD (Universe of Discourse).

An object system may be described in natural language. However, as pointed out in Section 2.3, descriptions in natural language suffer from such shortcomings as ambiguity and redundancy. To avoid the deficiencies of natural language, we shall focus on formal and structured description languages when modelling an object system. Recall that a language is formal if it has a grammar specifying which sentences belong to the language and which do not. A language is *structured* if a certain fact about the real world can be expressed in the language in only one way, or (exceptionally) in a very small number of ways. In the latter case the equivalence between formulae that express the same fact must be explicitly stated.

The following sections introduce a number of basic modelling concepts, which can be used to create formal and structured descriptions of a UoD. Also discussed, though in an informal way, are various notations for such descriptions, both textual and graphical. Chapter 5 more formally introduces a language for conceptual modelling.

3.1 Objects and Classification

3.1.1 Objects and Attributes

In conceptual modelling, the object is the basic modelling construct around which all other modelling constructs are defined. An *object* is a thing or phenomenon in the real world. Objects can be concrete, such as trees, people, cars, and buildings, or they can be abstract, like numbers, integrals, symphonies, and diseases. We shall sometimes use the term *entity* as a synonym for "object".

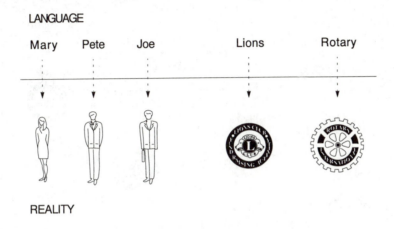

Figure 3.1 *Objects and object identifiers*

In order to reason about an object system, we need linguistic symbols that can be used to refer to particular objects; such symbols are called *object identifiers*. Their purpose is to provide handles to the objects in an object system. Some objects and their object identifiers are depicted in Figure 3.1, where the fact that a certain object identifier denotes a certain object is represented by a dotted arrow. The figure emphasises the distinction between language and reality: the objects belong to the object system (a part of reality), whereas the object identifiers belong to the language used in reasoning about the object system.

Objects do not exist in isolation, but are related to each other through various kinds of associations. Examples of such associations are one person being married to another, or a person being a member of a club. In order to represent associations, we need linguistic symbols for denoting them; such symbols are called *attributes*. Some examples of attributes are MARRIED TO and IS MEMBER OF. To represent a particular association between two objects, the corresponding object identifiers are tied together by means of an attribute. An example is Pete MARRIED TO Mary, which states that Pete is married to

Mary. The expression `Pete MARRIED TO Mary` is an example of an attribute statement, and the object identifiers `Pete` and `Mary` are called arguments. An *attribute statement* is defined as the composition of an attribute and two object identifiers, and it denotes how the two corresponding objects are associated with each other. In the context of an attribute statement the object identifiers are referred to as *arguments*. Note that the order of the arguments in an attribute statement usually affects the meaning of the statement; `John LOVES Mary` does not mean the same as `Mary LOVES John`.

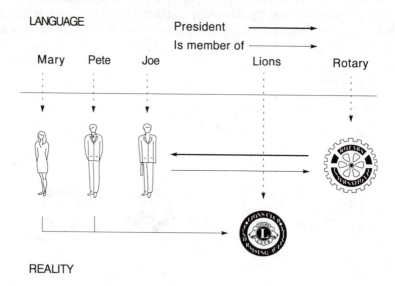

Figure 3.2 *Objects and attributes*

Example 3.1   In natural language, the associations in the object system depicted in Figure 3.2 could be described as follows. The person Mary is a member of Lions, as is Pete. Joe is a member of Rotary and he is also its president. Using some quasi natural language notation, the associations can be described by the following attribute statements:

```
Mary IS_MEMBER_OF Lions
Pete IS_MEMBER_OF Lions
Joe IS_MEMBER_OF Rotary
Rotary PRESIDENT Joe
```

In a Prolog-style notation (cf. Appendix 5) we would write:

```
is_member_of(mary, lions).        is_member_of(pete, lions).
is_member_of(joe, rotary).        president(rotary, joe).
```

Objects may have properties, such as a car being red, a person being tall, or a trip being long. Properties of objects can also be modelled by attributes. For instance, the fact that a person has a certain salary can be seen as an association between the person and an integer. The example below illustrates how properties are represented by attribute statements.

Example 3.2   We continue the previous example by considering some properties of the objects. Suppose Joe's salary is 12,000, Pete's is 11,000, and Mary's 14,000. In a Prolog-style notation these facts are represented by the following attribute statements:

```
earns(joe, 12000).
earns(pete, 11000).
earns(mary, 14000).
```

It is often convenient to talk about the *value* of an attribute. Consider an attribute statement A(O1, O2), where A is an attribute, and O1 and O2 are object identifiers. We then say that the *value* of attribute A for object O1 is O2. In the example above, we would say that the value of the attribute salary for joe is 12000.

3.1.2   Types and Classes

Objects judged as being similar to one another in some respect are often grouped together, and are said to belong to the same category or class. To represent categories, we need linguistic symbols for denoting them; such symbols are called *types*. Some examples of types are PERSON, COMPANY, CAR, and CITY. In order to represent that a particular object belongs to a certain category, we use a *type statement*, which consists of a type and an object identifier, called the *argument* of the type statement. An example of a type statement is John PERSON, where John is an object identifier and PERSON a type. We shall often use the term *instance*, and given a type statement we say that the argument is an instance of the type. For the example above, we would say that the object identifier John is an instance of the type PERSON. In the following, we shall use *object type* as a synonym for type.

Example 3.3   It seems natural to divide the objects in Figure 3.2 into two categories: persons and clubs. In Prolog-style notation we would represent the classification of the objects by the following type statements:

```
person(joe).          person(mary).          person(pete).
club(lions).          club(rotary).
```

To summarise, we regard an object system as consisting of a set of objects. These objects belong to different categories, have several distinct properties, and are associated with each other in various ways. The objects populating the world are neither unchanging nor immortal. They are born at certain points in time; they acquire properties and lose them; they connect and disconnect in relationships with other objects; and eventually they die. It can be helpful to think of a continuously changing object system as a series of snapshots. Each snapshot, or *state,* consists of a set of objects with properties and relationships with each other at a certain point in time. An object system does not remain in the same state for ever but changes from state to state as time passes. That which causes one state to change into another is called an *event*. An event occurs at a specific point in time and introduces new objects, properties, and relationships, or removes them. Some examples of events are weddings, bank transactions, and sales.

In order to describe a state of an object system, we use a *state description*, which consists of a set of type and attribute statements. The *extension of a type* in a certain state is the set of all object identifiers that are instances of the type in the corresponding state description. The *extension of an attribute* in a certain state is the set of all pairs of object identifiers, connected to each other by the attribute in the corresponding state description.

Example 3.4   If Figure 3.2 is regarded as depicting a state, then the set of the following type and attribute statements constitutes the corresponding state description:

```
person(joe).                is_member_of(joe, rotary).
person(pete).               is_member_of(pete, lions).
person(mary).               is_member_of(mary, lions).
club(lions).                president(rotary, joe).
club(rotary).
```

The extension of the type `person` in the state is {`joe`, `pete`, `mary`}, the extension of `club` is {`lions`, `rotary`}, the extension of the attribute `is_member_of` is {⟨`joe`, `rotary`⟩, ⟨`pete`, `lions`⟩, ⟨`mary`, `lions`⟩}, and the extension of `president` is {⟨`rotary`, `joe`⟩}.

In most cases, an attribute cannot connect objects of arbitrary types. As an example, consider an attribute `president`, used to represent clubs having presidents. If the object identifiers `joe` and `pete` denote persons and `rotary` and `lions` denote clubs, then the statement `president(rotary, joe)` is a meaningful statement expressing that a certain club has a certain person as its president. However, the following attribute statements would not be reasonable: `president(joe, rotary)`, `president(lions, rotary)`, `president(joe, pete)`. The reason for not allowing these statements is that persons cannot have clubs as presidents, clubs cannot be presidents of other clubs, and people cannot be presidents of other persons. These restrictions can be summarised by requiring that for every attribute statement involving `president`, its first argument must be an instance of CLUB and its second argument must be an instance of PERSON. Generalising the observations above, we see that an attribute can only connect arguments of certain types. If the first argument of an attribute A is always required to be an instance of the type D, then D is said to be the *domain* of A; if the second argument of A is always required to be an instance of the type R, then R is said to be the *range* of A. In the preceding example, CLUB is the domain of `president`, and PERSON is its range.

It is often valuable to obtain an overview of what kinds of attribute statements can be made in a language. One way to obtain this is by using type descriptions. A *type description* of a type T specifies each attribute that has T or a supertype of T as its domain (supertypes are described in Section 3.1.4). Furthermore, the range for each attribute is specified. An attractive feature of type descriptions is that they can easily be represented graphically. Two simple type descriptions are shown in Figure 3.3 (cf. Figure 3.2); each type name is written inside an ellipse, and each attribute name is written beside an arrow pointing from the domain of the attribute to the range. Using the terminology introduced above, the figure expresses that the domain of the attribute president is CLUB and its range is PERSON, whereas the domain of is_member_of is PERSON and its range is CLUB.

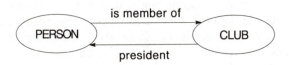

Figure 3.3 *Graphical representation of a type description*

Sometimes it is useful to be able to talk about the set of all object identifiers that are, have been, or will possibly become instance s of a certain type. Recall that an object system exists over an extended period of time, and that during this time it repeatedly changes from state to state. In this context, the *class* of a type is used to mean the union of the extensions of the type in all the states of the object system during its lifetime .

3.1.3   Lexical and Non-lexical Objects

The subject matter of object systems may vary widely, and the kinds of objects encountered in one system can be utterly different from those in another system. However, certain objects seem to occur in virtually all object systems. These objects are the numbers and the strings. They are so ubiquitous because they are used for naming, describing, and measuring other objects, activities that are required in modelling any system. For example, a string can be used to denote a person's name or address and an integer can indicate an employee's salary. Numbers and strings are called *lexical objects* (or *data values),* all other objects being *non-lexical objects.* Accordingly, we divide types into lexical and non-lexical types, where all instances of a lexical (non-lexical) type denote lexical (non-lexical) objects. Finally, an attribute is lexical if its range is lexical.

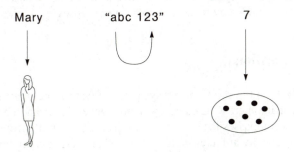

Figure 3.4 *Lexical and non-lexical objects*

An important feature of lexical objects is the existence of established and universally accepted linguistic symbols for denoting them. For numbers we use the well-known decimal system, based on the characters of the Arabic alphabet. Where strings are concerned, the situation is even simpler because strings are linguistic objects and are commonly included in the language used to model an object system. Consequently, strings simply denote themselves. Figure 3.4 shows two lexical objects and one non-lexical, together with the linguistic symbols used to denote them (the number 7 is a most abstract object, and hence its pictorial representation should not be taken too seriously). Note that strings can also contain digits, e.g. "abc123". It is often useful to introduce types whose extensions are strict subsets of lexical objects, such as "Article-code", instances of which should be strings of, say, at most four characters.

Another characteristic of lexical objects is that we do not usually make statements *about* them; they are only used to describe other objects. However, this distinction is not always true. Consider for example a mathematician's or an etymologist's database, where statements about numbers and strings are prevalent.

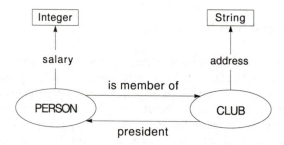

Figure 3.5 *Graphical representation of lexical types*

The distinction between lexical and non-lexical objects is so important that we make it explicit in the graphical representation. Figure 3.5 shows a type description, where the lexical types are surrounded by rectangles instead of ellipses.

3.1.4   Generalisation

When classifying the entities in an object system, it often turns out that certain categories are more general than others. One category is more general than another if the extension of that category encompasses the extension of the other, and if all properties relevant to the more general category are relevant also to the other. VEHICLE, for example, is a more general category than CAR, since every car is a vehicle, and every property relevant to vehicles is also relevant to cars. To represent this kind of relationship between categories, we introduce the concept of a generalisation relationship between types. A type G is a *generalisation* of a type S if the following two conditions are satisfied:

1. In any state, the extension of S is a subset of the extension of G.
2. The type description of G is included in the type description of S.

If G is a generalisation of S, we say that S is a *specialisation* of G, that S is a *subtype* of G, and that G is a *supertype* of S. In a graphical representation, generalisation is shown by a dotted arrow, labelled "ISA", pointing from the subtype to the supertype, see Figure 3.6.[1]

Example 3.5   Figure 3.6 shows the type CAR as a subtype of the type VEHICLE. VEHICLE is conversely a supertype of CAR. CAR is a specialisation of VEHICLE, and VEHICLE is conversely a generalisation of CAR. The type description of VEHICLE contains the following three attributes (with domains and ranges specified):

Attribute	Domain	Range
reg_no	vehicle	string
weight	vehicle	integer
owned_by	vehicle	person

The type description of CAR contains the following five attributes; note that three of them are inherited from VEHICLE:

Attribute	Domain	Range
weight	vehicle	integer
owned_by	vehicle	person
horsepower	car	integer
reg_no	vehicle	string
driven_by	car	person

---

1) Some authors reserve the label "ISA" for instantiations and instead use the label "A KIND OF" where we use "ISA".

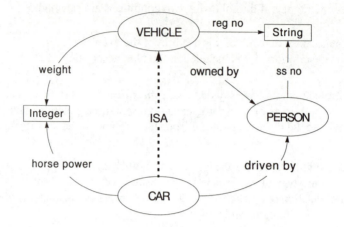

Figure 3.6 *An example of generalisation*

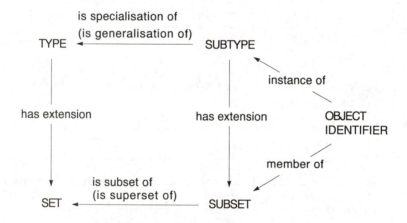

Figure 3.7 *Relationships between types and sets*

If a type s is a subtype of another type g, we say that s *inherits* the attributes belonging to (the type description of) g. This way of speaking emphasises the idea that a subtype is derived from a supertype; the subtype inherits all the attributes of the supertype, and in addition it acquires some new ones. In Figure 3.6, CAR inherits reg_no, weight and owned_by from VEHICLE. Notice that in the graphical representation the attributes of CAR inherited from VEHICLE do not have to be shown by arrows pointing from CAR; it is sufficient that they are displayed emanating from VEHICLE. This use of inheritance is warranted for the same reasons as in object-oriented programming in that it modularises code and allows for code reuse.

There are some simple relationships between types and sets, where subtypes correspond to subsets and instantiation to set membership; these relationships are summarised in Figure 3.7. Arrow labels in parentheses specify the meaning of the inverse arrow (cf. Figure 3.8 which shows a concrete example of Figure 3.7). The figure should be read as, for example, MAN is a specialisation of PERSON.

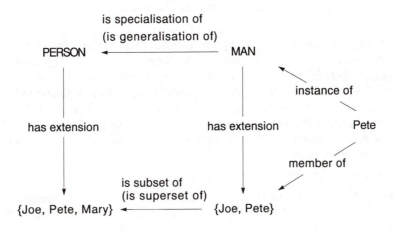

Figure 3.8 *An example of relationships between types and sets*

3.2 Time and Events

In this section, we shall outline how to model the behavioural aspects of an object system. As pointed out in Section 3.1.2, an object system is normally not static but is continually subject to changes; objects are born and die, and their properties and relationships to each other change as time passes. When modelling an object system it is therefore not sufficient to describe only its static aspects; it is essential also to model the dynamic aspects of the system. Dynamics means change over time, and we will therefore begin by recalling some basic mathematical characteristics of time.

Our point of departure will be that time can be thought of as a sequence of points, where the distance between two consecutive points is constant. We further assume the existence of a calendar for specifying each point in time, such as the traditional Gregorian calendar with years, months, days, etc. An illustration of this view of time is shown in Figure 3.9, where the distance between two consecutive points in time is one day. We assume that events can be associated with a specific point in time, and thereby receive a time stamp within the bounds of the calendar. This view of time is simplified in two important ways.

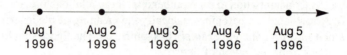

Aug 1   Aug 2   Aug 3   Aug 4   Aug 5
1996   1996   1996   1996   1996

Figure 3.9 *Time's arrow*

The first simplification is the assumption that each event can be associated with an absolute time point in a calendar. For most administrative and technical object systems this is a reasonable assumption, but there are cases where this does not hold true, e.g. medical information systems. In such a system, a patient's account of an illness may contain many statements that are ordered chronologically. The patient will probably be unable to remember the precise dates of symptoms, but may remember their order in time. In other words, the patient cannot associate the events with absolute points in time, but may be able to provide their relative order.

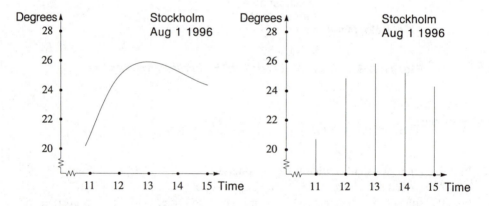

Figure 3.10 *Continuous time*   **Figure 3.11** *Discrete time*

The second simplification is the assumption of a discrete time structure. For each point in time we assume there is a unique "next" point in time that directly follows it. To express this more precisely, for each point T1 on the time scale there is a unique point T2, such that T1 < T2, and there is no point T3 such that T1 < T3 < T2. In some contexts this is an unnatural conceptualisation, and it may be more natural to view the set of points in time as a continuum, i.e. for any two distinct points in time T1 and T2 with T1 < T2, there is always a third point in time T3 between T1 and T2; that is, T1 < T3 < T2. The temperature during a day is depicted in Figure 3.10, based on the view of time as a continuum, while Figure 3.11 gives a corresponding representation of the temperature, but based on a discrete time structure. In this example, the continuous representation may seem to be the most attractive, since it provides temperatures for an infinite set of points in time, whereas the discrete representation only shows temperatures for a small number of points in time. However, the discrete representation can be improved by shortening the distance between two consecutive points in time. Instead of hours we could have chosen minutes, seconds, or even fractions of seconds. The suitability of the chosen scale depends on the object system in question. For a banking system the appropriate scale may be one day, whereas a system at a nuclear power plant may require a fraction of a second.

3.2.1   A Conceptual Model of Time

To conclude the discussion in the previous section we provide here a simple conceptual model of time. Utterances often contain references to time points or time periods. As indicated in the previous section, those references can be absolute or relative, and more or less exact. Some examples are:

1. Just now there is a great demand for personal computers
2. Prices will soon rise again
3. The first time I met you
4. The first day of next month
5. Each Friday afternoon
6. During spring
7. The winter 1975
8. 1982-04-20 23:53:37
9. When Charlie was fired
10. Before Tom was born and after our wedding

Some of those time references are hardly possible to formalise, e.g. 2. Some, e.g. 1 and 6, are imprecise. As mentioned previously, reasoning about more or less indeterminate temporal intervals may be of interest in certain types of applications. Historical information is often of this kind. In normal business contexts we are, on the other hand, used to dealing more exactly with time points and intervals. For this we will now introduce a simple model of time, i.e. a calendar system. Our model of time (see Figure 3.12) comprises two main object types:

1. The object type `time_point`, the instances of which correspond to points in time chosen to some preferred granularity, e.g. ms.
2. The object type `time_interval` with subtypes `second`, `minute`, `hour`, `day`, `week`, `month`, and `year`, the instances of which correspond to those regular intervals in the real world. In this case `second` has been chosen as the interval with the shortest duration. This choice is, however, application dependent.

Time points are related to the second during which they occur, as seconds are related to the minute to which they belong, etc. Furthermore, time points are ordered by means of the attribute `precedes`. The set of time points is finite, i.e. there is a first and a last time point. In consequence, the attribute `precedes` is partial since no time points precede the first one.

Time intervals are related to the time points at which they start and end. Each time point and time interval of the mentioned types is numbered according to some calendar system. In other words, the instances of those types correspond to calendar seconds, minutes, etc. In order to keep the model finite, we do not allow arbitrary time intervals, such as a month from now, etc.

A date can be constructed by combining `year_no`, `month_no`, and `day_no`. In addition to this, `day` is, for practical reasons, also related to a complete date of the form YYM-MDD by the attribute `dt`. As a matter of fact, a number of such date attributes, corresponding to the various day numbering schemes used throughout the world, may be needed.

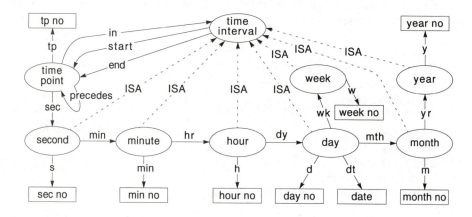

Figure 3.12 *A conceptual model of time*

To keep the model simple, `precedes` is the only attribute expressing relative time reference. However, attributes `before` and `after` can easily be derived for time points as well as time intervals by means of the attributes `precedes`, `start`, and `end`. Also other attributes expressing relative time can be derived in similar ways. Furthermore, the attributes `in`, `sec`, `min`, etc., can also be derived from `precedes`, `start`, and `end`.

3.2.2   State Changes and Event Types

Based on a conception of a discrete time structure, it is natural to view the evolution of an object system as a series of state changes. Recall that the state of an object system was defined as the set of objects occurring in the system at a certain point in time, including the properties of the objects and their relationships to each other. Thus, a state can be thought of as a snapshot of the object system at a particular point in time. An object system does not normally remain in a single state for its entire life span. At certain points in time it changes from one state into another, and when that happens, we say that a *state change* occurs. That which causes a state change is called an *event*. We take the view that an event is not extended over time, but that it occurs at a specific point in time and does not extend for any length of time.

Example 3.6   Examples of events:

1. Mary S. marries Peter R. at 960810.
2. Mary S. joins Rotary at 960705.
3. Mary S. joins Lions at 960705.
4. John C. joins Rotary at 960305.
5. Mary S. leaves Rotary at 970705.
6. John C. is elected president of Rotary at 960811.

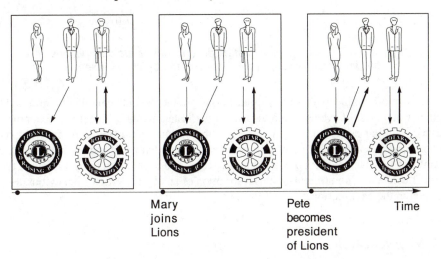

| Mary joins Lions | | Pete becomes president of Lions | Time |

Figure 3.13 *A sequence of states (states shown inside boxes, events represented by filled circles)*

At each point in time there are two alternatives for an object system: either nothing happens and the system remains in the same state as before, or an event occurs, causing the system to change from one state into another. The object system will then stay in its new state for some period of time, until a new event occurs, prompting the system into yet another state. This process continues until the system has reached the end of its life span. This view of the behaviour of an object system is illustrated in Figure 3.13. Note that states persist over periods of time, whereas events occur at specific points in time.

For each state of an object system, there is a corresponding state description. If we think of the life span of an object system as a sequence of states separated by events, we find a corresponding sequence of state descriptions. This point of view is depicted in Figure 3.14, which represents the events of Figure 3.13.

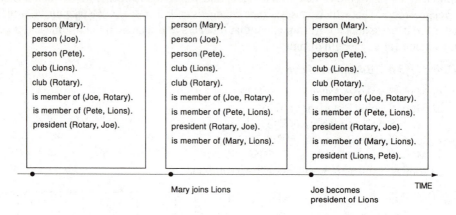

Figure 3.14 *A sequence of state descriptions (state descriptions shown inside boxes, events represented by filled circles)*

As with other objects that are similar to one another, events can also be grouped together. Categories of events are called *event types*. Statements 2, 3, and 4 in Example 3.6 describe similar events, namely joining a club, which is an example of an event type. Other examples are the hiring of an employee, the depositing of money into a bank account, the marriage of a couple, and the departure of a train. The concept of event types is an effective tool for structuring the description of an object system's behaviour, as will be seen in the next section.

3.2.3   Event Rules

A major problem with modelling the dynamics of an object system is to find a structured way of specifying changes between state descriptions. In order to handle this problem we make the simplifying assumption that there is a finite set of event types, such that every possible event in the object system can be seen as an occurrence of exactly one of these event types.[2] The problem is now reduced to that of modelling event types.

We will describe event types by means of *event rules*, which are functions that map state descriptions into state descriptions. In order to motivate this point of view, we first

---

2) That this is indeed a significant simplification can be seen by comparing it with the discussion in Section 4.4 below.

informally discuss an example. Consider an event type "Increase salary". When an event of this type occurs, a person's salary will be increased by a specified percentage. To describe this event type, we need certain information. First, we must be able to refer to the person whose salary is to be increased. This, we assume, can be done with a social security number. Secondly, we must specify the positive integer signifying the percentage by which the salary will be increased. Thirdly, we need to know the present state of the object system, and in particular the person's present salary. This information allows us to infer the state description of the state obtained after an occurrence of an event of type "Increase salary". This inferential ability means that the event rule for this event type can be seen as a function:

"Increase salary": $SD \times \text{String} \times \text{Integer} \to SD,$

where SD is the set of all possible state descriptions of the object system in question. So, the function takes as arguments a state description, a string containing a social security number, and an integer signifying the percentage increase. The function then yields a new state description, which will be identical to the previous one, except that it specifies a different salary for the person who has received a raise.

Generalising the example above, we claim that any event rule can be thought of as a function. The domain and range of different event rules may vary. The signature of an event rule has the form

"Event type X": $SD \times T_1 \times ... \times T_m \to SD,$

where SD is as above, and $T_1, ... ,T_m$ are types. (In the example, $T_1 = \text{String}$, and $T_2 = \text{Integer}$.)

When an event occurs in an object system, only a minor part of the present state is changed. This observation suggests that it is a good idea to describe the effect of an event by specifying the (small) differences between the state before the event and the state after it. The differences can be expressed by means of two sets of statements: one to be added and one to be deleted from the state description before the event in order to obtain the new state description. These statements are usually called *postconditions*. Furthermore, an event rule includes a set of statements, called *preconditions*, which function as checks before the postconditions are applied. More precisely, preconditions consist of a set of statements, which if satisfied in the state description before the event allow the postconditions to give the new state description, otherwise the new state description remains identical to the present one. Example 3.7 informally describes the event type "Increase salary".

Example 3.7   An example of an event rule.

- EVENT TYPE
  Increase salary
- DECLARATIONS
  Ss_no: String
  Increase: Integer

- PRECONDITIONS
  - Increase > 0
  - There is an instance X of Employee with ss_no = Ss_no
- POSTCONDITIONS
  - Old_Sal := the value of the attribute Salary for X
  - Delete the attribute statement giving the salary of X
  - Add an attribute statement specifying that the salary of X is Old_Sal*(1+Increase/100)

3.3 Rules

The primary purpose of conceptual modelling is to create a formal and structured language for reasoning about an object system. In this activity, it is essential to establish the semantics of the language, i.e. to arrive at a consensus on what the different expressions in the language mean. The meaning of the expressions, i.e. how the language is interrelated with the object system, is usually difficult to grasp if we are given only the syntax of the language. For example, a type or an attribute of the language can always be interpreted in different ways. This is illustrated in Figure 3.15 which shows two types, PERSON and CREDIT_CARD, and an attribute for. The attribute for can be given at least two interpretations: either it means that a credit card is licensed to a certain person who holds the legal responsibility for the card, or it means that a card can be used by a person. One way to make the meaning clear is to choose a better name for the attribute, e.g. is_owned_by and can_be_used_by, respectively. Another way is to specify some property of the attribute for that must hold for every state. If we were told that several people could be associated with each credit card through the attribute for, then we would be able to rule out the interpretation of for meaning legal owner.

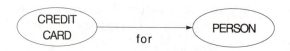

Figure 3.15 *A graph allowing multiple interpretations*

An effective way to clarify the semantics of a language is to specify rules that describe how the language may be used. Such rules can be thought of as natural or human laws that are to hold true in an object system. We define *rule* as meaning a linguistic expression declaring which state descriptions are allowable, or which changes between state descriptions are permissible. This definition is admittedly somewhat vague, so we shall spend a large part of this section identifying various types of rules in order to clarify our definition.

3.3.1 The Origin of Rules

The rules discussed here are sometimes referred to as *business rules*. We take, here, the word *business* to mean the processes conducted within some organisation, be it a huge company or some small organisational subunit, in order to achieve the goals that have been formulated for that organisation. The business can be characterised by the fact that it deals with certain things and that this dealing with is controlled by certain rules restricting what it is possible to say or do, and describing what actions to take given that certain situations arise. The things dealt with are represented in the conceptual model by the object types, attributes, and data types that are introduced in the model. The rules may be represented by statements formulated according to some language. It should be noted, though, that since the business rules talk about the things dealt with in the business, their exact formulation in the conceptual model is strongly dependent on precisely which concepts are introduced in the model. This will be further discussed in Chapter 6. As indicated above, the purpose of rules is to control and guide the activities of an organisation, so that its goals are achieved. Rules may express any of the following:

- Vague high-level objectives and policy statements.
- More precise statements describing the way that an organisation has chosen to achieve its goals and implement its policies.
- Various restrictions imposed on the organisation from the outside world, such as laws and collective wage agreements.

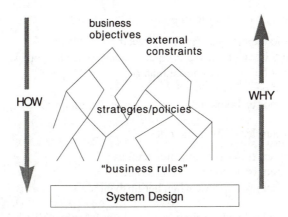

Figure 3.16 *Levels of rules*

The objectives range from vague overall statements of the type "the goal of the business is to maximise its profit in the long run" to more precise statements defining the various means by which the overall goal is to be accomplished. In order to identify the goals and to specify the strategies for realising them, a structural refinement is sometimes performed, resulting in a hierarchy of goals and means for reaching them. At each level of such an analysis, there is a shift in perspective so that what at one level was considered part of a strategy to reach a higher level objective is later considered a goal in itself, a goal which should be reached by some other, even more precise, measures. Hence, a subgoal is seen as a means to bring about a superior goal. The further we get in the analysis and the lower the level we reach, the easier it becomes to formulate rules that define when a goal is fulfilled.

The rules forced upon the business from the outside world are not much different, since they could, in principle, be arrived at by a similar decomposition of general constraints for the business such as "every company is obliged to observe the laws of the country in which it is operating". Figure 3.16 illustrates the relationship between the various levels of abstraction. At the bottom level, some business rules may be implemented and embedded in a computerised information system.

3.3.2   Static and Dynamic Rules

Certain rules concern the static properties of an object system, whereas others describe its dynamics. A *static rule* is an expression which only takes a single state into account. Static rules put restrictions on objects, their properties, and relationships within a single state. A *dynamic rule,* on the other hand, takes several states into account. Dynamic rules put restrictions on changes from one state into another one.

Example 3.8   Examples of static rules:

1. The salary of an employee may not exceed 100,000 euro.
2. The net salary of an employee is equal to total salary less taxes.
3. A car may not be owned by more than one person.
4. A man cannot be father to himself.
5. A person cannot be both a man and a woman simultaneously.

Example 3.9   Examples of dynamic rules:

6. The salary of an employee must not decrease.
7. A person cannot be fired unless employed.
8. A woman becomes a widow when her husband dies.

Note that rule 8 is indeed a dynamic rule, since in order to establish whether a salary has decreased, we need to take into account the state both before and after the change in salary. Rule 1, however, is static, since we only need to consider a single state to determine whether that rule is satisfied.

3.3.3   Derivation Rules

A *derivation rule* is an expression that specifies how certain statements can be derived from other statements. A derivation rule can be used to derive type statements as well as attribute statements.

Example 3.10   Examples of derivation rules:

1. The net salary of an employee is equal to total salary less taxes.
2. The GNP per capita of a country is equal to the GNP of the country divided by the number of inhabitants.
3. The weight of a piece of furniture is equal to the sum of the weights of its parts.
4. An employee is a high-income employee if earning more than 50,000 euro.

The first three of these derivation rules are concerned with deriving attribute statements, whereas the fourth describes how type statements can be derived. Derivation rules can naturally be expressed in a Prolog notation. For example, the first rule above could be expressed:

```
net_salary(Emp, Net):- earns(Emp, Sal), taxes(Emp, Tax),
Net is Sal - Tax.
```

The fourth rule could be expressed:

```
high-income_employee(H):- employee(H), earns(H, Sal), Sal > 50000.
```

The examples above show static derivation rules. There are also dynamic derivation rules that express how statements can be deduced from two or more states.

Example 3.11   An example of a dynamic derivation rule:

A woman becomes a widow when her husband dies.

3.3.4   Integrity Constraints

Integrity constraints express what states and behaviour are legitimate for an object system. A static integrity constraint expresses a condition that must hold in every legal state. A dynamic integrity constraint specifies a condition that should be satisfied at every legal state change. Again, these definitions are not strict owing to the use of the unclarified term "legal". An important issue is to distinguish between different meanings of the term "legal", and we will consider this question at the end of this section.

Certain classes of static integrity constraints are especially helpful in order to obtain understanding of an object system. We shall discuss three such classes of integrity constraints: typing constraints, mapping constraints, and extension constraints.

Typing constraints have already been implicitly introduced in Section 3.1.2. A *typing constraint* for an attribute specifies the domain and the range of the attribute, i.e. it specifies the types of the arguments required in order to make a statement using the attribute.

An example of a typing constraint is "the domain of the attribute president is CLUB and the range is PERSON". This constraint implies that if a statement president(c1, p1) occurs in a legal state description, then c1 must be an instance of CLUB and p1 must be an instance of PERSON.

Mapping constraints specify basic set-theoretical properties of the extensions of attributes. We distinguish four types of mapping constraints:

1. An attribute is *single valued* if for each instance of its domain, the attribute has at most one value. (An attribute that is not single valued is *multi-valued.*)
2. An attribute is *total* if the attribute must have a value for each instance of its domain. (An attribute that is not total is *partial.*)
3. An attribute is *injective* if two different instances of the domain cannot have the same value.
4. An attribute is *surjective* if each instance of the range is the value of the attribute for some instance of the domain.

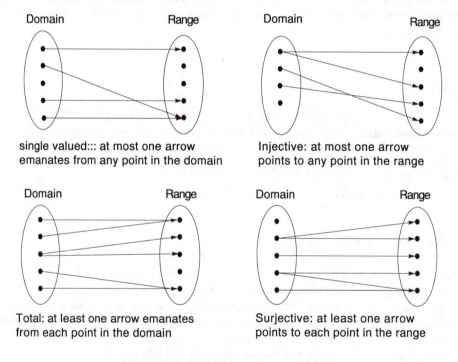

single valued::: at most one arrow
emanates from any point in the domain

Injective: at most one arrow
points to any point in the range

Total: at least one arrow emanates
from each point in the domain

Surjective: at least one arrow
points to each point in the range

Figure 3.17 *Mapping constraints*

These notions are illustrated graphically in Figure 3.17. The following questions provide a simple means to determine the mapping constraints of a given attribute. Suppose that the domain of the attribute is A and that its range is B.

1. Can one A be associated to several Bs? If so, then the attribute is not single valued.
2. Must every A be associated to a B? If so, then the attribute is total.
3. Can one B be associated to several As? If so, then the attribute is not injective.
4. Must every B be associated to an A? If so, then the attribute is surjective.

An attribute is called 1–1 (one-to-one) if it is single valued and injective, 1–m (one-to-many) if it is single valued and not injective, m–1 (many-to-one) if it is multi-valued and injective, m–m (many-to-many) if it is neither single valued nor injective.

A convenient notation for mapping constraints is the quadruple *(m|1, m|1, t|p, t|p)*. The first component of this quadruple indicates whether the attribute is single valued or not. When single valued, this component is set to *1*, otherwise to *m* (for *multi-valued*). The second component of the structure indicates whether the attribute is injective, in which case the component is set to *1*, otherwise to *m*. The third component indicates the totality of the attribute. A *t* indicates totality, a *p* partiality. The fourth component indicates the surjectivity of the attribute. When surjective, this component is set to *t*, otherwise to *p*. See Figure 3.18 below.

Let an object type person have an attribute address, the mapping constraints of which are specified by (1, m, t, p). Here each person has exactly one address (components 1 and 3), several people may live at the same address (component 2), and there are addresses where no one lives (component 4).

	First component: Single valuedness	Second component: Injectivity	Third component: Totality	Fourth component: Surjectivity
1	single valued	injective	-	-
m	multi-valued	not injective	-	-
t	-	-	total	surjective
p	-	-	partial	not surjective

Figure 3.18 *Notation for mapping constraints*

Extension constraints concern simple set-theoretical relationships between the extensions of subtypes. We distinguish between two types of extension constraints:

1. A supertype's subtypes are *disjoint* if their extensions are disjoint.
2. A supertype's subtypes are *exhaustive* if the union of their extensions is equal to the extension of the supertype.

If a supertype's subtypes are disjoint and exhaustive, then their extensions constitute a partition of the extension of the supertype.

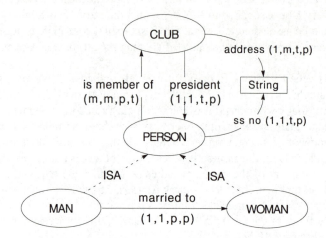

Figure 3.19 *Persons and clubs*

Example 3.12   We shall determine here the mapping constraints of some of the attributes occurring in Figure 3.19.

- The attribute `is_member_of` is not single valued, since one person may be a member of many clubs. Neither is it total, since not every person has to be a member of a club. The attribute is not injective, since more than one person can be a member of the same club. The attribute is surjective, since every club must have at least one member.
- The attribute `ss_no` is single valued, since one person can have at most one social security number. It is also total, since everybody has a social security number. The attribute is injective, since two people cannot have the same social security number. The attribute is not surjective, since there may be strings that are not social security numbers.
- The attribute `married_to` is single valued, since a man can be married to at most one woman. It is not total, since some men can be single. The attribute is injective, since a woman can be married to at most one man. The attribute is not surjective, since there may be women who are single.
- The types MAN and WOMAN are disjoint, since no person can be both a man and a woman simultaneously. MAN and WOMAN are exhaustive for PERSON, since every person is either a man or a woman.

For any object system, there is usually a large number of typing, mapping, and extension constraints, but there may certainly exist other types of constraints.

Example 3.13   Examples of static integrity constraints that are not typing, mapping, or extension constraints:

1. A person may not have a larger salary than the boss.
2. A person may not own more than three cars.
3. A person cannot be married to himself.
4. A person younger than 18 may not drive a car.

The rules introduced above can often be represented graphically. The reason for using graphical descriptions in conceptual modelling is that a graph can provide a clear overview of a schema. Unlike natural language descriptions, a graph is two dimensional and can therefore offer several different points of departure for browsing a model. The two-dimensionality also makes it easy for a group of people to view and manipulate the graphical description jointly. Graphs are therefore used extensively as an effective means of communicating about object systems. Since graphical description techniques are easy to learn and understand, they are particularly well suited for facilitating communication between systems designers and users who lack extensive knowledge of modelling techniques. In order for a graph to function well as a means of communication, it is essential that the graph is not cluttered with excessive details. For that reason it is customary to represent only a few types of rules in graphs.

Different modelling approaches employ different graphical signs for representing mapping constraints. Non-functionality is frequently denoted by forks on the end points of arrows. A fork at the head of an arrow indicates that the corresponding attribute is multi-valued, whereas a fork at the tail of the arrow shows that the attribute is not injective. Filled dots are often used to represent totality. A filled dot at the head of an arrow means the corresponding attribute is surjective. A filled dot at the tail of the arrow means the attribute is total.

Example 3.14   Consider Figure 3.20. `is_member_of` has the mapping constraints:

Multi-valued	(the fork at the head of the arrow)
Not injective	(the fork at the tail of the arrow)
Not total	(no filled dot at the tail of the arrow)
Surjective	(the filled dot at the head of the arrow)

For `president` the following constraints hold:

single valued	(no fork at the head of the arrow)
Not injective	(the fork at the tail of the arrow)
Total	(the filled dot at the tail of the arrow)
Not surjective	(no filled dot at the head of the arrow)

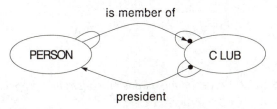

is member of

president

Figure 3.20 *Representing mapping constraints graphically*

Some entities are dependent for their existence on other entities, i.e. they cannot exist without being associated to certain other entities. For example, a club membership cannot exist unless a particular person and a particular club exist and are associated through the club membership. As soon as either the person or the club ceases to exist, so does the membership. Intuitively, one can think of these kinds of entities as relationships, which bind other entities with one another. For that reason we shall call entities of this kind relationship types. More precisely, an object type is a *relationship type* if it is the domain of two total attributes with non-lexical types as ranges. Graphically, diamonds are often used to represent relationship types, see Figure 3.21.

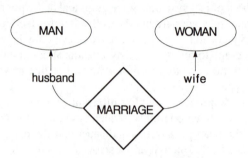

Figure 3.21 *Graphical representation of relationship types*

Figure 3.22 shows how extension constraints can be depicted graphically. To show that subtypes are disjoint, the ISA arrows emanating from the subtypes are joined in a small unfilled circle, connected to the supertype. If the subtypes are not only disjoint but also exhaustive, the circle is filled.

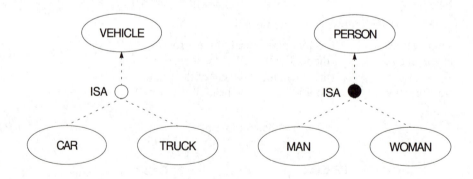

Figure 3.22 *Representing extension constraints graphically*

Integrity constraints express conditions that should hold true for every legal state of an object system, and for every legal state change. To clarify what we mean by "legal", we distinguish between two types of integrity constraints: necessary constraints and deontic constraints. *Necessary constraints* specify conditions which necessarily and without exception must hold true. For example, "A person's age must be greater than zero". This constraint is an analytic truth, which follows directly from the meaning of the word "age". Necessary constraints can also have an empirical basis: for instance, "A person's age must be less than 150". Strictly speaking, the last example is not a necessary truth, since a person might become more than 150 years old. If, however, we consider an object system for a limited period of time, we may well regard the constraint as a necessary one. Somewhat simplified, necessary constraints can be thought of as natural laws, which hold true without exception.

Deontic constraints, on the other hand, are construed by some human agent such as a business manager, or a legislator requiring the constraints to be satisfied. A deontic constraint might be "The salary of an employee may not exceed 100,000 euro", or "A book may not be borrowed for more than six weeks". A deontic constraint is not necessarily satisfied in every state; if a state violates a deontic constraint, it only means that the state is regarded as undesirable by the party responsible for formulating the constraint. One can think of deontic constraints as human laws, which can be violated.

Figure 3.23 summarises the various types of rules introduced in this section: static versus dynamic rules, derivation rules versus integrity constraints, and necessary versus deontic constraints.

	STATIC RULES		DYNAMIC RULES	
DERIVATION RULES	STATIC DERIVATION RULES "Net salary = Salary - Tax"		DYNAMIC DERIVATION RULES "A woman becomes a widow when her husband dies"	
INTEGRITY CONSTRAINTS	STATIC INTEGRITY CONSTRAINTS		DYNAMIC INTEGRITY CONSTRAINTS	
	NECESSARY	DEONTIC	NECESSARY	DEONTIC
	"A person has at most one father"	"The salary of a person may not exceed 100 000 euro"	"A person can't be fired unless employed"	"The salary of a person may not decrease"

Figure 3.23 *Classification of rules*

3.4 Conceptual Modelling and Information Systems

The primary purpose of an information system is to provide a model of an object system, thereby enabling people to obtain information about reality by studying the model. In this respect, an information system works as a passive repository of data that reflects the structure and behaviour of the object system. However, an information system may also be active in the sense that it can perform actions that influence the reality of the system's environment. For example, a library information system may automatically send reminders to borrowers who have not returned their books on time.

We shall view an information system as consisting of three components: a conceptual schema, an information base, and an information processor. The conceptual schema describes the language used to reason about the object system and determines which statements may be included in the information base. The conceptual schema also specifies the behaviour of the object system through a set of event types. The information base consists of statements describing the current state of the object system. The information processor is a software component, whose purpose is to enable users to query and update the conceptual schema and the information base, see Figure 3.24. For the rest of this section we shall elaborate on these three components of an information system.

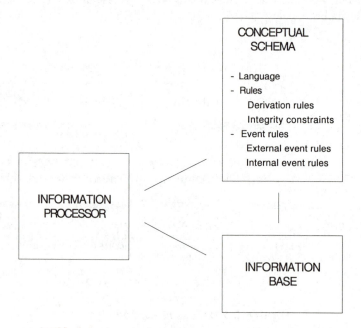

Figure 3.24 *Architecture of an information system*

3.4.1 The Conceptual Schema

A *conceptual schema* consists of three parts:

1. A language specified using an alphabet and a grammar. The alphabet is partitioned into five classes of symbols: types, attributes, object identifiers, variables, and punctuation marks. Often the language of a conceptual schema is specified by enumerating only the types and attributes, since the other symbols and the grammar are seen as given implicitly.
2. A set of derivation rules and a set of integrity constraints. These rules are linguistic expressions in the language given in 1. The purpose of the derivation rules is to make it possible to derive new statements from the statements already contained in the information base. The purpose of the integrity constraints is to restrict which statements may be contained in the information base.
3. A set of event rules describing the behaviour of the object system. These are partitioned into external and internal event rules.

Events are usually initiated by an agent in the object system, e.g. a person or a company. Some events, however, can be initiated by an information system. Such events are called *internal events,* while events caused by an agent in the object system are called *external events.* Characteristic of internal events is that one can specify rules that determine when they are to occur. Based on these rules, the information system decides when to initiate internal events.

Example 3.15 Examples of internal events:

1. A club member who has not paid the fee by the expiry date, is sent a reminder.
2. If the air conditioning is off and the temperature rises above 25°C, the air conditioning is turned on.
3. A person who has violated traffic regulations more than three times in the course of a year, will have his or her driver's licence invalidated.

In order to initiate an internal event, the information system usually needs to be physically connected to the object system. In the second of the examples above, a physical connection must exist between the information system and the air conditioning equipment, otherwise the information system cannot switch on the air-conditioning. In some cases, however, an internal event can be performed without directly causing any physical changes to the object system. Such cases occur when the internal event corresponds to a speech act (see Section 2.2.3). The event then consists of the information system making a statement that by itself changes the object system. The statement does not change the physical reality, but it does change the social reality, e.g. by creating obligations or permissions. In the third example above, the information system in some sense performs a speech act, thereby invalidating a driver's licence.

Internal event types can be described in a similar way to external event types, as discussed in Section 3.2.3. The description of an internal event type consists of two parts: an *occurrence rule* and an *action rule*. The occurrence rule specifies a condition for when an event of the given event type is to occur, for instance "The temperature rises above 25° C". The action rule corresponds to the postconditions of an external event rule and specifies how the new state description can be obtained from the present. In addition, the action rule can contain instructions that do not concern state descriptions, such as sending signals to devices in the object system. An informal description of an internal event type is given below.

Example 3.16   An example of an internal event rule:

- INTERNAL EVENT TYPE
  Activate air conditioning
- OCCURRENCE RULE
  Temperature rises above 25°C
  Air conditioning is off
- ACTION RULE
  Send_signal(Switch on air conditioning)

3.4.2   The Information Base

A conceptual schema provides a language for reasoning about an object system, and it specifies rules for the structure and behaviour of the system. However, the conceptual schema does not describe any particular state of the object system. A description of a particular state is given in an *information base*, which is a set of type and attribute statements expressed in the language of the conceptual schema. However, an information base usually does not in itself completely describe a state of the object system. Some statements describing a state can be derived from the information base using derivation rules. By the *state description corresponding to an information base* we mean the union of the information base and the set of statements we can derive from the information base and the derivation rules.[3] The elements of an information base are called *base statements*. Statements that can be derived from the information base using derivation rules are called *derived statements*. By a *conceptual model* is meant a conceptual schema together with a corresponding information base.

Example 3.17   Consider an information base containing the following statements:

```
employee(joe).        earns(joe, 12000).      tax(joe, 4000).
employee(joe).        earns(mary, 15000).     tax(mary, 5000).
```

---

3) The reader familiar with logic programming may note the following analogies: information base = ground facts, static derivation rules = normal clauses, state description corresponding to an information base = least (minimal) Herbrand model.

Suppose there is a derivation rule in the conceptual schema stating that net salary is equal to salary less tax. The state description corresponding to the above information base would then be:

```
employee(joe). earns(joe,12000). tax(joe,4000). net_salary(joe,8000).
employee(mary).earns(mary,15000). tax(mary,5000).net_salary(mary,10000).
```

Integrity constraints state conditions that an information base should satisfy. We say that an information base *violates* an integrity constraint if the constraint is not satisfied in the state description corresponding to the information base. If an information base violates an integrity constraint, some action should be taken. Which action to take depends upon the type of constraint: necessary or deontic. An information base that violates any necessary integrity constraint is incorrect and should be corrected. But an information base that violates a deontic constraint is not necessarily incorrect in the sense that it does not faithfully reflect the present state of the object system. It may be the case that the object system is in what is regarded as an undesirable state, in which case action may be taken to alter its state. For example, a person who has borrowed a book for more than six weeks could be sent a reminder. One way to effectuate such action is to utilise the mechanism of internal event rules.

Example 3.18 Suppose for the information base in the example above that there is an integrity constraint stating that the net salary of an employee must not be less than 9,000 euro. This constraint is violated, since `net_salary(joe, 8000)` belongs to the state description corresponding to the information base.

For negative statements, we make the assumption that if a statement cannot be derived from an information base using the derivation rules, then the statement is false. Consequently its negation is true. This assumption is called the *Closed World Assumption*. Using the information base in Example 3.17, the following statements become false, for instance: `salary(joe, 13000)`, `tax(mary, 2000)`. The advantage of the Closed World Assumption is that negative statements need not be explicitly stated in the information base, the size of which is thereby significantly reduced.[4]

3.4.3 The Information Processor

Given a conceptual schema and an information base, it is important for a user to be able to query and manipulate them. These activities are supported by the third component of an information system, the *information processor*. A user may ask about the current state of the object system by submitting a query to the information processor. A *query* is a formula, possibly containing variables, expressed in the language of the conceptual schema. Given a query, the information processor will check for an answer using the state de-

---

4) In order for the concept of size to become meaningful, recall that we have a finite number of types in our domain, and that we do not use function symbols.

scription corresponding to the information base. In other words, the answer to a query depends not only on the information base, but also on the derivation rules of the conceptual schema.

When an event occurs in the object system, this should be reported to the information system, in order for the information base to be changed so that it correctly reflects the current state of the object system. The user informs the information processor of the occurrence of an event by submitting an *event message*. An event message consists of the name of the event type and a parameter list. The parameter list contains one instance of each of the components occurring in the domain of the event rule in question, see Section 3.2.3. An example of an event message corresponding to the event type in Example 3.7 is ⟨"Increase salary", ["600101-1234", 12]⟩. This represents an event in which the salary of a person with social security number 600101-1234 has been increased by 12 per cent. Upon receiving an event message, the information processor will perform the appropriate updates on the information base. The information processor determines which updates to perform by considering the event message as well as the appropriate event rule; the updates are called a *transaction*.

There is usually a delay between the occurrence of an event and the submission of the corresponding event message. The point in time of an event is called its *intrinsic* time, and the point in time of the submission of the event message is called its *extrinsic* time.

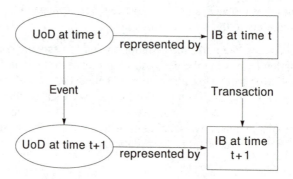

Figure 3.25 *Events and transactions*

The functionality of the information processor is shown pictorially in Figure 3.25 and Figure 3.26. When an event occurs in the UoD, it changes from one state into another one. This change will be reflected by the information base, which is updated through a transaction, as shown in Figure 3.25. The transaction is executed by the information processor. A concrete example of this is given in Figure 3.26, where the information base is updated by adding information about a marriage.

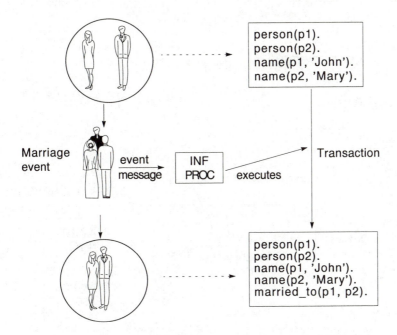

person(p1).
person(p2).
name(p1, 'John').
name(p2, 'Mary').

Marriage event   event message   INF PROC   executes   Transaction

person(p1).
person(p2).
name(p1, 'John').
name(p2, 'Mary').
married_to(p1, p2).

Figure 3.26 *A marriage and the corresponding transaction*

It is important that the information processor checks that updating the information base does not lead to a state in which an integrity constraint is violated. If a user submits an event message to the information processor, the resulting updates may cause the information base to violate a necessary constraint. In this case the information processor should refuse to perform the updates and inform the user of the reason for rejecting the message. If, on the other hand, a deontic constraint were to become violated, the information processor should perform the updates and notify the user of the violations. The information processor must also monitor internal event rules, executing corresponding action rules as required.

In Figure 3.27, we summarise the interrelationships between an object system and an information system. The current state of the object system is reflected in the information base, which consists of statements that are expressed in the language of the conceptual schema and obey its rules. When an event occurs in the object system, an event message is sent to the information processor which updates the information base accordingly. The information processor may also take actions on its own initiative and thereby influence the object system. Finally, a user can submit queries to the information processor and receive answers.

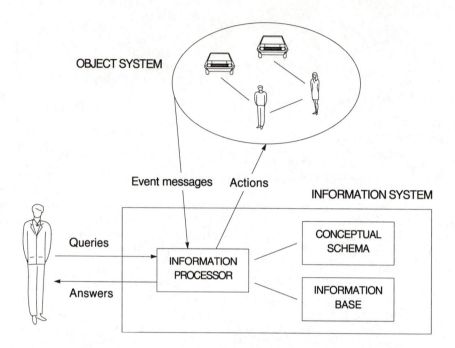

Figure 3.27 *The information system models and influences the object system*

3.5 Some Relevant Literature

Many different approaches to conceptual modelling have been proposed, among the most important are: the original Entity–Relationship approach [Chen76]; the extended Entity–Relationship approach [ElMasri85]; the functional model [Shipman81]; the semantic data model [Hammer81]; and NIAM [Nijssen89]. A formal semantics for a conceptual modelling language is presented in [Gogolla91]. General surveys of the field of conceptual modelling are given in [Hull87] and [Peckham88]. Many notions from conceptual modelling have been incorporated into methods for object-oriented analysis and design, e.g. [Booch91], [Rumbaugh92].

3.6 Exercises

3.1   Using the sentences below, draw a graph of a conceptual schema, which can be used to reason about sentences of this type.
a) Donald is a duck.
b) The colour of Donald's eyes is blue.
c) Chip is a squirrel.
d) The colour of Chip's hair is brown.
e) The length of Chip's tail is 2 cm.
f) Chip lives in Ducksburg.

3.2   For each type of object system listed below, discuss what kinds of entities and rules may occur. Sketch a graph of a conceptual schema and using natural language, express a number of rules. (Be sure to include static and dynamic rules, derivation rules, integrity constraints, necessary and deontic constraints.)
a) A travel agency
b) A library
c) A book keeper
d) A computer manufacturer
e) A car dealer

3.3   Draw a graph of a conceptual schema that allows the following type of sentences to be expressed: Peter exchanged his apple for Lisa's orange.

   Using the schema, give a set of type and attribute statements (i.e. an information base) that represents the above statement.

3.4   Adventure games are often based on maps with a set of nodes that represent locations. There is a set of directions (these are not limited to N, E, S, and W; there could be NE, UP, etc.). Given any node n and any direction d, there is at most one other node that can be reached by going in direction d from n. Draw a graph of a conceptual schema for representing such maps. Indicate the mapping constraints for all the attributes.

3.5   Try to counter the following argument, which is against the use of generalisation in conceptual modelling. "Generalisation is a superfluous concept which only complicates conceptual schemas! A schema with generalisation can always be replaced by a schema without generalisation, and the two schemas can express exactly the same information. For example, if we have a schema with a type VEHICLE and two subtypes CAR and BOAT, then we could replace this schema with a schema containing only one type, VEHICLE. All attributes of CAR and BOAT would then be 'moved to' VEHICLE, and we would include an extra attribute vehicle_type to take the values car and boat. This new schema can represent just as much information as the original schema. So, generalisation relationships are unnecessary and should be banished from modelling."

3.6   Try to counter the following argument, which is against the use of derivation rules in conceptual schemas. "Derived attributes are always redundant. Derived attribute statements do not contain any new information, they only paraphrase what is already contained in other statements. So, derivation rules are unnecessary and should be banished from all modelling."

3.7   The properties of relationships are important when describing integrity constraints in a conceptual schema. Give an example of a relationship that is transitive, but neither reflexive nor symmetric. Show how knowledge of the relationship can be used to simplify a constraint on that relationship.

3.8   For each attribute in the schema below, determine whether it is
  a) single valued
  b) injective
  c) total
  d) surjective

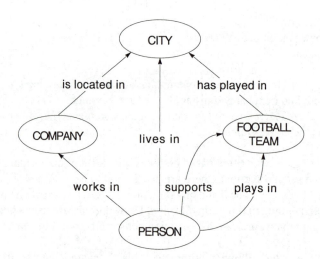

3.9   Give a concrete example of a conceptual schema containing a type E and two attributes B and C, so that
  a) The domain of B and C is E
  b) The range of B and C is E
  c) B is total and single valued
  d) C is injective

3.10   Consider the following two sets of integers:
  $F = \{x \mid x < -1\}$
  $G = \{x \mid x > 4\}$

We introduce an attribute `square`, where `square(X, Y):- Y is X*X`. Suppose that square has the domain F and the range G. Specify the mapping constraints of square.

3.11 For each of the statements below, determine whether it is

1. a static or a dynamic rule
2. a derivation rule or an integrity constraint
3. a necessary or a deontic constraint (if indeed it is an integrity constraint)

a) A member of the EU may not leave the union.
b) American countries may not be members of the EU.
c) The GNP per capita of a country is equal to the GNP of the country divided by its population.
d) Every country has a capital.
e) A country that has left the United Nations may not rejoin the union.
f) A country cannot have two capitals.
g) The Father of the House of the English Parliament is the oldest man in Parliament.

3.12 For each of the object systems in Exercise 3.2, give examples of at least two internal events, and discuss if their action rules can be regarded as speech acts.

3.13 Let C1 and C2 be two conceptual schemas that are identical, except for the fact that the set of integrity constraints in C1 is strictly included in the set of integrity constraints in C2. Let B1 be the set of all information bases that do not violate C1. Let B2 be the set of all information bases that do not violate C2. Determine which of the following statements is true:
a) $B1 \subset B2$
b) $B2 \subset B1$
c) $B1 = B2$
d) None of a)–c) is true

3.14 Let CS be a conceptual schema that does not contain any derivation rules. Let A and B be two different information bases. Let $C = A \cup B$. Is the following statement true?
If neither A nor B violates any integrity constraint in CS, then neither does C.

3.15 Let CS be a conceptual schema. We define a relation "<" over the set of all integrity constraints expressed in the language given by CS. Let C1 and C2 be two integrity constraints. C1 < C2 if every information base that violates C2 also violates C1; we say that C1 is weaker than C2. Which of the following properties holds for the relation "<"?
a) symmetric
b) transitive
c) anti-symmetric
d) total

3.16 When constructing a conceptual model, we deliberately restrict our attention to a specific part of reality, i.e. the object system. In doing so we sometimes consciously disregard certain aspects of reality that are otherwise seen as important. Give an example of an application and two types that satisfy the following two conditions:

a) One of the types is a subtype of the other.
b) In the context of the application, it is preferable that the two types be amalgamated into one.

3.17 Construct a graph of a conceptual schema for the object system outlined in the following description of a programming support environment. "In the environment programmers produce programs, which are written in different programming languages. Each program is written by a single programmer. Each program can call other programs, and can be used by given users. The programmers, as well as the users, are identified by the name with which they log in. Several versions of a given program may exist and it is important to keep track of the date when a certain version of a program is created. Some programs interact with database management systems (DBMSs). Each DBMS maintains stored data in the form of relations, with a number of attributes and a primary key. It is necessary to know which relations and attributes each program affects." Specify mapping constraints.

3.18 Given two information bases, IB1 and IB2, such that IB1 satisfies all its static integrity constraints, i.e. is consistent, but IB2 is inconsistent, answer the following questions.

a) Is the difference IB1 – IB2 necessarily inconsistent?
b) Is the difference IB1 – IB2 necessarily consistent?
c) Is the difference IB2 – IB1 necessarily inconsistent?
d) Is the difference IB2 – IB1 necessarily consistent?
e) Is the intersection IB1 ∩ IB2 necessarily inconsistent?
f) Is the intersection IB1 ∩ IB2 necessarily consistent?
g) Is the union IB1 ∪ IB2 necessarily inconsistent?
h) Is the union IB1 ∪ IB2 necessarily consistent?

3.19 The sentences below are examples of information that it should be possible to represent in a geographical information system:

- Sweden is a country with an area of 400,000 km^2. It has 8.5 million inhabitants and its capital is Stockholm which has 1.2 million inhabitants.
- In 1989, Sweden's GNP was 130 billion euro and in 1990, 132 billion euro.
- Sweden borders on Denmark, Norway and Finland.
- Manchester is a city in the UK with 0.9 million inhabitants.
- The distance between Manchester and Birmingham is 75 kilometres.
- Denmark has been a member of the United Nations since 1947.
- In 1987, Japan exported cars to France for 2 billion euro.

- In 1990, Denmark exported butter to the United Kingdom for 0.3 billion euro.
- The River Danube, which is 1200 kilometres long, flows through Austria, Hungary, and Romania.
- The River Rhine flows through Düsseldorf and Bonn.
- The Danube flows into the Black Sea, which has an area of 200,000 km^2.

a) Draw a graph of a conceptual schema in which it is possible to represent the statements above.
b) State a number of rules (both derivation rules and integrity constraints) that could be contained in the schema. Specify all mapping constraints.

3.20 Suppose a user gives the information processor in an information system a message about the occurrence of an event. If the information processor were to update the information base according to the event message, this would violate a necessary constraint. Does this mean that the event that the event message pertains to cannot in fact have occurred, or could there be another explanation for the constraint violation?

CHAPTER 4

Logic for Conceptual Modelling

Knowledge can be expressed in numerous ways: as atomic propositions; very complex sentences; formulae of some formal language; mindmaps; the list seems almost endless. This chapter investigates the use of logic to represent knowledge. It examines further the languages of *first-order logic (FOL)* and *Prolog,* and also the Prolog meta-interpreter thoroughly examined in Chapter 5. It is assumed that the reader has had some experience of both FOL and Prolog (cf. Appendix 5).

4.1 Simplicity vs. Complexity in Models

Since most users of conceptual modelling techniques and tools have a fairly weak background in formal sciences such as logic and mathematics, it is desirable to keep the representation of knowledge simple. Just by looking briefly at the contents in the information base and the conceptual schema, every user should gain a good overview of the UoD and, what is more important, be equipped to manipulate the knowledge in it. One of the simplest, least formal methods of knowledge representation is mind mapping. *Mindmaps* are completely informal graphs usually used during the very first stage of modelling. Mindmaps do not compare very easily with other mindmaps, not least because they have no uniform notation. This makes it difficult to detect and remove errors from mindmaps, particularly from sets of mindmaps where errors may not necessarily be apparent in any individual mindmap. In the club example, one mindmap may be developed from the club's point of view and so primarily describe abstract objects like how pleased the member was with some weekend arrangement, value for money, and how the user perceives the organisation of the club. Another mindmap may consist mainly of descriptions of different databases to be used for enrolment, such as lists of registration days, and waiting lists. Integrating the two resulting mindmaps (see Figure 4.1) is almost impossible, since they use different levels of abstraction, and there is no way of specifying a procedure for their integration. There is a compromise here between simplicity on the one hand, and completeness on the other. *Completeness* and its related concept *soundness* are important logical concepts that respectively mean that every fact true in the UoD can be proven to be true in our model, and that no fact false in the UoD can.

Ideally, our club case should be represented *adequately* in the sense that the implemented model is a sound and complete model of the UoD. If this holds true, the model becomes an adequate mirror representation of the reality under study.

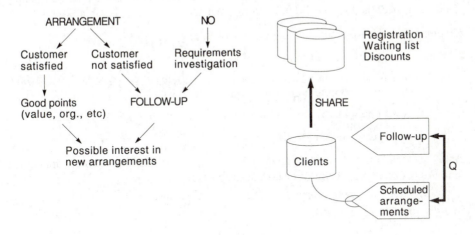

Figure 4.1 *Two incommensurable graphs which both qualify as mindmaps*

4.2 Propositional Logic for Conceptual Modelling

4.2.1   Analysing Natural Language Using Propositional Logic

Recapitulating Chapter 2 above, propositional logic is used to make statements in a language which is often called *the propositional calculus*, and to calculate the truth or falsity of these statements. It is the simplest form of formal logic, in the sense that all common forms of logic are extensions of it. The propositional calculus consists of symbols from some alphabet, for instance the set $\{a, ..., z\}$, and connectives which operate on the symbols. The alphabet symbols are used to form constants that are then combined by means of the connectives. Together with the left and right parentheses the constants and the connectives constitute an *object language* in which statements can be written down and analysed. The analysis often has the form of a (partial) translation from some natural language into the object language of propositional logic. To be able to talk about such analyses we need another language, called a *metalanguage*. This is because it is impossible to describe our work inside a propositional logic only in terms of its object language. Instead, we define a convenient metalanguage in which we have another set of symbols, e.g. $\{A,B,C,D,A_1,A_2,A_3, ...\}$, and also special symbols like $\Rightarrow$ and $\Leftrightarrow$. Now we can make statements about the logic in the metalanguage, like $(A \wedge B) \Rightarrow C$, which means "The statement corresponding to the letter C is a logical consequence of the conjunction between the two statements corresponding to the letters A and B". This is an example of a metalanguage statement that is true or false, depending on what A, B, and C stand for. If A, B, and C are different atomic sentences, for instance, it is false.

Example 4.1   Using metalanguage symbols.

> `Let A represent Alice is a member,`
>
> `let B represent If Alice becomes a member within ten days, she will receive the club's weekly paper, and finally`
>
> `let C represent Alice will receive the club's weekly paper.`

In the above interpretation, $(A \wedge B) \Rightarrow C$ holds.

Another formula in the metalanguage is $A \Leftrightarrow D$, which means that A and D are equivalent. With A as above, D could for instance represent

> `It is not the case that Alice is not a member`

in order for $A \Leftrightarrow D$ to be true.

4.2.2   Limitations of Propositional Logic for Knowledge Representation

The limitations of propositional logic, which make it unsuitable for the representation of knowledge, are probably most easily realised by means of some examples. Suppose that after some effort, we have acquired a lot of information about the club UoD, and we are now interested in representing this information adequately. Our first statement might be `Every person younger than 19 receives a ten per cent discount on the membership fee`. This actually expresses a rule, but in the knowledge acquisition phase we will normally not yet have separated knowledge into subgroups like atomic formulae, rules, etc. Our second statement is a straightforward fact, represented by the sentence `Mr. Jones is head of the club's complaints department`. Let us investigate the propositional logic representation of these two statements.

In the first example, we first encounter the words `Every person younger than 19`. This immediately shows that we are dealing with a classification of a set of objects, namely a set of young people, by describing some important common characteristic of them in the UoD. In this case, the characteristic is a ten per cent discount. The statement is now analysed as follows. We rewrite it as an implication: `If a person is younger than 19, then that person receives a ten per cent discount on the membership fee`. What we would like to do next is use the implication connective and rewrite the sentence as: `A person is younger than 19` $\rightarrow$ `A person receives a ten per cent discount on the membership fee`. But here we run into trouble, since `A person younger than 19` does not denote any definite object in the UoD but rather it is a predicate taking variables, which range over some set of objects, as its arguments. But propositional logic cannot handle variables! This also renders it impossible to ensure that A person in the antecedent denotes the same (set of) object(s) as A person in the consequent. Propositional logic connects *atomic sentences* using connectives, and atomic sentences are completely analysed; they have no internal structure, no connections to other atomic sentences, and they do not contain any connectives. They are thus the primitives of the representation, but still not small enough for our needs, since we are interested in breaking down atomic sentences into even smaller objects like entities, attributes, and data types.

This is even more clear in the example Mr. Jones is head of the club's complaints department. Earlier, we called it a straightforward fact, and it is really an atomic sentence, but this entails that it does not contain any logical connectives. So there is no difference between the representation of this fact in propositional logic and its English form. This is not an unusual case, and it means that we are unable to represent certain forms of logical reasoning. Consider for instance the conclusion of Socrates is mortal from the two premises Socrates is a man and All men are mortal. All three sentences are atomic, so there is no way to prove that the first sentence is a logical consequence of the two other sentences. These are not the only problems with using propositional logic for knowledge representation, but they are indeed severe enough to motivate a search of more expressive formalisms.

4.3 Predicate Logic for Conceptual Modelling

4.3.1 Analysing Natural Language Using Predicate Logic

Predicate logic utilises variables, and to bind variables, *quantifiers* are used, as was briefly explained in Section 2.2 above. They can be combined in various ways to range over formulae, as shown in the following example.

Example 4.2 Translations from natural language to FOL formulae.

```
Every membership number is a number.
translates to: ∀x(MN(x) → N(x)),
given the lexicon:
MN(x) = x is a membership number;
N(x) = x is a number.
```

We can investigate the expressive power of FOL by carrying out a new analysis of the two sentences in the previous section. Now the partially analysed sentence A person is younger than 19 → A person receives a ten per cent discount on the membership fee can be further analysed into It is true of all people that if they are younger than 19, then they receive a ten per cent discount. If we choose the variable x to represent any person and let Y(x) be interpreted as x is younger than 19 and D(x) as x receives a ten per cent discount, then we can translate the first sentence into ∀x(Y(x) → D(x)).

In the second example, by using constants, and by letting H(x,y) represent x has head y, we reach the formula H(cd, jones). No quantifiers are required here since this atomic formula contains no variables. Finally, the inference example translates to: from Man(socrates) and ∀x(Man(x) → Mortal(x)), conclude Mortal(socrates). How the actual inference is carried out varies with the formalisation, but generally speaking, the constant socrates is first substituted for x in ∀x(Man(x) → Mortal(x)) to give Man(socrates) → Mortal(socrates). This is indisputable since if something is true for every man it must be true for Socrates in particular. The conclusion is then reached by utilising the basic logical rule, *modus ponens*: from *A*, and *A → B*, *B* can be inferred.

4.3.2   Limitations of Predicate Logic for Knowledge Representation

From the previous section, it seems the expressive power of full FOL is impressive. It is not powerful enough, however. Some very simple natural language sentences are not expressible as formulae in FOL. One example is Most swans are white, as we will see below. Moreover, FOL is not equipped for describing intensional sentences, as discussed in Chapter 2. The most common escape from this problem of lack of expressive power is to resort to higher order logics like second-order logic, or to so-called *modal logic* especially designed to handle intensional contexts. The standard argument against this escape route is that this is only achievable if one accepts a complex and hence slow inference procedure. So, there is a trade-off between expressive power and tractability. We will comment below on one way of diminishing this problem by making the observation that all our models are, in some sense, finite. Another drawback of FOL is that it is hard to understand for people without a background in mathematics or other formal subjects.

In order for our conceptual models to grow dynamically into adequate models of the UoD, it is not sufficient to find ways of representing knowledge and rules that pertain to the UoD. We must also maintain consistency in the model over time. Consistency is a necessary condition for soundness, and inconsistencies should be kept out by implementing integrity constraints, as was explained in Chapter 3. Checking that a given integrity constraint has not been violated in practice entails access to some sort of integrity checking mechanism. One of the best candidates, and the one we will use, is the Prolog inference engine.

Even after an inference mechanism has been successfully adopted, the most serious problem with using FOL, and (consistent) extensions of it, remains: FOL is only semi-decidable. This means that if something is false in the model, then we can prove that this is in fact the case. But if something is true in the model, and we ask the implemented decision procedure about this particular formula, then we might never receive an answer. What is worse, we cannot know whether the mechanism is just having a hard time finding a proof of the truth of the formula, or if it is lost in an infinite loop of some sort. We will solve this problem by using a famous trick that lets us pose all interesting questions as questions about falsity (and never about truth), as will be explained below.

4.4 Conceptual Models as Logic Programs

This section suggests solutions to the problems explained in the previous section by introducing logic programs for representing our conceptual models. The rest of this chapter will, together with Appendix 5, provide a background for understanding the logical aspects of the Prolog meta-interpreter in the following chapter.

4.4.1 On the Lack of Expressive Power in FOL

First-order logic is extensional. Intensional analyses are simply left out; the semantics is based on the truth values of formulae. This can be seen as a voluntary limitation of language; if one wants to represent intensional aspects of formulae, one should use modal operators. Such operators, and their logics, have been described for the modalities knowledge, belief, necessity, possibility, provability, desire, obligation, and many more (including several modalities related to the passing of time). Our own approach to conceptual modelling is extensional. In other words, we have chosen not to describe any of the modalities of the kinds just mentioned. There is good evidence for the fact that we can well do without them. On the other hand, if any particular UoD should seem to require reasoning about intensional aspects, nothing in our approach deems this inappropriate. The grammar for our modelling language (cf. Appendix 1) would have to be extended, however, and we have chosen not to describe such extensions in this book.

If we investigate the example `Most swans are white` quoted above, its elusiveness is due to its use of the comparator "most". To a linguist, "most" is a quantifier. It is related to another quantifier, "few", in much the same way as $\forall$ is related to $\exists$. One could argue that the example sentence could be reasonably rewritten as `The number of white swans is larger than the number of non-white swans`. A problem is that the elements with the two properties `white` and `swan` are selected from the universal domain, i.e. the entire existing universe with all its elements.[1] For the sentence to be meaningful, the number of swans must be finite, so we are dealing with a finite subset of the universe. But we also need to know the cardinality of this set, i.e. how many swans there are. Something like the Closed World Assumption can help us here: the swans that we have data about in our information base are the only swans that exist! Logicians only became

---

1) Thankfully, we do not have to include neither all the elements that ever were, nor all the elements that will ever be, since this requires modal operators such as "it was once true that", and this is in the realm of temporal modal logic which constitutes one of the intensional logics we just defined away.

interested in the question of finite domains, i.e. limitations to finite UoDs, very late in the history of logic. The main reason was that, strange as it may seem, logic gets much harder to describe, and in particular it gets much harder to prove things about the logic, in finite domains. Happily, this is of less concern to the computer scientist who should instead feel that finite domains are more natural than infinite domains, since implemented programs have a finite number of procedures, databases have a finite number of records, etc. Implemented portions of logic, such as the parts of logic used for logic programming, therefore have a semantics that is different from standard (Tarski) semantics. This new kind of semantics is called Herbrand semantics.

If the domain is finite, the quantifiers can be understood in terms of logical connectives. The universal quantifier over some variable x ($\forall x$) becomes conjunction ($\wedge$), and the universal quantifier ($\exists x$) becomes disjunction ($\vee$). Thus, it seems like large parts of FOL collapse into propositional logic, which makes it possible to represent formulae in the language of "finite FOL" which were not possible to represent in FOL. If, on the other hand, a compact representation is the chief objective, one may turn to second-order logic, in which the quantifiers may range not only over variables, but also over the predicates of a formula.[2] The reason that the highly expressive second-order logic is not our first choice as a representation language is that we then cannot check the adequacy of our conceptual models using the soundness and completeness criteria. A discussion of why this is so is beyond the scope of this book. We will, however, briefly re-encounter second-order logic below as we discuss the language of Prolog, which has some higher order features.

4.4.2   On Maximising Readability in FOL

In Chapter 3, the introduction of a graphical notation for representing conceptual models was motivated. When we strive to make our representation as easily understandable as possible, we should take into account that it is normally supplemented by graphs. It thus remains to choose a textual representation in which it is easy for the user to see the connection between it and the corresponding graphs.

Example 4.3   Graphical representations of FOL.

Let us consider the attribute `is_member_of` introduced in Section 3.3 above to denote that a person is a member of a club. The graphical notation (cf. Figure 3.19) maps easily into the FOL formula

$\forall x \forall y$(Is-member-of(x,y) $\rightarrow$ (Person(x) $\wedge$ Club(y))).

Each attribute in a graph thus becomes a dyadic (two-place) predicate in FOL, while object types become monadic (one-place) predicates. That predicates may take a maximum

---

2) In second-order logic, we can express properties of relations, and so Most swans are white could be represented by the existence of a relation that is an injective, but not surjective, function from the non-white swans to the white swans (cf. Section 3.3.4).

of two arguments is not an actual limitation on the expressive power, since every *n*-place predicate may be replaced by a collection of two-place predicates. Note that if we would like to describe the graphical notation itself on the type level, propositional logic would suffice. The proposition corresponding to the graph at hand would be

Is-member-of $\rightarrow$ (Person $\wedge$ Club).

The direction of the arc from PERSON to CLUB is lost in this formula but this is in fact irrelevant. Just as $\wedge$ is a commutative connective, the arc may be reversed without loss of information; the only thing that might be affected is the appropriateness of the mnemonic name on the attribute.

The connection is not made between the graphical notation of our modelling language and pure FOL, but between its graphical notation and Prolog, the reasons for which will become apparent below. This mapping is perhaps the most straightforward imaginable, as shown by the following example.

Example 4.4   From graphical conceptual schema to Prolog.

Instances of the is_member_of relation, e.g.

```
John is a member of Rotary
```

are described by a series of facts:[3]

```
person(john).
club(rotary).
is_member_of(john,rotary).
```

or if one prefers:

```
person(p1).
person_name(p1,john).
club(c1).
club_name(c1,rotary).
is_member_of(p1,c1).
```

Rules are also easy to understand (cf. Appendix 5); in particular inheritance is natural. Consider, for example, Every woman is a person (cf. Figure 3.19):

```
person(X) :- woman(X).
```

Just as we decided above that intensional aspects of formulae could be left out of the conceptual model representation, we may argue that we do not need the full power of expression of FOL. To be specific, we can do without functions. This insight is very important to the readability aspect, since the understanding of function symbols is the most difficult part of using the language of FOL. Functions complicate things immensely even in the Herbrand semantics discussed in the previous subsection. The absence of

---

3) Note that Prolog has the opposite notation from FOL in that predicate names, and names for constants, start with lower-case letters and variable names with upper-case letters. Quotes allow for *John* to become a constant, as in 'John'.

functions allows us to work with a proper subset of Prolog that is often called *Database Prolog* and that has a relatively clear-cut Herbrand semantics.[4]

4.4.3   Logical Foundations of Prolog

With the creation of Prolog, two dreams met. The first dream was to construct an efficient theorem prover for as large a subset of logic as possible . The second dream was to construct a programming language with a *declarative semantics* based on set theory and logic, in contrast to the *operational (procedural) semantics* based on the behaviour of programs written in programming languages like Pascal. The declarative semantics of a logic program focuses on which values are true in a model of the program, much like standard model theory for FOL. The operational semantics, by contrast, focuses on how to compute values using the program.

The use of an established programming language as a basis for a conceptual modelling language has obvious advantages compared with inventing an entirely new language. Specifically, the inference engine of Prolog can be used to enforce integrity constraints and to maintain consistency in conceptual models. Most importantly, Prolog takes care of the problem that FOL is semi-decidable, in the following way.

We want our modelling language to be decidable, so one idea could be to search for a decidable subset of FOL. One such subset is monadic FOL in which all predicates are monadic, i.e. only properties (and not relations) can be described. But in conceptual modelling, being able to represent relationships between objects is pivotal to the quality of the models. A better idea might be to study *clausal form logic*. A *clause* is an implication $A \to C$, where the antecedent A is a conjunction of atomic formulae and the consequent C is a disjunction of atomic formulae. We mention clauses mainly as parts of Prolog programs and so use the stylised backward arrow, as in c :- a. Since it holds for propositional logic that $(A \to C) \Leftrightarrow (\neg A \vee C)$,

$$c_1, c_2, c_m :- A_1, A_2, A_n$$

is the clause form of $\neg A_1 \vee \neg A_2 \vee \neg A_n \vee C_1 \vee C_2 \vee C_m$. As one would expect, an *atomic formula* is just a predicate and its arguments, which are all terms. Our definition of terms

---

4)   In practice, it is convenient to allow for certain (sometimes predefined) Prolog predicates, e.g. *sum*, *count*, and *unique*, to be used when specifying rules in our modelling language, and the implementation of the language in fact allows for the insertion of a full Prolog program just about anywhere. Derivation rules in particular then become decidedly less complicated (with respect to clarity) to define and to understand. Using that possibility takes one away, however, from the simpler, but useful, examples that we discuss in this book, and we have therefore chosen to see this possibility as an extension to be used with good judgement. Hence, it is not covered by the discussion of the semantical properties of the language either in this chapter, or in Appendix 1. We adopt a similar liberal view on the arity of predicates; although a limitation to unary and binary predicates, representing entities and relationships respectively, would be an option, we recognise the freedom of having the possibility to use predicates of higher arity, e.g. findall. Like modal operators, the introduction of functions could, if desired, be made by expanding the grammar.

here differs from the one for FOL in Chapter 2. It adheres instead to the theory of logic programming. Given a finite set of constants (and, in logic programming, functions applied to these) we arrive at what is called a *Herbrand universe*, consisting of all ground terms which can be formed from the constants (and the functions). The predicates of the language can now form ground atomic formulae using the terms in the Herbrand universe, and the collection of all such formulae forms the so-called *Herbrand base*. A *literal* is an atomic formula or a negated atomic formula. We thus group the so-called positive literals of our original disjunction in the consequent of the clause and the negative literals in the antecedent of the clause. The indices m and n above may be 0, i.e. the consequent as well as the antecedent may be empty. All FOL formulae can be rewritten into clauses, and the rewriting is usually fairly simple (there is plenty of literature on such rewriting, see Section 4.7 below).

The next breakthrough from a computer science point of view came with *Herbrand's theorem* in 1930, which read something like the following. A set of clauses is inconsistent only if there is a finite subset of ground clauses of the original set which is inconsistent. This result yields a procedure for investigating whether a set of formulae logically entails another formula or not, if it is combined with a so-called refutation method. The notion of entailment, or logical consequence, can now be used in the following way. Let us assume that we wish to know whether the formula A_1 follows from the two formulae A_2 and $A_2 \rightarrow A_1$. We first negate A_1 and move it to the set of premises. Informally, this move is justified by the fact that A_1 follows logically from A_2 and $A_2 \rightarrow A_1$ only if the set $\{\neg A_1, A_2, A_2 \rightarrow A_1\}$ is unsatisfiable, i.e. if it is impossible to assign truth values to the atoms involved in such a way that all three formulae in the set evaluate to true. To put it yet another way: an unsatisfiable set has no model and it must therefore be inconsistent. Next, we rewrite all three formulae as clauses to get the set $\{:- A_1, A_2 :-, A_1 :- A_2\}$. We then check whether the set is satisfiable or unsatisfiable. In the 1950s and early 1960s much effort was put into finding such sets of rules, and in 1965 Robinson presented the *resolution rule* which contained a set with only one rule. In propositional logic, one can think of the resolution rule as saying: if $\neg A$ is true and $A \vee B$ is true, then B is true.

The resolution rule is very efficient compared with many other rules, but still not fast enough to constitute the basis for a modern programming language. The creators of Prolog therefore limited the expressive power of the language by declaring that Prolog would not handle general clauses, but only so-called Horn clauses. A *Horn clause* is a clause with at most one literal in its consequent. This rarely presents a constraint in practice to the typical Prolog programmer, and certainly not to the user of our modelling language, as will be seen in the following chapter.

4.4.4 Declarative Semantics for Prolog Programs

Prolog does not treat negation in the same way as classical logic where $\neg\neg P$ is equivalent to P, but rather in Prolog evaluating not(not(P)) is different from evaluating P. This difference can be traced back to Prolog's use of the syntactic rule *negation as failure*, which says that if some goal cannot be proven by Prolog, then the negation of this goal is true. The "semantic counterpart" is the Closed World Assumption introduced in Section 3.4 above, which says that if something is not in the information base, then it is considered false.[5] The quantifiers have simpler mappings. Variables used in queries are implicitly existentially quantified, while variables in facts are universally quantified. We illustrate some declarative readings in a simple example.

Example 4.5   An example Prolog program with clauses and interactions read declaratively.

```
person(john).
person(mary).
```

John and Mary are persons. Declarative reading: `Person(john) ∧ Person(mary)`.

```
club(rotary).
club(lions).
```

Rotary and Lions are clubs: `Club(rotary) ∧ Club(lions)`.

```
member(john,rotary).
```

John is a member of Rotary: `Member(john,rotary)`.

```
member(mary,X).
```

Mary is a member of every club: $\forall$x`Member(Mary,x)`.

```
hon_mem(X,Y) :- person(X), club(Y), person(Z), rec(X,Y,Z).
```

A person X is an honorary member of a club Y if there is a person Z who has recommended X:

```
∀x∀y∀z((Person(x) ∧ Club(y) ∧ Person(z) ∧ Rec(x,y,z)) →
Hon_mem(x,y)).
```

This formula was obtained by mechanically universally quantifying all the free variables. That this is in fact the formal version of the above sentence can be seen by transforming the formula to its equivalent formulation:

```
∀x∀y((Person(x) ∧ Club(y) ∧ ∃z(Person(z) ∧ Rec(x,y,z))) →
Hon_mem(x,y)).
```

```
?-member(john,X).
    X=rotary, yes
    ; no
```

The logical query "Is John a member of anything?": $\exists$x`Member(john,x)` is answered by "Yes, he is a member of Rotary" and then "No, he is not a member of anything else".

```
?-member(Y,Z).
```

---

5) It should be noted in this context that, as a computation rule, the Closed World Assumption is more powerful than negation as failure.

```
Y=john, Z=rotary, yes
; Y=mary, Z=X, yes
; no
```

The logical query "Is anybody a member of anything?": ∃y∃zMember(y,z) is answered by "Yes, John is a member of Rotary" and then "Yes, Mary is a member of everything", and finally "No, nobody else is a member of anything else".

Theorem provers are often hard to use, and since Prolog's aspirations included being more than an ordinary theorem prover, Prolog provides some built-in predicates, like any other programming language. Some of these, e.g. `findall`, can be shown not to belong to FOL, but to second-order logic, because it quantifies over predicates instead of over variables as in FOL. These built-in predicates thus facilitate the use of Prolog as a programming language whilst making the semantic analysis of Prolog programs complex. For this reason, and also because there are so many variants and dialects of Prolog, the language is often approached without the built-in predicates. The name of the language obtained from Prolog in this way is `Datalog`. Referring simply to `Datalog` assumes exclusion not only of the built-in predicates of Prolog, but also of all its function and negation symbols.

For many tasks, amongst which is conceptual modelling, extensions of Prolog provide a surprisingly simple way of representing different UoDs. However, Prolog is not typed, and there is no obvious way of enforcing constraints on an information base. It is therefore necessary to impose a structure on Prolog that has been developed especially for conceptual modelling. There are several such modelling languages, common to which is the fact that they can be used to structure modelling in Prolog. We argue that our modelling tool described in the following chapter has the desired properties. It is based on the modelling language CMOL [Bubenko84], developed by Janis Bubenko Jr and Eva Lindencrona for educational purposes, and originally not intended for machine implementation. We have collected some interesting sets of predicates mentioned in this section into a Venn diagram in Figure 4.2. The set CMOLP is included for historical reasons. Looking at the diagram, one might get the impression that using our modelling language (MOLOC in the diagram) incorporates programming in full Prolog. This is not the case: it can be used successfully with a minimal knowledge of the Prolog language. However, our liberal view explained earlier in this chapter makes us refrain from excluding any particular predicate of Prolog. This freedom is also demonstrated in the grammar in Appendix 1. What neither that grammar nor Figure 4.2 shows, however, is that a typical textual conceptual schema, as exemplified by the two cases in Appendices 2 and 3, essentially uses Prolog in two ways only. First, to map the graphical conceptual schema into textual form in a straightforward way, and secondly, to make the definition of rules as simple as possible. The grammar in Appendix 1 is context free, and so it does not show, for example, that every use of a ternary Prolog predicate sooner or later has to be linked to a binary predicate representing an attribute in the conceptual model, or to a unary predicate representing an entity. Similarly, the diagram in Figure 4.2 fails to convey the information that instances from the intersection containing the instance `var`, for example, are very rarely chosen for inclusion in conceptual schemata.

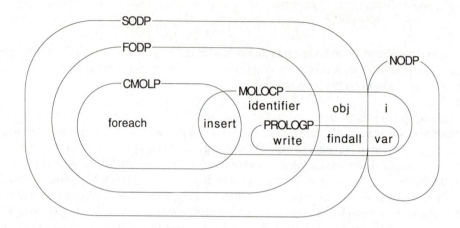

FODP = First Order Definable Predicates
SODP = Second Order Definable Predicates
NODP = NO Declarative semantics for Predicates
CMOLP = CMOL Predicates
MOLOCP = MOLOC Predicates
PROLOGP = Prolog Predicates

Figure 4.2 *Some interesting sets of predicates*

4.5 Related Areas of Interest

4.5.1　Artificial Intelligence

Using general formulae to reach particular conclusions is characteristic of deductive reasoning. An *inductive method* instead infers a general principle or *law* as its conclusion, with particular instances as its premisses. In a valid *inductive inference*, the truth of the premisses does not entail the truth of the conclusion. A valid deductive inference, by contrast, is truth preserving since it contains a conclusion such that it would be contradictory to assert the premisses and deny the conclusion. As everyone knows, computers are extremely good at complicated tasks that involve storing proof-structures, applying algorithms, matching, etc. Such features make it possible for computers to handle inductive inferences. The problem is then partly reduced to determining the applicable rules or laws of probability in order to make useful inductive inferences. Since such systems handle only probable truths, they should supply functions for changing premisses and for "making inferences undone". Such *non-monotonic reasoning* methods constitute the core of most artificial intelligence tools developed within areas such as inductive logic programming and explanation-based learning. In conceptual modelling, the knowledge acquisition phase, in which all relevant information is identified and represented as data, typically requires inductive reasoning. Because of the complexity of this task, tools that support knowledge acquisition are scarce. This has been an active subarea of research in artificial intelligence since the 1970s.

4.5.2   Software Engineering

Software engineering and conceptual modelling advocates are sometimes described as looking at the same coin from two different sides, unable to flip the coin around. This is untrue. The two areas do, however, use different formal theories for their foundations. The foundations of software engineering are to some extent provided by dynamic logic. Moreover, software engineering is more dependent on modalities related to time than is conceptual modelling. A vital part of software engineering is the ability to verify the correctness of programs by means of pre- and postconditions of assignments, described in so-called *Hoare triples*. A Hoare triple might describe a loop invariant, for instance. A deductive system called *Hoare logic*, whose formulae are inductive assertions, can be used to prove properties of programs. Software engineering techniques are normally applied in the design phase of systems development, after the specification of an information system. They can be used independently of whether conceptual modelling has been used to provide the specification or not.

One way of comparing the two approaches is perhaps to look at the event concept (described in Section 3.2 above, and further in Section 5.3 below), whose preconditions are similar to those used in Hoare triples, and for which postconditions may also be easily formulated. The two approaches share the notion of information state, and the view that the passing of time may change this state, creating a dynamic and complex representation.

4.6 Some Relevant Literature

A classic introductory text on logic is [Lemmon87]. A more advanced textbook is [Hamilton78]. Deeper ideas and results can be found in [Chang90], but be prepared to spend a month on each chapter. A nice philosophical essay on logic is [Haack78]. The best first book on modal logic is [vonWright51]; then one can go on to study [Chellas80]. Prolog has been described in dozens of books. A good beginner's introduction is [Clocksin90]. The bible on logic programming in general, and Prolog in particular, is [Lloyd87]. If one is interested in the logical properties of `Datalog`, and other pure logic programming and deductive database issues, a good collection of research papers is [Minker88]. The mechanisation of logic is investigated in the area of automated reasoning. [Chang73] is the classic here, modern alternatives to which are [Gallier87] and [Lalement93]. These books are all hard to read, but serve well as references for finding out more about rewriting to clausal form, refutation methods, or Herbrand's theorem. A recent textbook on artificial intelligence is [Russell95], the first chapter of which is an excellent introduction to the field. The book that perhaps best captures the spirit of the field is [Kurzweil90]. Textbooks more oriented towards logic programming in artificial intelligence are [Lukaszewicz90] and the easy-to-read [Rowe88]. A good textbook on the formalisation of programs and program verification is [Gries81].

4.7 Exercises

4.1   Suppose that a given atomic fact q is not derivable from an information base IB1. The query ?-q. is then answered in the negative, given IB1. Suppose further that q is not derivable from another information base IB2.
   a) Is it necessarily the case that q is not derivable from the intersection of the two information bases? Formally, is (IB1 ∩ IB2) ⟹ q necessarily false?
   b) Is it necessarily the case that q is not derivable from the difference IB1 − IB2? Formally, is (IB1 − IB2) ⟹ q necessarily false?

4.2   Suppose that a given atomic fact q is derivable from an information base IB1, and also from another information base IB2.
   a) Is it necessarily the case that q is derivable from the intersection of the two information bases? Formally, is (IB1 ∩ IB2) ⟹ q necessarily true?
   b) Is it necessarily the case that q is derivable from the difference IB1 − IB2? Formally, is (IB1 − IB2) ⟹ q necessarily true?

4.3   Just like FOL, Prolog has limited expressive power. This means that there are interesting sentences that one cannot express within the language. If one considers, for instance, the sentences below about various relationships between people:

   1. Adam loves Eve
   2. Eve loves Adam
   3. Anne loves Adam
   4. Adam is married to Eve
   5. Eve is married to Adam
   6. Anne is not married

one finds that sentences 1 to 5 are easily represented as Prolog facts:

```
loves(adam,eve).          married_to(adam,eve).
loves(eve,adam).          married_to(eve,adam).
loves(anne,adam).
```

while sentence 6 cannot be translated in any straightforward way.

If one writes

```
not(married_to(anne,X)).
```

it does capture the meaning of 6, but it will in no way affect the results of any query. If, for instance, someone were to ask

```
?-married_to(anne,X). or
?-married_to(anne,adam).
```

these queries will be answered by "no" by the Prolog interpreter, regardless of whether

```
not(married_to(anne,X)).
```

is in the information base (or Prolog program) or not! If one instead tries

```
single(anne).
```

it again captures the meaning of 6, but now the user must bear in mind the relationship between the predicates `married_to` and `single`, and the natural definition of `single` in Prolog is

```
single(X) :- not(married_to(X,Y)).
```

and we are back at square one...

Explain which of the following sentences are expressible in Prolog and which are not, and why.

7. Adam is married to someone.
8. Nobody likes Anne.
9. Many people like Eve.
10. Most men like women.
11. If a person is married to another, then that other person must also be married to the first person.
12. Every class of classes of sets has infinitely many subclasses that each consists of an uncountably infinite number of classes of sets.
13. Everybody likes themselves.

CHAPTER 5

Logic Programming
for Conceptual Modelling

In this chapter, we show how logic programming can be used for conceptual modelling. Our approach is based on the logic programming language Prolog, which means that a conceptual schema and an information base are defined in terms of a Prolog program. As discussed in Chapter 4, there are major advantages in using Prolog as a basis for a conceptual modelling language, in particular the fact that Prolog provides a homogeneous environment by allowing base statements, rules, and queries to be expressed in the same language. In the next section we give an overview of the architecture of an information system. The following four sections describe its components in detail.

5.1 Information Systems Architecture

The architecture of an information system (depicted in Figure 5.1) is based on the view of an information system as consisting of three parts: a conceptual schema, an information base, and an information processor, cf. Section 3.4.

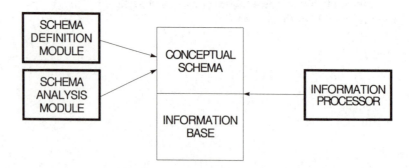

Figure 5.1 *Information systems architecture*

The conceptual schema contains the definitions of entity types, data types, attributes, event types, and rules. The information base describes entities, data objects, and associations between them. The information processor is used to query the conceptual schema and information base, and to change the information base in accordance with the event types and rules defined in the schema. A schema definition module is used to specify a conceptual schema, and a schema analysis module contains tools for the verification and validation of the conceptual schema.

The information processor, the schema definition module, and the schema analysis modules are used to build, manipulate, and query a conceptual schema and an information base. The following sections give a detailed description of each component. We shall use the schema shown in Figure 5.2 as an example throughout this chapter.

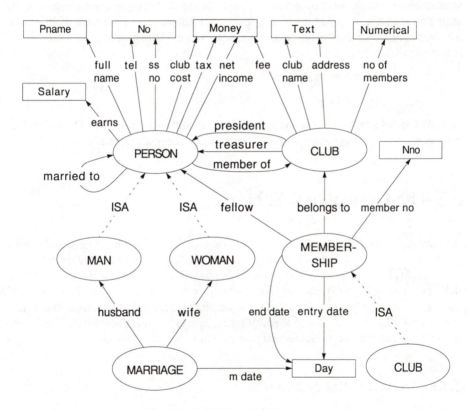

Figure 5.2 *The club schema*

5.2 The Information Base

An information base consists of a set of type statements and attribute statements, expressed as Prolog facts. For example:

```
man(joe).
man(pete).
woman(mary).
```

The first of these facts says that the object identifier `joe` denotes an entity of the type `man`. Now for some attribute statements:

```
earns(joe, 9000).
earns(pete, 8000).
president(rotary, joe).
```

If an attribute is multi-valued, several facts may be needed to represent the values of that attribute for an entity. For example, supposing an attribute `child_of` were multi-valued, the following facts might occur in an information base expressing that Joe has the children Mary, Sally, and Pete:

```
child_of(joe, mary).
child_of(joe, sally).
child_of(joe, pete).
```

Note that an information base consists of only one- and two-place facts. One-place facts correspond to type statements, and two-place facts to attribute statements.

5.3 The Conceptual Schema

A conceptual schema is represented by a Prolog program consisting of facts and rules. A problem in this context is that a Prolog program is a flat structure of clauses, which implies that Prolog does not support any kind of modularity. In order to overcome this deficiency, at least partially, we lay down certain conventions for the declaration of a conceptual schema that give the schema declaration a clear and modularised structure. A schema consists of declarations of entity types, data types, and event types. The following sections describe declarations and provide a number of examples.

5.3.1 Declaring Entity Types

The first clause of an entity type declaration is a fact with the form `entity(entity_id)`, where `entity_id` is an entity type. For an example, see the first line of Example 5.1.

Example 5.1   An entity type declaration.

```
entity(person).
attribute(ss_no,
                domain(person),
                range(no),
                mapping(1, 1, t, p)).
attribute(full_name,
                domain(person),
                range(p_name),
                mapping(1, m, t, p)).
attribute(tel,
                domain(person),
                range(no),
                mapping(m, m, t, p)).
attribute(earns,
                domain(person),
                range(salary),
                mapping(1, m, t, p)).
                transition_violation :-
                before(earns(Per, Before_sal)),
                after((earns(Per, After_sal),
                After_sal<Before_sal)).
                /* The salary of a person may not decrease */
attribute(tax,
                domain(person),
                range(money),
                mapping(1, m, t, p)).
attribute(net_income,
                domain(person),
                range(money),
                mapping(1, m, t, p)).
                net_income(Person, Net):- earns(Person, Sal),
                tax(Person, Tax), Net is Sal - Tax.
```

Generalisation relationships are specified by means of Prolog rules. To express the idea that person is a supertype of man, the following rule would be used:

```
person(P):- man(P).
```

Note that the body of such a rule may be a conjunction. For example:

```
flying_creature(X):- bird(X), not(penguin(X)).
```

Virtual entity declarations, i.e. static derivation rules concerning type statements, can be given by specifying a rule that defines which entities belong to an entity type. Suppose there is a subtype high-income_employee to person. A virtual entity declaration for high-income_employee might then be

```
high-income_employee(H):- person(H), earns(H, S), S > 100000.
```

The main part of an entity type declaration consists of the declarations of the attributes of the entity type. For each attribute its domain, range, and mapping constraints must be specified. In addition a derivation rule, an initialisation rule, and integrity constraints may be specified. To specify the mandatory part of an attribute declaration, one fact is stated. An example of such a fact is the following:

```
attribute(earns,
                domain(person),
                range(salary),
                mapping(1, m, t, p)).
```

The first component of this structure specifies the attribute itself. The second specifies its domain, the third its range, and the fourth its mapping constraints. The domain must always be the entity type currently being specified. The range must be an entity type or a data type (see Section 5.3.2 for data types). The mapping constraints of the attribute have the format

mapping(**m|1, m|1, t|p, t|p**)

The first component of this structure indicates whether the attribute is single valued or not. When single valued, this component is set to *1*, otherwise to *m* (for *multi-valued*). The second component of the structure indicates whether the attribute is injective, in which case the component is set to *1*, otherwise to *m*. The third component indicates the totality of the attribute. A *t* indicates totality, a *p* partiality. The fourth component indicates the surjectivity of the attribute. When surjective, this component is set to *t*, otherwise to *p*.

The next clause to be specified is a static derivation rule describing how the values of the attribute can be computed, if such a rule exists. The example below specifies how the net income of a person is calculated by subtracting tax from the person's salary:

```
net_income(Person, Net):- earns(Person, Sal),
                tax(Person, Tax),
                Net = Sal - Tax.
```

Sometimes more than one rule may be required for the definition of a derived attribute:

```
married_to(Man, Woman):-
                marriage(Mar), husband(Mar, Man), wife(Mar, Woman).

married_to(Woman, Man):-
                marriage(Mar), husband(Mar, Man), wife(Mar, Woman).
```

Derived attributes are often used for aggregated information, like sums and averages. The rule below states that the total cost incurred for club membership is calculated by summing the fees of the clubs of which a person is a member:

```
club_cost(Per, Cost):-
                findall(Fee,
                (membership(Memb), fellow(Memb, Per),
                belongs_to(Memb, Club), fee(Club, Fee)),
                Fees),
                sum(Fees, Cost).
```

Sometimes it is useful to assign a value to an attribute automatically as soon as an entity has been created. This is achieved by means of initialisation declarations. For example:

```
initialize(earns(Person, 7000)).
```

Including this clause in the declaration of the entity type `person` sets the value of the attribute `earns` to `7000` as soon as an instance of the type is created (see the `new_entity` predicate, Section 5.3.3).

In order to enable the information system to enforce integrity constraints, we use a special device to express these constraints. A static integrity constraint is declared by a rule with the form

```
inconsistent :- body.
```

where **body** is the negation of the constraint. In other words, **body** specifies a condition that should not hold in any state. The following constraint says that the president of a club may not be married to its treasurer:

```
inconsistent :- president(Club, Pres),
                treasurer(Club, Treas),
                married_to(Pres, Treas).
```

The following constraint expresses the fact that a person cannot be both a man and a woman (the types `man` and `woman` are disjoint):

```
inconsistent:- man(P), woman(P).
```

The next constraint states that every person is either a man or a woman (`man` and `woman` are exhaustive for their supertype `person`):

```
inconsistent:- person(P), not(man(P)), not(woman(P)).
```

This way of expressing static constraints makes it simple to check if a constraint has been violated: if at any time `inconsistent` is derivable, the information base will have violated an integrity constraint.

A dynamic integrity constraint is declared by a rule with the form

```
transition_violation :- before(before_body),
after(after_body).
```

where `before_body` describes a state before a state change takes place and `after_body` the state after the state change has taken place. If `before_body` is true in the state before the state change and `after_body` is true afterwards, then a dynamic integrity constraint has been violated. The constraint below says that the salary of a person must not decrease:

```
transition_violation :- before(earns(Per, Before_sal)),
                after(earns(Per, After_sal),
                After_sal < Before_sal).
```

We have now covered the declaration of attributes. The next part of an entity type declaration is the optional identifier declaration, which has the form

```
identifier(entity_name, attribute_list).
```

The attributes in `attribute_list` uniquely identify an entity of type `entity_name`. For example:

```
identifier(person, [full_name, tel]).
```

In this case two people are not permitted to have the same name and phone number.

Any integrity constraint that does not naturally belong to a certain attribute can be stated at the end of an entity type declaration. The syntax of such a constraint is exactly the same as the rules described above.

5.3.2   Declaring Data Types

The declaration of the entity types is followed by the declaration of the data types (lexical types). A declaration of a data type consists of a fact and a rule. The fact is of the form `data_type(identifier)`, which states that `identifier` is a data type. For example:

```
data_type(salary).
```

The rule specifies the basic type (i.e. atom, integer, or number) of the data type and the range of values it may take. In order to specify that `salary` is a number between 0 and 500,000, we write

```
salary(S):- number(S), S > 0, S < 500000.
```

5.3.3   Declaring Event Rules

In Prolog, a program can be updated by means of the built-in predicates `assert` and `retract`. In order to model the dynamics of an application more naturally, updates of the information base should only be allowed through a set of predefined rules in the schema. These are called event rules, cf. Section 3.2.3. An event rule specifies a set of update operations. Upon invocation of an event rule, either all of its update operations are performed, or none of them. In other words, the execution of an event rule either commits or aborts its operations on an all or nothing principle.

We now turn to the syntax of event rule declarations. The declaration of an event rule consists of a Prolog rule (see Example 5.2), the head of which has the form

```
event(event_name, argument_list, interface_list)
```

as in the first row of Example 5.2.

Example 5.2 An event declaration.

```
event(join_club, [Ss, C_name, Date], ['Ss_no', 'Club', 'Date']):-
        precondition((ss_no(P, Ss), person(P))),
        precondition((club_name(Club, C_name),club(Club))),
        precondition((not((membership(Mem),
                           belongs_to(Mem,Club),
                           fellow(Mem, P))))),
        new_entity(membership, M),
        insert(belongs_to(M, Club)),
        insert(fellow(M, P)),
        insert(date_joined(M, Date)).
```

The head of the rule gives the form for event messages concerning the event type being described. The first component of the structure is the name of the event type, `join_club` in our example. The second component is a list of variables, corresponding to the parameter list of an event message. The third component is a list of constants, corresponding to the variables of the second component. These constants are used for the interface described in Section 5.4.

The body of an event rule consists of two parts: preconditions and postconditions. The preconditions specify conditions that must hold true for the event to commit. The postconditions specify how the information base must be changed.

The syntax of a precondition is `precondition(body)`, where **body** specifies a number of facts that must hold true in the state in which the event has been invoked. If any of the facts in **body** are false, the execution of the event rule will be aborted. The first precondition in Example 5.2 says that a person with the social security number specified in the event message must exist. The second precondition says that a club with the specified name must exist, and the third precondition that the person must not already be a member of the club. (The qualification of variables with unary predicates `club(Club)`, `person(P)`, `(membership(Mem)`, is in fact not necessary in order to bind them to instances. It is merely a clarification intended to make the code easier to read.)

There are seven types of postconditions: three of them manipulate attribute values, two create and delete instances, and two change the type of instances. The predicate `insert` is used to assign values to attributes. For example, `insert(tel(joe, '123456'))`. The opposite of `insert` is the predicate `delete`, which is used to remove values from attributes: `delete(tel(joe, '123456'))`, for example. If `delete` is used with a variable, all matching attribute statements will be deleted. For example, `delete(tel(joe, T))` deletes all the telephone numbers of Joe.

For convenience there is also a predicate `replace` which can be seen as a combination of `delete` and `insert`. For example, `replace(earns(joe, 9000))`. The effect of this clause is to remove the old value of Joe's salary and replace it with 9,000. The same effect would have been obtained with the following two clauses:

```
delete(earns(joe, E)).
insert(earns(joe, 9000)).
```

In the case of a multi-valued attribute, `replace` will remove all the old attribute values before inserting new ones.

To create a new instance of a type the predicate `new_entity` is used. For example:

```
new_entity(person, P).
```

When this clause is executed the variable P becomes bound to a brand new object identifier thus creating an instance of the type `person`.

The predicate `remove` is used to remove an instance from the information base. For example, `remove(joe)`.

It is possible to change the type of an instance by means of the predicates `include` and `exclude`. The predicate `include` is used to add an instance to a type, while `exclude` is used to remove an instance from a type. For example, the following would change the gender of Mary:

```
exclude(woman, mary).
include(man, mary).
```

The postconditions of event rules have a very simple form; they simply consist of a sequence of insert, delete, replace, remove, exclude, or include operations. There are no special constructs for selections and iterations. However, it is easy to introduce such constructs, and different ways to do so are discussed in Exercise 5.13.

Example 5.3 Consider an information base containing the following statements:

```
woman(mary).
ss_no(mary, '4567_89').
full_name(mary, 'Mary Roberts').
tel(mary, '222222').
earns(mary, 12000).
tax(mary, 4000).
club(lions).
club_name(lions, 'Lions').
address(lions, '22 Covent Garden').
fee(lions, 200).
```

Now, suppose that Mary joins Lions. Our information system is informed of this event by the submission of the following event message: ⟨join_club, ['4567_89', 'Lions', '910810']⟩. The information base is now updated, and the new information base contains the following statements:

```
woman(mary).
ss_no(mary, '4567_89').
full_name(mary, 'Mary Roberts').
tel(mary, '222222').
earns(mary, 12000).
tax(mary, 4000).
club(lions).
club_name(lions, 'Lions').
address(lions, '22 Covent Garden').
fee(lions, 200).
```

```
membership(ms1).
fellow(ms1, mary),
belongs_to(ms1, lions).
date_joined(ms1, '910810').
```

We now introduce a restricted form of internal events. Recall that an event rule consists of two parts: an occurrence rule and an action rule. When a state change occurs that satisfies the occurrence rule, the action rule must be executed. The occurrence rule is expressed as a condition embracing two states: the state before the change and the state after.

The following example of an internal event type says that a message is to be printed if a person's salary has more than doubled:

```
internal_event(high_increase,
            before((earns(P, S))),
            after((earns(P, N), S2 is 2*S, N>S2))):-
                            write('The salary of'),
                            write(P),
                            write('has been more than
                            doubled.').
```

The syntax of an internal event type is

```
internal_event(Event_name,
            before(Before_condition),
            after(After_condition)):-
            Action_rule.
```

Informally, the semantics of an internal event rule is that if there is a state change, and

`Before_condition` is true in the state before the change, and
`After_condition` is true in the state after the change, then
`Action_rule` is to be executed.

If several internal events are invoked by a single state change, they are executed in the order in which they appear in the schema. The execution of each internal event induces a state change.

5.4 The Information Processor

We now describe how a user interacts with the system. In the rest of this section, we assume that a Prolog program containing a schema and a corresponding information base has been consulted. A user can then query the schema and information base and modify the information base. To query the schema and the information base, the user asks ordinary Prolog queries. A useful predicate is `obj`, the syntax of which is `obj(S)`, where `S` is an object identifier. This query will produce all the values of the entity's attributes. A transcript showing how the user may interact with a conceptual model is shown in Figure 5.3.

```
?-full_name(P,N),salary(P,S).
     P = pete,  N = 'Peter Roberts',  S = 9000;
     P = pete,  N = 'Peter Roberts',  S = 9000;
     P = mary,  N = 'Mary Roberts',   S = 12000;
     P = sally, N = 'Sally Jones',    S = 6000 ;
     no
?-findall(M,married_to(M,P),Married).
     M = _0, P = _1, Married = [pete,mary]
?-findall(Name,
        (president(C,P),full_name(P,Name)),
        Presidents).
     Name = _0, C = _1, P = _2,
     Presidents = ['Peter Roberts','Joe Smith']
?-e.
Event> change_salary.
Ssnum> '4567_89'.
New salary> 8000.
Before the event the following holds:
salary(mary,12000)
After the event the following would hold:
salary(mary,8000)
8000<12000
This implies a violation of a dynamic constraint
and no updates have been performed.
yes

?- e.
Event> elect_treasurer.
Ssnum> '4567_89'.
Club> 'Lions'.
If the updates were performed a constraint
would be violated:
president(lion,pete)
treasurer(lion,mary)
married_to(pete,mary)
Since consistency violations have been detected
no updates have been performed.
yes
```

Figure 5.3 *A transcript of a session (user input italicised)*

As mentioned earlier, a user is not allowed to update an information base using Prolog's assert and retract predicates directly. Instead all updates must be performed via an information processor, written in Prolog. This makes it possible to enforce integrity constraints and to ensure that the information base is only updated using the event rules in the schema. If the preconditions of an event rule are not satisfied, or the execution of the event rule would violate an integrity constraint, then no updates will be performed. In such a case the information processor would also inform the user of the reason for the abortion of the event rule.

To invoke an event the user types an *e* and is then prompted for an event message. Figure 5.3 shows the transcript of a session on a terminal where three queries are submitted, and two event rules are invoked. The first query asks for the names and salaries of all the people registered in the system. The second query asks for everybody who is married. The third query asks for the names of everybody who is a president. The first event message specifies a change of salary to 8,000 for the person whose social security number is "4567_89". However, the salary of that person is currently 9,000, and since there is a dynamic integrity constraint forbidding salary decreases, the event message is rejected. The second event message specifies that the person whose social security number is "4567_89" is elected treasurer of Lions. However, this would mean that the treasurer of Lions would be married to its president, and since there is a static integrity constraint forbidding this, this event message is also rejected, and no updates are performed.

5.5 The Schema Definition and Analysis Modules

The most straightforward way to define a conceptual schema is to edit a file containing a Prolog program according to the conventions in Section 5.3. The schema definition module provides the convenience of a graphical interface for specifying a schema. The user enters a graphical schema, which is then transformed into a Prolog program. Those parts of the schema that cannot be represented graphically can be added as Prolog clauses after the transformation.

The schema analysis module assists a user in checking the correctness of the conceptual schema. The problem of correctness of conceptual schemas has two aspects: verification and validation. Verification concerns the mutual consistency of the defined concepts. Validation concerns the consistency of the model with the object system.

An important part of the verification of a schema consists of checking to see that the static constraints are not contradictory. Verification is also concerned with those dynamic aspects of a schema that are expressed by events and dynamic constraints. Specifically, a schema should satisfy the following properties:

- For each event rule, there must be a state in which the event rule can be invoked and successfully committed.
- For each entity type, some sequence of event rule executions must exist that leads to a state where an instance of the entity type exists.
- For each attribute, some sequence of event rule executions must exist that leads to a state, where a value of the attribute for some instance exists.

Validation of a conceptual model cannot be performed automatically since it concerns the relationship of the model to reality. One way to check the consistency of the model with the UoD is to generate a prototype database system from a description of the UoD. This enables the user to confront the conceptual model with data from the real world and test the generated system, thereby ensuring that the model fulfils expectations. The schema analysis module provides facilities for prototyping even when the specified schema is not complete. For instance, a user may construct an information base without using any event rules and this information base can then be checked for violation of integrity constraints. This may be useful when constructing a prototype of a system, since it is not often obvious at the outset which event types are required, and it may therefore be desirable to declare event rules later. It is often useful to be able to fill an information base with facts, despite a lack of event rules.

5.6 Meta-schemas

It is essential for almost any organisation to keep information about its business. In many cases, it is also important to keep track of this information itself, and many companies view their business information as one of their most valuable assets. This business information is often dispersed across many different locations, such as databases, files, programs, or even old-fashioned card indexes. In order to obtain an overview of all that scattered information, it is customary to describe it with a conceptual model, usually called a *meta-schema*. A meta-schema does not describe the business of an organisation; instead it describes *information about* the business. This means that a meta-schema can be viewed as being on a higher level than an ordinary conceptual schema, see Figure 5.4. Meta-schemas have become so important that there now exist specialised computerised tools for managing them; such tools are called *data dictionaries* or *repositories*.

We now turn to a meta-schema for conceptual schemas. This means that we take conceptual modelling notions as our object system and create a schema for them, see Figure 5.5. The object systems encountered in most of the examples earlier in this book have been fairly concrete ones containing objects like people, companies, cities, and countries. However, the creation of a schema for a conceptual modelling language involves modelling linguistic symbols and linguistic expressions that are far less tangible. For example, the object type NON-LEXICAL_OBJECT_TYPE in the meta-schema above could have the following instances: PERSON, DEPARTMENT, and CAR. ATTRIBUTE could have: salary, ss_no, and colour. The schema of Figure 5.5 only models linguistic symbols and a few simple rules, such as typing and mapping constraints. A more complete schema would need to model general integrity constraints, derivation rules, event rules, type statements, and attribute statements. In Exercise 5.10, we discuss how to extend the schema above to include such constructs.

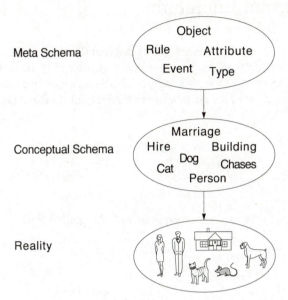

Figure 5.4 *Schema levels*

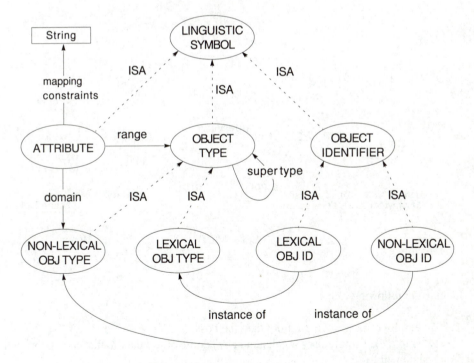

Figure 5.5 *A meta-schema*

5.7 Some Relevant Literature

This chapter is based on the paper [Johannesson90]. A general survey of the application of logic to information and database systems is given in [Gallaire84]. [Gallaire78] is a classic collection of papers on this topic, whereas [Minker88] is a more recent collection. The logical database language LDL, an extension of relational database languages, is presented in [Naqvi89].

5.8 Exercises

5.1 Specify a conceptual schema that corresponds with the graph below.

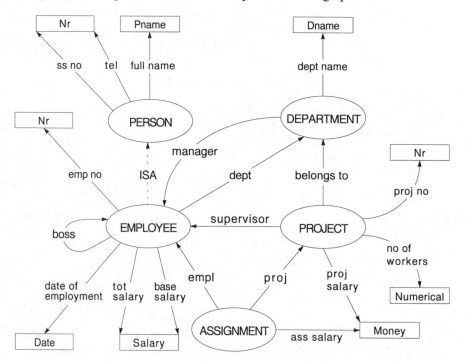

Include the following rules:

- An employee may not earn more than the boss.
- An employee's total salary is calculated by adding base salary to that earned through assignments.

- The manager of a department must work for that department.
- The salary of an employee may not decrease.
- The attribute `no_of_workers` is calculated by counting the number of employees assigned to a project.

Specify event rules for the following events:

- Hire an employee
- Sack an employee
- Change an employee's salary
- Change the department of an employee
- Assign an employee to a project

(A solution to this exercise is found in Appendix 3.)

5.2 We have introduced a special syntax for specifying typing and mapping constraints. However, these constraints could be expressed by the ordinary construction `inconsistent:-` . Using `inconsistent`, give rules that express typing and mapping constraints and show how extension constraints can be represented. This exercise shows that the special syntax for mapping constraints and extension constraints is only a form of 'syntactical sugar'.

5.3 An attribute is called *stable* if it receives its value upon the creation of an entity, and its value does not change during the entire lifetime of the entity. Sketch an algorithm that analyses the event rules in a schema and determines whether an attribute is stable or not.

5.4 An event type is called *irreversible* if an occurrence of the event type changes the state of the object system into a state from which it is impossible to return to the original state. For each event type in Exercise 5.1, determine whether it is irreversible. Give examples to motivate your answers.

5.5 Necessary as well as deontic constraints have been defined in the same way; for static constraints the construction `inconsistent:-` was used. Recall that if the execution of an event rule implies a violation of an integrity constraint, then no updates are performed. Explain why this is a limitation. Suggest an extension that could overcome this problem.

5.6 Read Exercise 3.18 and its solution. Write integrity constraints and derivation rules for the rules suggested in the solution.

5.7 Examine the graphical representation of the schema below.

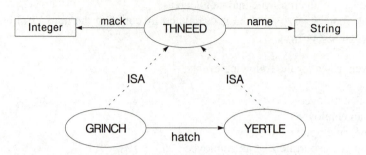

The mapping constraints for both the attribute `hatch` and the attribute `mack` are (1, m, t, p). The schema also contains the following integrity constraints:

```
inconsistent :- grinch(G), yertle(Y), hatch(G, Y), mack(G, Gm),
                mack(Y, Ym), Gm < Ym.
inconsistent :- grinch(G), mack(G, M), M > 1500.
inconsistent :- yertle(Y), mack(Y, M), M < 2000.
```

Consider the information base below:

```
grinch(g1).
grinch(g2).
yertle(y1).
yertle(y2).
hatch(g1, y1).
hatch(g2, y2).
mack(g1, 1000).
mack(g2, 2000).
mack(y1, 2000).
mack(y2, 1000).
```

a) Explain why the information base above violates the integrity constraints.
b) Is it possible to modify the attribute statements in the information base in such a way that the information base no longer violates any of the constraints? You may not modify any of the type statements. (Hint: the attribute `hatch` is total.)

5.8 Examine the graphical representation of the schema below.

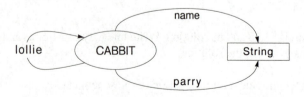

The schema includes the following mapping constraints:

```
name (1, 1, t, p)
parry (m, m, t, p)
lollie (1, 1, p, p)
```

The schema contains the following event rules:

```
event(loll, [Name1, Name2], ['Name1', 'Name2']):-
            precondition((name(C1, Name1), name(C2, Name2))),
            insert(lollie(C1, C2)).
event(delete_parry, [Name, Parr], ['Name', 'Parr']):-
            precondition((name(C, Name))),
            delete(parry(C, Parr)).
```

Consider the following information base:

```
cabbit(c1).
cabbit(c2).
cabbit(c3).
name(c1, 'Peter').
name(c2, 'John').
name(c3, 'Steve').
parry(c1, 'XYZ').
parry(c2, 'XYZ').
parry(c2, 'QWERTY').
parry(c3, 'XYZ').
lollie(c1, c2).
```

Specify what the contents of the information base would be after the updates caused by each of the following event messages. In each case, you should start with the original information base as printed above.

a) ⟨loll, ['John', 'Steve']⟩
b) ⟨loll, ['Peter', 'Steve']⟩
c) ⟨loll, ['John', 'Robert']⟩
d) ⟨delete_parry, ['John', 'XYZ']⟩
e) ⟨delete_parry, ['Peter', 'XYZ']⟩

5.9 Write down an information base representing the schema in Figure 6.8 using the schema given in Figure 5.5.

5.10 Extend the schema in Figure 5.5 by including general integrity constraints, derivation rules, event rules, type statements, and attribute statements. The schema should be sufficiently detailed for the following queries to be expressed in the language given by the schema:

- Is there any attribute statement for the attribute XYZ?
- Is the object identifier ABC involved in any attribute statement?
- Which event rules create instances of the type XYZ?
- Which event rules update the attribute XYZ?

- Which attributes are derivable?
- Which attributes are used to compute the attribute XYZ?
- Which deontic constraints concern the attribute XYZ?
- Which dynamic integrity constraints concern the attribute XYZ?

5.11 Consider the following conceptual schema:

```
entity(jabber).
attribute(ss_no,
                domain(jabber),
                range(string),
                mapping(1, 1, t, p)).
attribute(wock,
                domain(jabber),
                range(integer),
                mapping(1, m, t, p)).
attribute(rick,
                domain(jabber),
                range(integer),
                mapping(1, m, t, p)).

rick(J,R) :- wock(J,W), R is W + 10.

event(change_wock,[SS_no, W],
                ['Social security number', 'New wock']) :-
                precondition((jabber(J), ss_no(J, SS_no))),
                replace(wock(J,W)).
```

Next, consider the following three information bases:
(i)
```
jabber(j1).            ss_no(j1,'123456').        wock(j1,200).
jabber(j2).            ss_no(j2,'345678').        wock(j2,300).
```

(ii)
```
jabber(j1).            ss_no(j1,'123456').        wock(j1,250).
jabber(j2).            ss_no(j2,'345678').        wock(j2,300).
```

(iii)
```
jabber(j1).            ss_no(j1,'123456').        wock(j1,200).
                                                  wock(j1,220).
jabber(j2).            ss_no(j2,'345678').        wock(j2,300).
```

a) Is there an event message that leads from (i) to (ii)?
b) Is there an event message that leads from (i) to (iii)?

5.12 Let a be an attribute with the mapping constraint (1, m, t, p), i.e. a is a total function, but neither injective nor surjective. Let b be the inverse of a, i.e. b is defined as

```
b(X,Y) :- a(Y,X).
```

What is the mapping constraint of b?

5.13

a) Define a new update operation `insert_set`. The meaning of `insert_set(Type, List)` is that every element in `List` shall become an instance of `Type`. Your definition should take the form of a Prolog rule (note that list handling is required).

b) Define an event rule that sets the tax of a person to 20 per cent if that person earns less than 20,000, and to 50 per cent if earning more. The event rule should take just one argument, the social security number of the person.

5.14 Consider the information base and the event rule below:

```
person(jim).
person(james).
person(jane).
ss_no(jim, '1234_56').
ss_no(james, '2345_67').
ss_no(jane, '3456_78').
name(jim, 'James Smith').
name(james, 'James Smith').
name(jane, 'Janet White').

event(marry, [Man, Woman], ['Man', 'Woman']):-
            precondition((person(M), name(M, Man),
            person(W), name(W, Woman))),
            insert(married(M,W)).
```

a) Which updates will be performed as a result of the event message ⟨'James Smith', 'Janet White'⟩?

b) There are two possible answers to the question in a). Explain why this situation is undesirable and how it could be corrected.

CHAPTER 6

Modelling Practice

The previous chapters introduced the fundamental, theoretical ideas of conceptual modelling. We shall now take a more practical stance by advising how a conceptual model of good quality can be constructed. The first section describes the form of modelling seminars and discusses how to model in groups. The second section introduces a number of tricky object structures that frequently occur in conceptual schemas. The third section outlines how to identify rules in an enterprise, and finally the notion of quality in conceptual modelling is discussed.

6.1 The Modelling Seminar

When developing information systems, systems analysts have traditionally tried to elicit user requirements by interviewing people individually. This way of working can be complemented with approaches based on group-work. An important form of group-work is the *modelling seminar* which is a session, or a sequence of sessions, during which a group of people construct a conceptual schema. There are several advantages of modelling in a group. First, many different views of the enterprise under consideration are put forward and can be discussed. Secondly, conflicting opinions and conflicts of interest are made explicit and can sometimes even be reconciled. Furthermore, participants can learn from each other and take joint responsibility for the rules and concepts they introduce.

If a modelling seminar is to be successful, it must be carefully prepared. Of particular importance is to identify the object system to be modelled and to demarcate it clearly. Furthermore, it must be ensured that the right people participate in the seminar. Finally, it is essential to determine the purpose of the schema to be constructed.

A schema can serve at least four different purposes. First, it can be used for clarifying the language used in an organisation. Secondly, it can be used for making explicit the rules that prevail in an organisation, which helps to criticise them and possibly to draw up new rules. Thirdly, a schema can be useful for reviewing existing information systems. Fourthly, a schema can be used for developing a new information system. The purpose of a conceptual schema heavily influences the modelling seminar. For example, if the purpose is to review an existing system it is important that computer and systems specialists participate, whereas this may not be required if the purpose is to investigate the rules that should prevail in an organisation.

Since a modelling seminar is typically short and intensive, usually between one and two days, the discussion has to be focused. Before the seminar it should therefore be made clear on which parts of the enterprise to concentrate and to exclude explicitly those parts which are not to be modelled. It is often useful to focus on a particular function of an organisation like marketing or production, and the tasks performed within that function.

The participants of a modelling seminar should come from different parts of the organisation and include computer professionals and end users, as well as middle management and, preferably, senior management. Letting people with different roles participate ensures that no important point is overlooked.

We now turn to the form of the modelling seminar. It is common to divide the seminar into a number of distinct steps:

- Education
- Checking focus and demarcations
- Listing concepts and objects
- Modelling

In most cases, it is advisable to provide the participants of the seminar with a brief education in conceptual modelling prior to the seminar. When this is not possible, the seminar should include an introduction to modelling together with a few exercises illustrating how modelling can be utilised in the enterprise of the participants.

In the second step of the modelling seminar, one should check that all participants agree on which parts of the enterprise to concentrate. Some useful guiding questions in this context are:

- What should the schema be used for?
- Which business functions should be focused on?
- Which tasks are performed within each relevant business function?
- Which business processes exist within each function?
- Which parts of the enterprise should not be modelled?

In the third step, objects and concepts are listed irrespective of their interrelationships. An important objective for this step is to find all the concepts that could be relevant to the enterprise, and one should therefore not be too restrictive in accepting concepts suggested during the seminar. In order to find suitable concepts, it is often helpful to consider the nouns and verbs people use to talk about the enterprise. If a text concerning the object system is available, a preliminary concept list can be obtained by underlining the nouns and verbs in the text. Some categories that frequently contain relevant concepts include: Persons, Places, Events, Time periods, and Agreements, see Figure 6.1. When listing concepts, the following questions can help spur the discussion:

- Which important concepts are we working with?
- What does the term X mean?
- Give a few concrete examples of X!
- Is concept X derivable from any other concepts?

PERSONS	PLACES	EVENTS	TIME PERIODS	AGREEMENTS
Employees	Countries	Marriages	Campaigns	Purchases
Authors	Cities	Divorces	Wars	Loans
Englishmen	Streets	Payments	Travels	Marriages
Women	Islands	Deposits	Holidays	Employments
Students	Mountains	Deliveries	Terms	Contracts

Figure 6.1 *Frequently occurring object types*

In the fourth step of the seminar, the participants construct a conceptual schema based on the concept list obtained in the previous step. Interrelationships between object types and their properties are introduced as well as simple rules such as mapping constraints. The documentation of the seminar should include: a graphical conceptual schema; natural language definitions of all object types; concrete examples of the instances of the object types, possibly in the form of tables, see Figure 6.2. A number of guiding questions are:

- What identifies the object type X?
- Can an instance of X be associated to several instances of Y?
- Give examples of the object type X!
- Do the object types X and Y have the same attributes?
- Is it possible to generalise the object types X and Y into a common supertype?

NAME	PART OF THE WORLD	CAPITAL	HEAD OF STATE
Sweden	Europe	Stockholm	Carl XVI Gustaf
New Zealand	Oceania	Wellington	H.M. Queen Elizabeth II
USA	North America	Washington DC	Bill Clinton
Nicaragua	Central America	Managua	Violeta Barrios de Chamarro
Bangladesh	Asia	Dhaka	Abdur Rahman Biswas
South Africa	Africa	Cape Town	Nelson Mandela

Figure 6.2 *Instances of the object type COUNTRY*

6.2 Prototypical Object Structures

Some types of object structures arise frequently in conceptual schemas. In this section, we shall describe five types of object structures that occur in many different contexts.

6.2.1 Hierarchical Object Structures

In order to describe situations where certain objects are subordinated to other objects, we use *hierarchical object structures*. Hierarchical object structures occur in such varying contexts as scientific classifications, organisational structures, version management, and geographical areas. An example of a hierarchical structure is depicted in Figure 6.3, and the corresponding structure of object types is shown in Figure 6.4. This figure also exemplifies how hierarchies are modelled. Note the mapping constraints, which express that each object at a particular level in the hierarchy is associated with exactly one object at the level above and possibly with several objects at the level below.

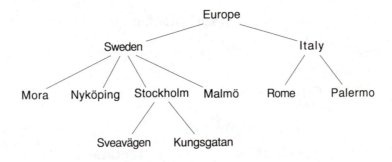

Figure 6.3 *A hierarchy of geographical entities*

6.2.2 Provider–Transfer–Acquisition–Recipient Structures

A modelling structure common to many conceptual schemas is that of a provider transferring an acquisition to a recipient. The graphical representation of an example of such a structure is shown in Figure 6.5, where producer corresponds to provider, consumer to recipient, purchase to transfer, and product to acquisition. This structure appears in many different forms, as illustrated in the example below:

Example 6.1   Examples of provider–transfer–acquisition–recipient structures:

- A person purchases a car from a car dealer.
- A person rents a car from a car renting company.

- A person borrows a book from a library.
- A football club buys a player from another club.
- A country imports oil from another country.
- A person borrows money from a bank.
- One person receives a Christmas present from another.

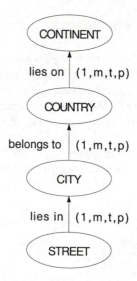

Figure 6.4 *A hierarchical object structure*

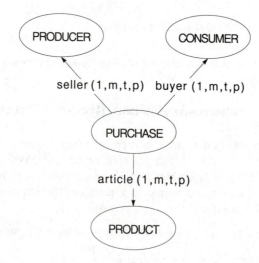

Figure 6.5 *Provider–transfer–acquisition–recipient structure*

Common to all these examples is one party acquiring something from another party. Note that the type of the provider can be the same as that of the recipient, see Figure 6.6. Frequently, the type corresponding to the purchase has attributes such as price and date.

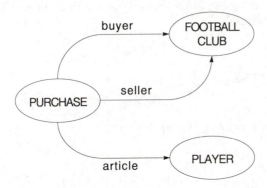

Figure 6.6 *Provider–transfer–acquisition–recipient structure where provider and recipient are of the same type*

6.2.3   Attribute Reification

An association between objects is usually modelled by an attribute. Sometimes, this is not sufficient because it is necessary to maintain information about the association rather than the associated objects. It may then become necessary to *reify* the attribute, which means converting the attribute into a type. (This is sometimes called introducing a *relational object*.) Let us illustrate this idea with an example.

Figure 6.7 shows the types PERSON and CLUB, and the attribute is_member_of. This attribute is multi-valued and not injective, since a person can be a member of many clubs, and a club can have many members. We call such attributes *m–m attributes* ("m–m" is read as many-to-many).

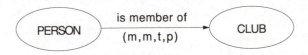

Figure 6.7 *Persons and clubs*

Suppose we want to keep information about when people joined a club. To do this we need an attribute, call it date_joined, that specifies the date a person joined a club. date_joined must not be an attribute of PERSON, since it does not model a property of PERSON alone, but concerns both PERSON and CLUB at the same time. Likewise, `date_joined` cannot be an attribute of CLUB. In other words, an enrolment date concerns neither an isolated person nor an isolated club, but rather the association between a particular person and a particular club. Consequently, we require a new type to act as the domain of `date_joined`. The idea is then to reify the attribute `is_member_of` and introduce a new type MEMBERSHIP, as shown in Figure 6.8. We can now let `date_joined` be an attribute of MEMBERSHIP.

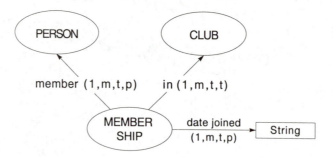

Figure 6.8 *Reification of attribute (cf. Figure 6.7)*

Generalising the example above, we arrive at the following heuristic rule: If a conceptual schema requires information to be kept about an association modelled by an attribute, then the attribute should be reified. Usually, reification only occurs for m–m attributes.

6.2.4   Recursive Structures

Recursive structures model objects that can be composed of other objects of the same type. These structures may occur when modelling articles and their components. For example, a cupboard may consist of five cupboard walls, two doors, four hinges, and twelve screws. A door, in its turn, may consist of a frame, a mirror, two door knobs, and four screws. An object structure for modelling this type of information is shown in Figure 6.9.

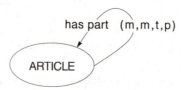

Figure 6.9 *A recursive structure*

To describe the composition of a cupboard and a door, the following statements would be used:

```
has_part(cupboard7, wall2).        has_part(cupboard7, door3).
has_part(cupboard7, hinge13).      has_part(cupboard7, screw19).
has_part(door3, frame1).           has_part(door3, mirror9).
has_part(door3, knob5).            has_part(door3, screw19).
```

The above statements describe which components a cupboard and a door are composed of. The statements do not, however, specify how many of each component are included in the cupboard and the door. To do this, a new attribute that takes integers as values is needed. A moment's thought should suffice to convince the reader that it is inappropriate to let the domain of this attribute be ARTICLE. Consequently, we need to introduce a new entity type. Using techniques from the previous section we reify the attribute has_part, see Figure 6.10. (Because the new type has two total attributes, contains and contained_in, it is a relationship type and we therefore draw it using a diamond.)

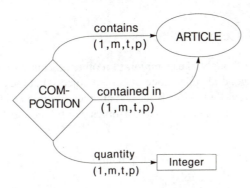

Figure 6.10 *Article structure*

The new type introduced through reification provides a domain for the attribute quantity that specifies how many components of each type an article contains. To state that a door contains two door knobs, we use an instance, say c1, of the relationship type COMPOSITION and three attribute statements:

```
contains(c1, knob5).      contained_in(c1, door3).      quantity(c1, 2).
```

Here an instance c1 of COMPOSITION ties together an instance of ARTICLE, door3, with another instance of ARTICLE, knob5, and with an integer, 2. By tying door3, knob5, and 2 together in this way, we are able to express the idea that a door has two knobs.

Example 6.2 A complete state description of the example introduced at the beginning of this section:

```
article(cupboard7).        composition(c1).
article(hinge13).          composition(c2).
article(screw19).          composition(c3).
article(wall2).            composition(c4).
article(frame1).           composition(c5).
article(knob5).            composition(c6).
article(door3).            composition(c7).
article(mirror9).          composition(c8).
```

```
contained_in(c1, cupboard7). contains(c1, wall2).   quantity(c1, 5).
contained_in(c2, cupboard7). contains(c2, door3).   quantity(c2, 2).
contained_in(c3, cupboard7). contains(c3, hinge13). quantity(c3, 4).
contained_in(c4, cupboard7). contains(c4, screw19). quantity(c4, 12).
contained_in(c5, door3).     contains(c5, mirror9). quantity(c5, 1).
contained_in(c6, door3).     contains(c6, frame1).  quantity(c6, 1).
contained_in(c7, door3).     contains(c7, knob5).   quantity(c7, 2).
contained_in(c8, door3).     contains(c8, screw19). quantity(c8, 4).
```

6.2.5   Template–Copy Structures

Certain objects can be thought of as *templates* for other objects, called *copies*. A template object prescribes the general appearance of copied objects, but the copies may have several individual traits and thus differ from one another. Templates are often abstract objects, whereas copies are concrete objects. Copies can be seen as "materialisations" of their template.

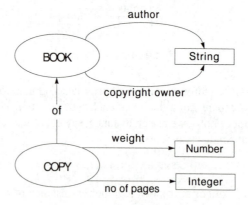

Figure 6.11 *Templates and copies*

A typical example of a template object is a book, regarded as a literary work. Here the copies are the individual copies of the book — concrete, physical objects. A structure like this could be modelled as in Figure 6.11. Some properties, such as author and copy-

`right owner`, should be attributed to the abstract book objects, and not to concrete copies. Others, such as `weight, number of pages, hard-` or `paperback`, should be attributed to `COPY` and not to `BOOK`.

Some other examples of templates and copies are:

- A course and a course offering
- A symphony, a recording of it, and a CD with that particular recording
- A painting and a reproduction

6.3 Rule Elicitation

Section 6.1 discussed the initial steps in the process of conceptual modelling, in particular how to identify object structures. We now turn to the question of how to discover the (business) rules that govern an organisation's activities. Those rules are reflected in a model by introducing certain entity types, attributes, and data types and then declaring rules over those concepts, using the various constructs offered by the language. We refer to this simply as "rules" and use in the sequel the term "business rule" only when we talk about natural language sentences expressing the requirements of the organisation. A straightforward way to elicit rules is to confront the domain experts with a set of guiding questions, such as those that follow.

For each object type, we ask: How do instances of this type come into existence? When do they cease to exist? Describe this in natural language and write it down. If a text is available, try to find rules hidden in the text.

For the enterprise as a whole as well as for its specific parts: Have any specific guidelines or policies been formulated? Are there any implicit (i.e. unwritten) rules? Are there any general restrictions that apply to the enterprise, either as a whole or some specific part of it?

Given a particular rule, one should ask:

- Which objectives does the rule contribute to fulfilling? How else is this objective realised?
- Is this rule a more specific variation of a more general rule?
- Is the rule valid for all instances of a certain type or are there exceptions?
- If a rule is valid for a certain kind of concept, does it also apply to all specialisations or generalisations for this kind of concept?
- If a rule is valid for a certain type which is a specialisation, does the rule also apply to other types based on the same criterion for specialisation?

In addition to general enquiries, such as those above, more specific questions can be formulated for particular classes of applications. Such questions may have to do with types of rules and policies that normally appear in a certain application area.

Rules may also be arrived at by repeatedly analysing the goals of an enterprise in order to specify how they should be accomplished. This means developing a detailed goal model. At higher levels, goals are general and vague, but through the analysis they are transformed and become more concrete in terms of objects and processes. Rules defined on less abstract levels will by necessity be more specific since they deal with more specific things. In the goal model you specify how to treat your customers, what the characteristics of your products should be in terms of quality, availability, use, etc. The goal model also describes what should guide business processes, what kind of policy the organisation should follow in relation to travelling expenses or tax regulations, for instance. The goal model may concern policy about personnel, investments, stocks, shares, etc. In Figure 6.12, a simple breakdown of high-level goals to more precise subgoals and rules is shown.

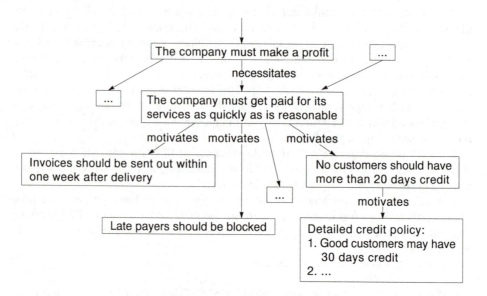

Figure 6.12 *Levels of goals*

From the above, it is obvious that goal modelling can be an important tool for capturing rules. However, it may not be possible to conduct such goal/rule analysis in a systematic way in practice for the entire UoD. The difficulty lies in the amount of information, the vagueness of high-level goals, and the fact that not all rules are derivable from primary objectives but from restrictions forced upon an enterprise by external sources. Instead, goal/rule analysis may be used for parts of the enterprise and as a means for justifying the presence of rules elicited in some other way. In addition, goal/rule decomposition is also an important framework for understanding rules.

6.4 Rule Representation

In Section 3.3.1, business rules are referred to as either being derived from requirements forced upon the organisation from the outside world (e.g. laws of nature or human laws and regulations), or describing how some organisation has chosen to implement its high-level objectives. In this section we will further discuss those rules and provide a set of examples demonstrating how various kinds of such rules are represented in logic programming. The rules apply to the club schema introduced earlier. In order to distinguish the business rules as expressed by natural language sentences from their representation in logic programming, we will sometimes refer to them as requirements. In order to bring about a better understanding of the nature of those rules and how they are represented in logic programming, we start by further elaborating and exemplifying the description provided in Section 3.3.

6.4.1   Types of Rules

Rules can be classified along several dimensions such as is done in Section 3.3. The most obvious is, perhaps, to distinguish between pure constraints restricting what is possible to do or to say in some business area, and event rules defining what actions to take given that some condition is fulfilled. However, the border between these classes is not clear cut. Quite often one has the choice between modelling some rule as a constraint or as an internal event rule (see the example about the registration of members below). In some cases one has the choice of representing a rule as a derivation rule, thereby avoiding storing the corresponding attribute or type statements in the information base. Along a different dimension one can distinguish, as is pointed out in Section 3.3.2, those rules that deal with a single state (static rules) from those that compare several states (dynamic rules). In Figure 6.13 (cf. Figure 3.23) we summarise this discussion and indicate which constructs in logic programming to use for the various categories.

For static constraints we can further classify rules according to whether the restriction concerns a whole set of elements, perhaps in relation to some other set, or specific instances of some set (cf. Section 3.3.1). More specifically, we distinguish the following categories.

Extension constraints

Extension constraints specify relationships between sets, e.g. one set is required to be a subset of another set such as in entity specialisation, or the intersection of two sets is required to be empty. Examples are

a) All men are persons
b) A person cannot be a man and a woman at the same time
c) There are no other persons than men and women
d) Salary is a special form of income

If PERSON, MAN, and WOMAN are modelled as different entity types a) would be expressed by a subtype rule (cf. Section 5.3.1). Furthermore, rules b) and c) would have to be represented by static integrity constraints. If, on the other hand, gender of persons is modelled as an attribute relating person to a data type with values male and female, then the fact that all men are persons would be represented by this data type having male as one of its values. Rule b) would be represented by the gender attribute being single valued, i.e. a person cannot be both a woman and a man. Finally, rule c) would be represented by the gender attribute being total, i.e. every person having to be either a man or a woman.

	Static A single state can be checked to determine whether the rule holds (or should trigger) or not.	Dynamic The current state and the state after an update has to be compared or a new state will be created.
Integrity constraints	Mapping constraints Identifier specification Subtyping rules Inconsistency rules	Transition violation rules (i.e. comparison states before and after a possible update)
Event rules	External event rules not affecting the information base (i.e. generating only external actions, e.g. write)	Internal event rules (i.e. comparison states before and after an update) External event rules updating the information base
Derivation rules	Rules deriving attributes or instances of some entity subtype	–

Figure 6.13 *Rule categories*

For the gender attribute solution to our example, it may seem wrong to classify a) and b) as an extension constraint (although c) could still be considered as an extension constraint since in this case it simply says the domain of gender equals the set of persons). In other words, the classification scheme is model dependent. On the other hand, this is a good example of a situation where one could introduce derived entity subtypes for man and woman. The MAN subtype would have the derivation rule

```
man(Person) :- gender(Person, 'male').
```

Hence, we have again a situation where it may be reasonable to talk about a) as being an extension constraint.

If we take `income` and `salary` to be attributes of employees relating to the same data type, d) would be an example of attribute specialisation. This might then be expressed by the following rule:

```
income(Person, Salary) :- earns(Person, Salary).
```

Note that `income` is defined here as a derived attribute. A corresponding derivation rule has to be included for each kind of income. Alternatively, we may choose to store income and salary separately in the information base. In that case the rule should be represented as an integrity constraint:

```
inconsistent :- earns(Person, Salary),
                not(income(Person, Salary)).
```

Such specialisation may, of course, occur also for relationships between entity types. Supposing, for instance, that `member_of` is a (derived) attribute relating persons to clubs, then `president` would be a specialisation of that attribute, i.e.

```
member_of(Person, Club) :- president(Club, Person).
```

Finally, d) may be interpreted to mean that the set of possible salary values is a subset of the set of possible income values. In this situation we realise the rule by defining the data type `salary` as

```
data_type(salary).
salary(S) :- income(S), S<10000.
```

We refer to this as "data type specialisation".

Cardinality constraints

Cardinality constraints specify limitations for the cardinalities of sets. The best examples are mapping constraints such as attributes being single valued or injective, but also restrictions on the cardinality of the extensions of entity types are quite common. Some examples of this type of rule would be

a) No club may have more than 1,000 members
b) A person has exactly one name

For a), the cardinality of the set of memberships for any club would have to be limited to 1,000. In Prolog this would be

```
inconsistent :- club(C), findall(M, belongs_to(M, C), Memberset),
                count(Memberset, N), N>1000.
```

The second rule would be represented by specifying the mapping (1, 1, t, p) for the `name` attribute.

Instance level constraints

An instance level constraint concerns specific instances of the universe of discourse. An example would, in our case, be

> The Rich Men's Club requires members to have a minimum annual income of SEK 1,000,000.

Here we have a rule that talks about a particular instance (Rich Men's Club) of the club entity type. It is probably desirable to avoid mentioning specific instances of rules which, in principle, should be kept as general as possible. Sometimes it may be difficult to avoid, though.

To conclude, the requirements of the outside world can be represented in a number of ways in the conceptual schema. It is, however, difficult to give any precise guidelines concerning what constructs to use in particular situations, except that in general it may be considered less flexible to introduce specialised entity types than to use attributes (cf. the gender example). This is due to the fact that in the former case we tailor the model to a particular situation, whereas in the latter case, the same information is represented as a value of an attribute, the definition and use of which could more easily be changed. On the other hand, using the entity subtype construct will show in a more explicit way the permissible types in the model, whereas in the attribute solution they will be hidden in the data type definition. In principle, though, it has to be left to the judgement of the people who design the model which constructs to use.

6.4.2   Sample Rules

Mapping constraints

Referring again to the club case introduced in Chapter 5, a common type of requirements statement would be

> Each club has a unique name

Now, what does this mean? First of all it tells us that there are entities called clubs and that those should be related to values called names. The word *each* tells us that all clubs have a name, i.e. the attribute is total. The word *a* indicates that each club has one name and not a set of names. Finally, *unique* means that every name is related to only one club, i.e. the attribute is injective. Whether the attribute is surjective or not, is not explicitly stated. Assuming that the attribute is not surjective, the complete mapping constraint would be (1, 1, t, p) (represented in the statement by respectively (a, unique, each, ...)).

Sometimes mapping restrictions range over a sequence of attributes, such as in the case

> A club assigns a unique number to each membership

This not only means that we have to assign a number attribute to the membership entity type, but it also indicates that the same numbers can be used by several clubs, as long as the combination <club, member_no> is unique. In other words, the attribute combination uniquely identifies entities belonging to this type. Hence, the mapping constraints of the attribute ought to be (1, m, t, p), whereas the uniqueness constraint can be represented by the constraint

```
identifier(membership, [belongs_to, member_no]).
```

A different and more complex way to represent it would be to state a rule that declares it inconsistent for members of the same club to have the same number, i.e.

```
inconsistent :- belongs_to(M1, C), member_no(M1,No),
                belongs_to(M2,C), member_no(M2,No), not(M1=M2).
```

Attribute dependencies

Quite often attributes depend on each other. In the simplest case one attribute can be derived from others. Those are rules stating a precise relationship between attributes. An example would be (cf. Example 5.1)

Net income = gross income − tax

Such a rule could be implemented either as a derivation rule deriving a "virtual" attribute from some other ones that are explicitly stored, or it can be implemented as a constraint or an internal event rule, provided that we have decided to store all the referenced attributes in the information base.

Assuming that gross_salary (in the example named earns) and tax, but not net_income, are stored in the information base, a derivation rule for net_income would be

```
net_income(P, Ns) :- earns(P, Gs), tax(P, T), Ns is Gs-T.
```

Assuming, on the other hand, that all three attributes are stored, then an integrity constraint could be defined as

```
inconsistent :- earns(P, Gs), Tax(P, T),
                not(net_salary(P, Ns), Ns is Gs-T.
```

This rule would prohibit the information base from being updated in a way that would violate the dependency between the three attributes. A different way to realise the dependency would be to have net salary automatically updated each time gross salary or tax is changed, i.e. we would specify internal event rules:

```
internal_event(tax_change,
               before(tax(P, T1)),
               after(tax(P,T2), not(T1=T2))) :-
               earns(P, Gs), Ns is Gs-T2,
               replace(net_income(P, Ns)).
```

The gross_salary_change event is specified correspondingly.

However, it is worth pointing out that the normal way to represent this dependency is as a derivation rule. The latter two cases were included to demonstrate possible alternatives.

Other kinds of dependencies simply restrict the way attributes may relate objects to each other. One example may be the following (cf. attribute specialisation above):

The president of a club must be a member of the club

Although this has in fact already been defined by specifying the `president` attribute as being a specialisation of (the inverse of) the `member_of` attribute, here we give an alternative definition:

```
inconsistent :- president(C, P), not(membership(M), fellow(M, P),
                belongs_to(M,C)).
```

A corresponding restriction would, of course, hold for treasurers.

Requirements involving time

Requirements involving time may take several forms. They may refer to time in absolute terms, e.g. stating that some event should take place at some particular point in time, or in relative terms, e.g. talking about some state occurring after another.

The constructs introduced in Section 5.3.3 allow us to refer to the time dimension in dynamic constraints and internal event rules, i.e. to compare information base states before and after an update. If, on the other hand, we have requirements demanding the system to keep track of, say, when something happened or the various values that an attribute has taken during its lifetime, then this has to be explicitly modelled by including temporal attributes. If this is done, then rules referring to time can be represented as static rules. In this context it will be useful to have a built-in model of time, such as is described in Section 3.2.1. Application entity types may then be related to entity or data types of this model as needed in order to represent temporal relationships or to state constraints, event rules, or derivation rules that refer to time. We give in the following a few such examples.

To be able to refer to the current time, we have included, in the conceptual model of time, unary predicates named `now(T)`, `this_second(S)`, `this_minute(M)`, `this_hour(H)`, `this_day(D)`, etc, giving access to the respective `time_point` and `time_interval` instances corresponding to current time.

Transition constraints

As indicated before, a type of constraint that does involve the temporal dimension is transition constraints, since those deal with two consecutive states of the information base. Consider, for instance, the following requirement:

Memberships can never be abandoned

Supposing we have a derived attribute `member_of` relating a person to all clubs of which that person is a member, this constraint would be represented by the following rule:

```
transition_violation :- before(member_of(P, C)), after
(not(member_of(P, C))).
```

However, since a schema is meant to describe the whole UoD, this proposition will implicitly hold if we do not include in the schema any means for removing memberships. From that point of view the rule is, hence, not necessary. Including it would only be a way to make it explicit, and also to enforce the rule for the case that later changes to the model would introduce events that might result in memberships being abandoned.

Historical constraints

Suppose that we allow people to leave clubs, but add instead the requirement

> Once having left a club, a person cannot re-enter

This means that we have to keep track of the membership history of people. We can do that by letting the instances of the membership entity type stay in the information base after they have ended. However, if we want the `member_of` attribute only to relate people to clubs of which they are currently members, we would have to change the derivation rule. Taking advantage of the attribute `end_date`, indicating the day when a membership ended, we can introduce a derived entity type `current_membership` with the derivation rule

```
current_membership(M) :- membership(M), not(end_date(M, D)).
```

The derivation rule for `member_of` can now be formulated according to the following:

```
member_of(P, C) :- current_membership(M), belongs_to(M,C),
fellow(M,P).
```

The integrity constraint that a person cannot re-enter a club can be stated either as a separate rule

```
inconsistent :- membership(M1), belongs_to(M1, C), fellow(M1, P),
membership(M2), belongs_to(M2, C), fellow(M2, P), not(M1=M2).
```

or as a precondition of the event introducing memberships, i.e. checking that the person has not been a member of that club before.

Rules or preconditions

It is quite common to have the choice between formulating a rule as a separate integrity constraint (static or dynamic) or as a precondition of an event. From an efficiency point of view it is obviously better to have it as a precondition since this will ensure the rule is checked at exactly the right time. On the other hand, one may, in this case, have to specify the rule in several places, since it may have to be checked in more than one event. This introduces the difficulty of keeping track of which preconditions influence the update of a particular fact. From a flexibility point of view it may therefore be better to have it as a separate rule, since if the rule changes one would need to change it in only one place.

Introducing both start and end dates for memberships means that we would have to add a rule stating that the membership cannot end before it started, i.e.

```
inconsistent :- entry_date(M,D1), end_date(M,D2), D2<D1.
```

Furthermore, a person cannot join a club again while currently a member. We state that as a precondition for the event rule introducing memberships:

```
precondition(not(member_of(P,C)))
```

Owing to the definition of the `member_of` attribute, this precondition allows for new memberships only for persons that are not currently members. To summarise, the `join_club` event would, if we go for the precondition solution, look as follows:

```
event(join_club, [Ss, C_name, Date, M_no], ['Ss-no', 'Club',
'Date', 'Member-no']) :-
            precondition((ss_no(Person, Ss), person(Person))),
            precondition((club_name(Club, C_name),club(Club))),
            precondition(not(member_of(Person, Club))),
            new_entity(membership, M),
            insert(belongs_to(M, Club)),
            insert(fellow(M, Person)),
            insert(member_no(M, M_no)),
            insert(entry_date(M, Date)).
```

For the date, here and in Figure 5.2, we might have let the `entry_date` and `end_date` attributes relate to the entity type day as defined in the conceptual model of time (Section 3.2.1). The correct day instance would then have been picked up by using the `dt` attribute of the time model.

Temporal attributes

To exemplify the use of the temporal attributes defined in the temporal model of Figure 3.12, suppose we have the following requirement:

> Only in January may a member be registered as having entered a club in the previous year

The date of entering a club is represented by the `entry_date` attribute for the membership entity type. The rule can be included as a dynamic rule declaring it illegal to enter a membership after January if it was started the previous year:

```
transition_violation :-
            before(not(membership(M))),
            after(membership(M), entry_date(M, D),
                        month(D, Mth),
                        year(Mth, Y), this_year(T_y),
                        Y<T_y, this_month(T_m), T_m>1).
```

This rule will prohibit memberships from being entered after January, should the `entry_date` be during last year.

This example illustrates an important point, namely that we have here *a requirement that contcerns the (temporal) relationship between the UoD and the information system.*

Such requirements should, in general, not be realised as necessary constraints. This is possible owing to their deontic nature, cf. Section 3.3.4. However, when asked to provide the rules of the object system, application experts sometimes formulate them as if they were laws of nature. This view is possible in a business run by humans, since they can deviate from rules when needed, based on, for example, what is usually referred to as common sense. In a computerised model of the object system, on the other hand, such exceptions have to be explicitly modelled.

In our case, representing the requirement as a necessary constraint is most certainly not the way one would want it to be implemented, since that would render it simply impossible to enter last-year members after January, should the registration by some reason have been delayed. Instead one would prefer to have it implemented in a softer way, e.g. by somehow reminding the club administrators in advance to report new members in such good time that it is possible to register without violating this requirement.

Temporal conditions can also be used to trigger internal events. Consider the following requirement:

A historical membership has to be kept until the end of the second subsequent year after it ended

This is again a requirement that concerns the relationship between the information system and the UoD, i.e. it is an information system requirement. Since each membership instance is timestamped, an internal event may trigger on the 1st of January each year the erasure of all memberships that ended more than a year ago.

```
internal_event(remove_membership,
               before(this_year(Y2)),
               after(this_year(Y3), Y3=Y2-1, membership(M),
                                    end_date(M, D), month(D, Mth),
                                    year(Mth, Y1), Y1<Y2) :-
               remove(M).
```

All attributes having the membership as their domain or range will automatically be deleted, provided there are no other integrity constraints (e.g. mapping constraints) preventing it. In the latter case, the removal of membership will also be prohibited.

Information base removals

As illustrated in the previous example, the removal of one instance may require the removal of one or several other instances. For example, if an attribute is surjective then the removal of one instance of the domain of the attribute may require the removal of instances in its range. Such removals may be carried out explicitly within the same event rule. Another possibility is to utilise internal event rules that take care of removing those related instances that should not stay in the information base after the removal of the first instance.

It should also be noted that static and dynamic constraints in the approach in Section 5.4 have the effect of hindering removal, should they be violated by removing an instance. Hence, all operations needed to prevent violation have to be included in the same event rule as the removal.

An example of a requirement that somehow would have to cascade removals is the following:

> People are known to the club register only if they are, or have been, members of clubs which are known to the register

Once again we have a rule that concerns the relationship between the information system, be it manual or computerised, and the UoD. More precisely, it concerns what the information system (the register) should know (or rather remember) about the real world. We interpret the rule such that members should be removed from the register if they do not fulfil the condition mentioned in the requirements statement. This means that as we remove clubs, all their memberships would also have to be removed. If this leaves a person as no longer a member of any club, it would consequently have to be removed. However, removing all the memberships of a club operates on a set of object identifiers. Since we have access only to insert, delete, and modify operations for single facts, we have to enhance the language with a predicate for removing sets of identifiers. Supposing the language contains such a predicate, named `remove_set`, cf. Exercise 5.13, we end up with the following rule:

```
event(remove_club, [C_name], ['Club name']) :-
            precondition(club_name(C, C_name),
                               findall(M, belongs_to(M, C),
                               M_set)),
            remove_set(M_set),
            remove(C).
```

Since the inverses of the `president`, `treasurer`, and `fellow` attributes are partial, people will stay in the information base regardless of the fact that the `club` and `membership` entities related to it are removed. Since what we wanted to specify in the first place was that people should be removed as soon as they are no longer members of any clubs, we define the following rule:

```
internal_event(remove_non_members,
            before(person(P)),
            after(not(fellow(M, P)), not(president(C, P)),
                               not(treasurer(C,P))) :-
            remove(P).
```

Literally, the rule says that whenever there is a person who is not a fellow, a president, or a treasurer, that person should be removed.

Rules with calculations

Sometimes rules may involve quite complex calculations. An example could be

> The club fee must not exceed 1% of the average salary of club members

This constraint is specified by the following rule:

```
inconsistent :- fee(Club, F),
               findall(Salary, (earns(Person, Salary),
               member_of(Person, Club)), Salaries),
               findall(M_ship, (current_membership(M_ship),
               belongs_to(M_ship, Club)), Memberships),
               count(Memberships, N),
               sum(Salaries, S),
               Average is S/N, Av01 is Average/100, F>Av01.
```

Note that the rule above counts only the current memberships of a club.

6.4.3 Deriving Conceptual Models from Requirements

When dealing with requirements formulated in natural language, one often runs into problems of interpretation. Using conceptual modelling forces one to penetrate the meaning of the requirements and to determine their semantics strictly. In that process one frequently has to go back to the application experts to have them clarify (or rather determine) what precisely those natural language statements mean.

Furthermore, it is difficult in a requirements specification for a real size application to avoid inconsistency. Here, the fact that logic programming models are executable and testable for consistency is a great help. In fact it would be more or less impossible to avoid inconsistency without such an engine. Being without it is perhaps the most important reason that so many mistakes are not discovered until the system is put into operation.

As exemplified by the "register before January" requirement presented earlier, rules are sometimes formulated in a way that does not correspond to how one would like to have them implemented, although it is perfectly possible to represent them directly. More precisely, this has to do with deontic rules, i.e. business rules that are introduced by people and that may (and most certainly will) be violated in the UoD. Hence, it is important that rather than being represented as a pure restriction, such a requirement has to be changed so as to specify what actions to take given that the restriction has been broken. It may even be the case that one rather wants the information system to take action in advance and try to influence its environment so as to avoid a violating situation appearing.

As has been shown by several examples above, the way business rules are represented in a conceptual model is strongly model dependent. This is due to the fact that those rules concern the things dealt with in the business, i.e. the phenomena represented in the conceptual model. Hence, their exact representation strongly depends on precisely which entity types, attributes, and data types are introduced. In general, one prefers the rules to be kept as simple as possible. For instance, derived attributes and entity subtypes may be introduced so as to correspond to precisely the concepts mentioned in the rules, rather than performing those derivations in the rules themselves. An example of this is the use of the derived entity type current_members.

However, specialising entity types and attributes so as to keep rules simple has the disadvantage that the object structures become more complex and that, hence, after database design (cf. Chapter 8) and implementation, the resulting database structure may become unnecessarily complex. Furthermore, it would be tailored to the way the business is currently run, i.e. the rules that are currently valid. This in turn may render changes to the model caused by changing requirements more difficult. In other words, there is a rather tricky trade-off between the generality of the object structures and the simplicity of rules.

6.5 Quality in Conceptual Modelling

Any object system can be modelled by many, in fact an infinite number of, different schemas. These schemas may vary in terminology and structure, in the number of types and attributes, in the layout of the graphical representation, etc. When systems analysts and users inspect these schemas of the same UoD, they often perceive that some schemas are, in some sense, better than others, but they may have difficulties in explaining why. An important concern is therefore to clarify what is meant by a "good" schema, a schema of high quality. In the context of conceptual modelling, the following quality criteria can be identified:

- Ease of understanding
- Semantic correctness
- Stability
- Completeness
- Conceptual focus

The following subsections explain each of these criteria and discuss how they can be achieved.

6.5.1   Ease of Understanding

When presenting a conceptual schema to a domain expert, it is essential that the representation is as easy to comprehend as possible. It is particularly important that the graphical schema be neat and clear. This can be achieved by placing the most important object types at the centre of the graph and by trying to avoid intersecting arrows. This advice works well for small schemas, but it does not always help for large ones that easily become too cluttered with details. When this happens it may be worthwhile reducing the complexity by removing all lexical attributes, retaining only the non-lexical object types and their interrelationships. Another way to get a better overview of a large schema is to remove all the subtypes, which will result in a less detailed schema in which only the most general object types remain. Finally, a large schema can be decomposed into smaller ones, often called local schemas (cf. Chapter 7).

A logical representation of rules, as in logic, is difficult to understand for most domain experts. It is therefore necessary to use more easily understood representations of rules. Certain simple types of rules can be shown graphically, as discussed in Section 3.3.4. Natural language can be used for expressing rules, but as discussed in Section 2.3, natural language is plagued with ambiguity. Two of the more successful techniques for expressing rules are decision tables and decision trees, which are able to express the conditions under which different actions should be carried out.

6.5.2 Semantic Correctness

A conceptual schema is said to be semantically correct if it accurately represents its domain, as perceived by a group of domain experts. The most important means for achieving semantic correctness is to conduct planned and structured walk-throughs of the schema as it evolves. The purpose of these walk-throughs is to ensure that no important part of the enterprise under consideration has been overlooked, and that the domain experts agree on the terminology and rules introduced in the schema. It may also be worthwhile experimenting with prototypes, which is simple to do if the conceptual schema is expressed in an executable modelling language.

6.5.3 Stability

It is desirable that a conceptual schema is as stable as possible. Adjusting a schema to reflect minor changes in the object system, or new information requirements, should not force major restructuring. One way to improve the stability of a schema is to introduce more object types than are strictly necessary. Then, if the schema has to be expanded later on, the chances are good that it will be sufficient just to add some attributes and that no new object types will be needed.

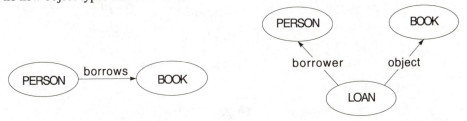

Figure 6.14 An unstable schema   **Figure 6.15** A stable schema

As an example, consider Figure 6.14 where the attribute `borrows` is m–m. As described in Section 6.2.3, the attribute can be reified resulting in the schema of Figure 6.15. The object type LOAN may seem unnecessary since it has no lexical attributes.

However, the schema of Figure 6.15 is more stable than the previous one; for if we need to keep track of the dates of loans, this would now only require the addition of a single attribute.

Another example where additional object types improve the stability of a schema is shown in Figure 6.16. The monthly sales of different products are represented by the attributes sales_jan, ..., sales_dec. This representation is clearly very clumsy, as it is inflexible. If we were to keep track of the sales for several years, we would be forced to add a large number of new attributes. A more flexible representation is given in the schema of Figure 6.17, where we have turned both months and sales into objects by introducing the object types SALES and MONTH. If we now wish to keep track of the sales for several years, only a single attribute need be added. The problem with the original schema is that, at the same time, each attribute represents two different concepts: both that of sales and that of the relevant month. The solution is to make these concepts explicit by additional object types, which results in the simpler and more flexible schema of Figure 6.17. The moral of this example is that an attribute in a conceptual schema must only represent a single and simple concept, and not a combination of concepts.

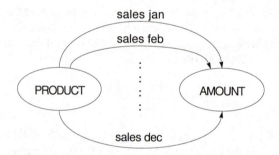

Figure 6.16 *One attribute—several concepts*

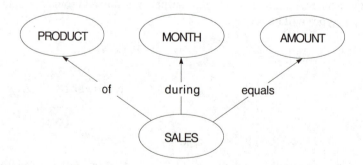

Figure 6.17 *One attribute—one concept*

Adding extra object types to a schema can also be useful for making the object types more homogeneous. Informally, an object type is said to have a high degree of *homogeneity* if the objects of that type are very similar to one another and all possess the same kinds of properties and interrelationships. For example, the object type DOG is more homogeneous than ANIMAL. An object type containing both persons and cars would have a very low degree of homogeneity. An object type that has one or several partial attributes is not very homogeneous, since some instances of the object type may have a value for the partial attribute(s), whereas others may not. Formally, we say that an object type is homogeneous if all its attributes are total. In order to increase the homogeneity, a new subtype can be introduced so that the partial attribute is applicable only to the instances of this new type. The partial attribute is then "moved to" the new subtype, i.e. the domain of the attribute is changed, making the attribute total. An example showing how to homogenize a schema is depicted in Figure 6.18 and Figure 6.19. Note that all attributes in the second schema are total.

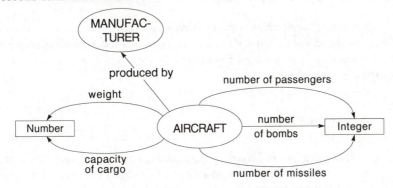

Figure 6.18 *A non-homogeneous object type*

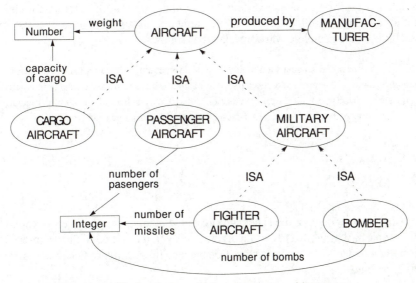

Figure 6.19 *A schema with homogeneous object types*

6.5.4   Completeness

An important guideline in conceptual modelling is the *100 per cent principle*, which says that all relevant aspects of an object system are to be described in the conceptual schema. When writing application programs, no extra information about the object system should be required; this information should already be contained in the schema. One motivation for the 100 per cent principle is that the model of an object system should be described by the people who have the best knowledge of it, i.e. by users and systems analysts, and not programmers. A consequence of this guideline is that a conceptual schema should be formally specified to the same degree of detail and with as much care as an application program. The 100 per cent principle was first proposed by an ISO working group (ISO/TC98/SC5/WG3), and in the report [ISO82], the principle was worded as follows:

> All relevant general static and dynamic aspects, i.e. all rules, laws, etc. of the universe of discourse should be described in the conceptual schema. The information system cannot be held responsible for not meeting those described elsewhere, including in particular those in application programs.

6.5.5   Conceptual Focus

Another important guideline is the *conceptualisation principle,* which states that a conceptual schema should include only those aspects of an object system that are conceptually relevant. The schema must not take those aspects into account that are primarily computer related, such as data representation, physical data organisation, or message formats. When modelling an object system, one should focus on the enterprise under consideration and not be influenced by implementation and performance aspects. In the report [ISO82], the principle was formulated as follows:

> A conceptual schema should only include conceptually relevant aspects, both static and dynamic, of the universe of discourse, thus excluding all aspects of (external or internal) data representation, physical data organisation and access as well as all aspects of particular external user representation such as message formats, data structures, etc.

6.6 Exercises

6.1   Using the language of the schema represented below, it is possible to express that certain people have travelled to certain cities. However, it is not possible to express when a person travelled to a city or the carrier used. Extend the schema so that this information can be expressed.

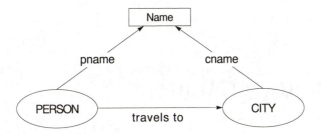

6.2 A certain schema contains only one non-lexical type: SHIP. SHIP is the domain of the following attributes: weight, length, horsepower, propeller_diameter, number_of_sails. The last three of these attributes are partial. Redesign the schema so that all the attributes become total.

6.3 Explain why a schema expressed in logic programming satisfies ISO's principle of conceptualisation.

6.4 In the club schema, the rule that salaries cannot decrease is expressed as a dynamic integrity constraint. Extend the schema in such a way that the rule can be expressed as a static integrity constraint.

6.5 Construct a conceptual schema that is able to represent the following information:

- Sausage contains 40 per cent meat and 20 per cent water
- Lasagne contains 30 per cent meat sauce and 20 per cent pasta
- Meat sauce contains 50 per cent tomatoes and 30 per cent meat

CHAPTER 7

Schema Integration

Schema integration involves merging several conceptual schemas into one global schema that represents all the relevant aspects of an object system. The first section of this chapter discusses how to organise the integration of several schemas. In the second section, we show which types of relationships may exist between conceptual schemas. The third section describes how conflicts between different schemas can be resolved. The fourth section shows how to merge two schemas. Finally, we illustrate the process of schema integration by means of a comprehensive example.

7.1 The Process of Schema Integration

When analysing a large object system by means of conceptual modelling, the task can become too complex for a single person or even a small group. For such a task, it is customary to apply a "divide and conquer" strategy. This involves dividing the task of modelling amongst several groups. Each group focuses on a particular part of the object system and constructs a conceptual schema, called a *local schema*, for that part. When the local schemas have been completed, they are integrated into a *global schema*, which describes the entire object system. In the context of information systems development, the integration of a number of local schemas into a global one is called *view integration*. A similar activity, called *database integration*, occurs in distributed database design, where a set of schemas for already existing information systems is merged into a single global schema. The main purpose of this integrated schema is to make it easier to submit queries involving several systems. To denote both view integration and database integration we use the more general term *schema integration*.

Fundamental to most problems with schema integration is that an object system can be modelled in many different ways. The same phenomenon may be seen from different levels of abstraction, or represented using different properties. Different terms can denote the same concept, and different modelling structures can represent the same reality. A certain phenomenon can often be modelled as an object type, an attribute, or as the composition of several attributes, all depending on the designer's perspective.

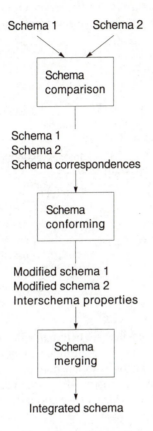

Figure 7.1 *The schema integration process*

Integrating a large number of schemas is a most complex process, and methods that prescribe how to carry out this activity are therefore valuable. Figure 7.1 shows an overview of the phases in the process of schema integration: schema comparison, schema conforming, and schema merging. *Schema comparison* involves analysing and comparing schemas in order to determine correspondences, in particular different representations of the same concepts. This step is the most difficult part of the integration process and requires close interaction with the designers and users who constructed the local schemas. *Schema conforming* involves modifying one or both schemas so that each phenomenon in the object system is represented in the same way in both schemas. *Schema merging* involves superimposing the schemas in order to obtain an integrated schema. This activity is very simple to do if schema conforming has been carried out correctly.

In large modelling projects, it is usual to construct tens or even hundreds of different schemas that must subsequently be integrated. Large-scale integration requires a strategy for integrating individual schemas in an appropriate order. Figure 7.2 shows a possible strategy where local schemas are integrated several at a time.

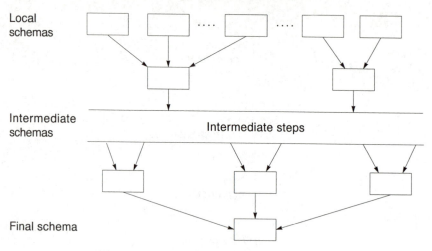

Figure 7.2 *A general approach to schema integration*

The resulting intermediate schemas are in turn integrated into a global schema. A disadvantage with this strategy is that it requires the comparison of several schemas at the same time. A better approach might be to integrate only one pair of schemas at a time, gradually accumulating all local and intermediary schemas into one global schema. This strategy is depicted in Figure 7.3, which shows how a local schema is integrated with an intermediate result at each step.

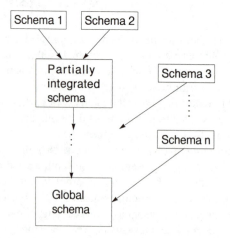

Figure 7.3 *A binary approach to schema integration*

For this strategy, it is important to choose the order in which schemas are integrated. The most important schemas should be considered in the first integration steps, i.e. one should first integrate the schemas that are most relevant, reliable, and complete. This policy will lead to better stability in the integration process.

7.2 Schema Comparison

The aim of schema comparison is to detect cases where the same aspects of reality are represented in different ways in the schemas to be integrated. Three main activities can be identified in this phase: name comparison, structure comparison, and the identification of interschema properties.

7.2.1   Name Comparison

People from different areas of the same organisation often refer to the same things using their own terminology which results in an abundance of names in the local schemas. The problematic relationships between names are of two types: synonyms and homonyms. Synonyms occur when the same object or relationship in the UoD is represented by different names in the two schemas. Homonyms occur when different objects or relationships are represented by the same name in the two schemas. Some examples of synonyms are BOY and LAD, VIOLINIST and FIDDLER, FUNNY and COMICAL. ARTICLE is an example of a homonym since this term may denote a written report in one schema and consumer goods in another.

In order to determine whether two terms are synonymous, it may be useful to compare the contexts in which they appear. The *context of an object type* is the following: its set of attributes; the object types to which it is related via attributes; and its subtypes and supertypes. The *context of an attribute* is its domain and range. If the contexts of two object types or two attributes are similar, this indicates that they are synonymous.

In addition to comparing contexts when determining synonymy, it is useful to consider integrity constraints. The reason for this is that if two object types or attributes are synonymous, then the same integrity constraints must apply to them. This observation can help us to check whether a proposed synonymy really holds or not. An example of this is given in Figure 7.4, where one might initially conjecture that the attributes lives_in and resides_in are synonymous. However, the attribute lives_in is single valued whereas resides_in is not. This shows that the terms are not synonymous, although they may have a similar meaning; resides_in might mean that a person has a residence in a city, while lives_in might mean that a person is registered in a city. If two object types or attributes are identified that seem to be synonymous but have constraints that mismatch, there are two possible explanations of this. Either the constructs are not synonymous after all, or an error exists in at least one of the local schemas. In the latter case, the design of the local schemas must be re-examined to see if the mismatch can be resolved.

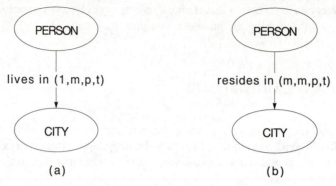

(a)   (b)

Figure 7.4 *Two attributes that cannot be synonymous*

7.2.2   Structural Comparison

The purpose of structural comparison is to identify cases where the same aspects of an object system have been modelled using different constructs. Owing to the difficulty in finding an exhaustive classification of semantically equivalent but structurally different modelling constructs, this section only provides examples of some of the most important ones.

Relationships between objects can often be modelled either by means of lexical attributes (attributes whose range is a data type) or by non-lexical attributes (attributes whose range is a non-lexical object type). Figure 7.5 illustrates this. The first schema represents the relationship between books and publishers as a lexical attribute, whereas the second schema uses PUBLISHER as an additional object type and represents the relationship as a non-lexical attribute.

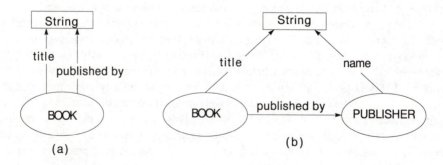

(a)   (b)

Figure 7.5 *Equivalent but structurally different constructs*

A relationship between objects can be modelled either directly as an attribute or indirectly by introducing an extra object that ties the associated objects together; compare the reification of attributes in Section 6.2.3. Two different ways of modelling the relationship of marriage between men and women are shown in Figure 7.6. In the first schema, the relationship is represented by a single attribute `married_to`, whereas in the second schema an additional object type `MARRIAGE` and two attributes `wife` and `husband` are used.

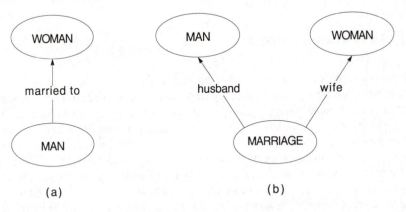

Figure 7.6 *Equivalent but structurally different constructs*

There are two ways to represent the classification of objects into categories in a conceptual schema. Either a number of subtypes of a given object type can be introduced or an attribute can be used that has a value indicating the category to which an object belongs. The first schema in Figure 7.7 represents the classification of people into male and female by means of an attribute `gender`, whereas the second schema uses two subtypes, `MAN` and `WOMAN`.

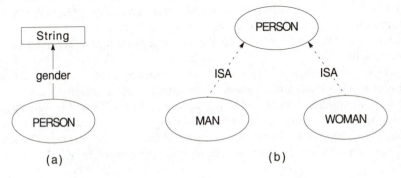

Figure 7.7 *Equivalent but structurally different constructs*

If distinct modelling constructs in two different schemas seem equivalent, checking whether the constraints applying to the constructs contradict each other can help to reveal whether they actually are equivalent. Detecting non-equivalence in this way is similar to name comparison, where the same constraints must apply to synonymous attributes and object types. However, defining when constraints are in contradiction within the context of modelling constructs that are structurally different is quite complex, so we refer the interested reader to the literature [Batini91], see also Exercise 7.2.

7.2.3   Interschema Properties

In the previous two subsections, we have discussed relationships between two schemas where constructs were equivalent, i.e. they were able to represent exactly the same information. However, more general correspondences may also exist where constructs appearing in different schemas have certain constraints in common. Such correspondences are commonly called *interschema properties.* More precisely, an interschema property is a formula expressed in the union of the languages belonging to the two schemas in question. An object type in one schema that is a subtype of an object type in another schema is an example of an interschema property, as is an attribute in one schema that is derivable from a set of attributes in another schema. These properties should be explicitly annotated during schema comparison, since they are used later during schema merging.

7.3 Schema Conforming

The aim of schema conforming is to transform schemas in order to increase their similarity, which facilitates the schema merging phase. For each synonym or homonym, we perform a renaming. When two object types, e.g. CUSTOMER and CLIENT, are synonymous, then one of them, say CLIENT, is selected and renamed CUSTOMER. Where homonyms are concerned, a new name must be introduced. Suppose ARTICLE meant report in one schema and consumer goods in another; ARTICLE could then be renamed REPORT in the first schema.

When modelling constructs are semantically equivalent but structurally different, it is impossible to provide any strict rules as to how to make them conform. Usually the schema containing the simpler construct is adjusted by replacing it with the equivalent construct from the other schema. The example in Figure 7.5 would be transformed by introducing an additional object type PUBLISHER into the first schema. The schemas would then acquire a similar structure, and merging them becomes trivial.

7.4 Schema Merging

Schema merging, which involves merging two or more schemas into a single one, is the final phase in the process of schema integration. If the schema conforming phase has been carried out correctly, discrepancies in terminology and structure should have been removed. In that case schema merging becomes a simple superimposition of schemas. Identical object types with identical contexts are superimposed directly. Identical object types with different sets of attributes are superimposed by adopting the union of their attributes. All interschema properties, such as subtype relations, are also included in the merged schema.

Having merged all the local schemas, it may be worthwhile restructuring the integrated schema. It is not unusual, once schemas are completely merged, to discover relationships between hitherto unconnected objects. For example, if one schema contains the object type COUNTRY and another schema the object type CITY, then an attribute lies_in can be introduced in the merged schema. Similarly, if the integrated schema contains the types RESEARCHER, TEACHER, and SECRETARY all originating from different local schemas, then a common supertype EMPLOYEE can be introduced. Furthermore, errors that have gone unnoticed in the local schemas might be detected in the integrated schema, in which case the original schemas will need to be reviewed and adjusted. As a consequence, the schema integration process becomes iterative moving back and forth between comparison, merging, restructuring, error analysis, and redesign. Performing schema integration therefore requires an extensive interaction between users and designers, and often results in new findings about the object system that were overlooked during construction of the local schemas.

7.5 An Example of Schema Integration

In this section, we shall illustrate schema integration by means of a more comprehensive example. Figure 7.8 and Figure 7.9 show two local schemas of an object system that deal with the management of a library. For the sake of brevity we specify neither the range nor the mapping constraints of the lexical attributes. In addition we only summarise the results of schema comparison, simultaneously indicating how the schemas should be made to conform. Note that the correspondences below cannot be discovered by merely studying the graphs; a thorough understanding of the object system in question is also necessary. In practice, this requires extensive interaction with users.

Synonyms:

1. PAPER and ARTICLE are synonymous. We rename ARTICLE as PAPER.
2. BOOK and MONOGRAPH are synonymous. We rename MONOGRAPH as BOOK.
3. TEXT and PUBLICATION are synonymous. We rename TEXT as PUBLICATION.

Homonyms:

1. PUBLICATION is a homonym. In the schema of Figure 7.8 it means a certain copy of a book, journal, or proceedings. In the schema of Figure 7.9 it means a book, journal, or proceedings considered as a template object, cf. Section 6.2.5. We resolve the homonyms by renaming PUBLICATION in the schema of Figure 7.8 as COPY.
2. TOPIC is a homonym. In the schema of Figure 7.8 it means the subject of a paper or a publication, whereas in Figure 7.9 it means the area in which a certain person performs research. We resolve the situation by renaming TOPIC in the schema of Figure 7.9 as RESEARCH_AREA.

Structural differences:

1. The attribute keyword in Figure 7.9 models the same relationship as treats in Figure 7.8, but the range of keyword is a data type whereas the range of treats is a non-lexical object type, cf. Figure 7.5. We resolve the differences by replacing keyword with a structure similar to that of Figure 7.8.
2. In order to represent authors, the schema of Figure 7.8 uses a lexical attribute, whereas the schema of Figure 7.9 uses a non-lexical attribute. We choose the representation of Figure 7.9.
3. In order to represent publishers, the schema of Figure 7.8 uses a lexical attribute, whereas the schema of Figure 7.9 uses a non-lexical attribute. We choose the representation of Figure 7.9.
4. In Figure 7.8, publications are classified into the three subtypes JOURNAL, PROCEEDINGS and MONOGRAPH. In Figure 7.9, an attribute type is used instead, cf. Figure 7.7. We resolve the differences by replacing the attribute type in Figure 7.9 with the subtypes of Figure 7.8.

Interschema properties:

1. The object type RESEARCHER is a subtype of EMPLOYEE.
2. The attributes appears_in and contained_in of Figure 7.8 are special cases of the attribute published_in of Figure 7.9.
3. If a book belongs to a series from a certain publisher (Figure 7.9), then the book is published by that publisher (Figure 7.8).

After schema conforming, we obtain the modified schemas of Figure 7.10 and Figure 7.11. The complete and fully integrated schema is depicted in Figure 7.12. Note that we have restructured it slightly by introducing an attribute between TOPIC and RESEARCH_AREA. Another plausible way to restructure the schema would be by introducing a supertype PERSON for the types AUTHOR and EMPLOYEE.

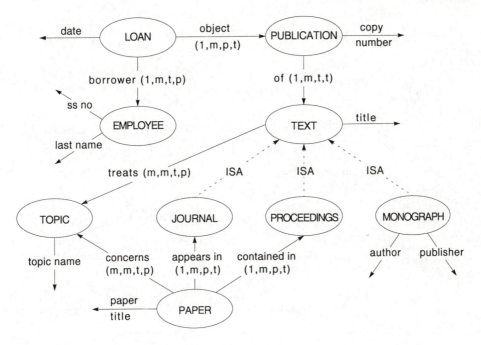

Figure 7.8 *Local schema 1*

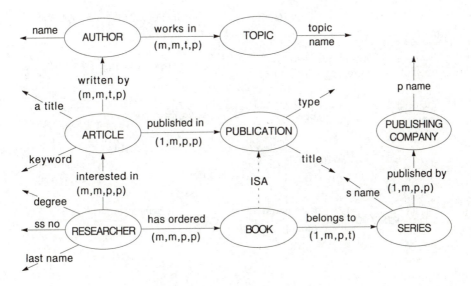

Figure 7.9 *Local schema 2*

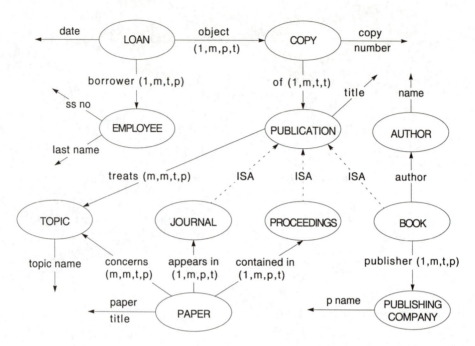

Figure 7.10 *Modified local schema 1*

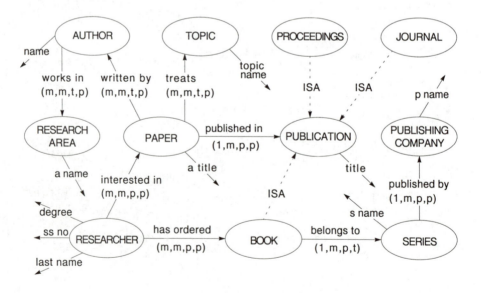

Figure 7.11 *Modified local schema 2*

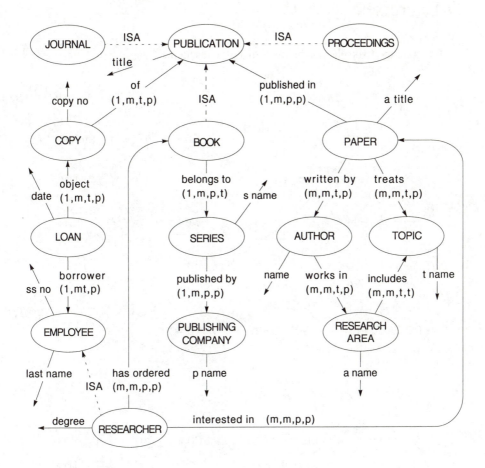

Figure 7.12 *Integrated schema*

7.6 Some Relevant Literature

A comprehensive survey of different approaches to schema integration can be found in [Batini86]. The textbook [Batini91] gives a good introduction to schema integration, and much of the material in this chapter is based on this source. More formal approaches to schema integration are presented in [Biskup86], [Johannesson93], and [Miller94].

7.7 Exercises

7.1   Integrate the two schemas below into a global schema.

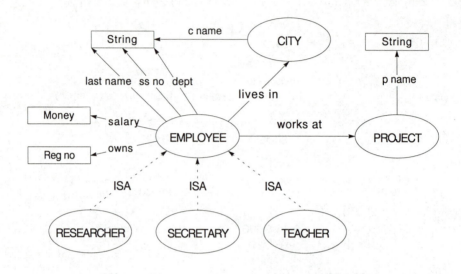

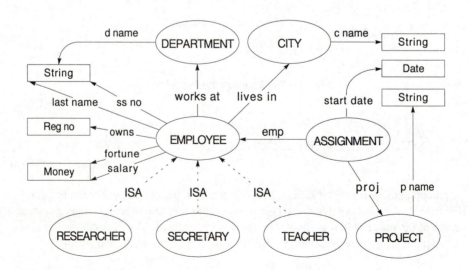

7.2 Assuming `att` can take only two values, then the two constructs below are equivalent, cf. Figure 7.7. Supposing `att` were single valued and total, which constraints would then apply to the subtypes of the second schema?

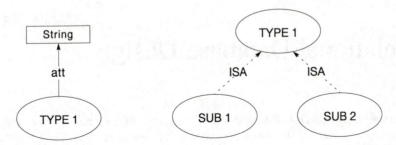

CHAPTER 8

Relational Database Design

Information systems are often realised by means of database management systems. It is therefore important to be able to translate a conceptual schema into a traditional data model, like the hierarchical, network, or relational model. This chapter describes how a conceptual schema can be translated into a relational schema. It is assumed that the reader is familiar with the basics of relational database theory. The first section introduces some of the terminology and notation of relational databases. In the following section, several examples are used to outline how a conceptual schema is translated into a relational one. Thereafter a formal algorithm for the translation is presented. Finally, there is a discussion on some of the fundamental differences between the relational model and the approach of conceptual modelling.

8.1 Basic Concepts of Relational Databases

This section introduces basic concepts and terminology in relational database theory; it can be skipped at first reading and referred back to as necessary. A *relation scheme* is a pair $\langle R_i, X_i \rangle$, usually denoted $R_i(X_i)$, where R_i is the name of the relation scheme, and X_i is a set of columns. Every column of a relation scheme is associated with a set, called its *domain*. We use the following notational convention: if $R_i(X_i)$ is a relation scheme with m columns, we write $X_i = A_{i,1}A_{i,2}...A_{i,m}$. The domain for $A_{i,j}$ is denoted by $D_{i,j}$. A *tuple* in the relation scheme $R_i(X_i)$ is an element of $D_{i,1} \times ... \times D_{i,m}$. A *relation* in a relation scheme $R_i(X_i)$ is a set of tuples in $R_i(X_i)$. If t is a tuple in $R_i(X_i)$ and Y is a subset of X_i, then $t[Y]$ denotes the subtuple of t corresponding to Y. Let $R_i(X_i)$ be a relation scheme, r_i a relation in $R_i(X_i)$, and Y a subset of X_i. The *projection* of r_i on Y, denoted by $\Pi_{Y}(r_i)$, is $\{t[Y] \mid t \in r_i\}$.

Let $R_i(X_i)$ be a relation scheme and r_i a relation in $R_i(X_i)$. A *functional dependency* over R_i is a statement of the form $R_i: Y \rightarrow Z$, where Y and Z are subsets of X_i. A functional dependency $R_i: Y \rightarrow Z$ is *satisfied* by r_i if $t[Y] = t'[Y]$ implies $t[Z] = t'[Z]$, for any two tuples of r_i, t, and t'. A *key* for R_i is a subset K_i of X_i, such that $R_i: K_i \rightarrow X_i$ is satisfied by any r_i associated with R_i, and no proper subset of K_i exists with this property. A relation scheme can have several *candidate keys* from which one *primary key,* denoted PK_i, is chosen.

Let $R_i(X_i)$ and $R_j(X_j)$ be two relation schemes. Let r_i and r_j be relations of $R_i(X_i)$ and $R_j(X_j)$, respectively. An *inclusion dependency* is a statement of the form $R_i[Y] << R_j[Z]$, where Y and Z are subsets of X_i and X_j, respectively. The inclusion dependency $R_i[Y] << R_j[Z]$ is *satisfied* by r_i and r_j if $\Pi_Y(r_i) \subset \Pi_Z(r_j)$. If $R_j[Z]$ is a key, the inclusion dependency is called a foreign key relationship, and $R_i[Y]$ is called a *foreign key*.

A *relational schema* is a pair $\langle R, F \cup I \rangle$, where R is a set of relation schemes, F is a set of functional dependencies, and I is a set of inclusion dependencies.

8.2 From Conceptual to Relational Schemas

Translating a conceptual schema into a relational one is basically a simple process consisting of the following steps. First, each object type in the conceptual schema gives rise to a relation scheme. Each attribute of the object type gives rise to one or several columns of the relation scheme. Each m–m attribute is translated into a relation scheme, and the columns of this scheme correspond to the identifiers (cf. Section 5.3.1 above) of the domain and range of the attribute. Each non-lexical attribute and each ISA relationship gives rise to a foreign key relationship.

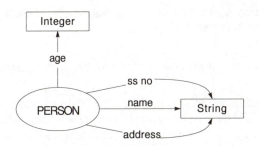

Identifiers for PERSON: [ss_no], [name, address]

Figure 8.1 *A schema without non-lexical attributes*

Example 8.1   Figure 8.1 shows a conceptual schema with two different identifiers for the type PERSON: [ss_no] and [name, address]. The object type PERSON gives rise to a relation scheme, and each attribute is mapped into a column in this scheme (we use the convention of underlining the primary key of a relation scheme):

PERSON(<u>SS no</u>, Name, Address, Age)

[Name, Address] will be a candidate key of PERSON.

The domains of the columns are derived from the ranges of the corresponding attributes:

```
domain(SS_no) = domain(Name) = domain(Address) = String,
domain(Age) = Integer
```

Each non-lexical 1–1 or 1–m attribute is mapped onto one or more columns, which should correspond to an identifier of the range of the attribute. If the identifier is composed of several attributes, then several columns are needed to represent the attribute, as illustrated in the following example.

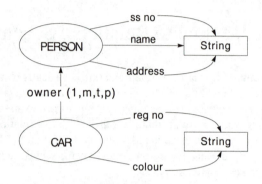

Identifiers for PERSON: [ss_no], [name, address]
Identifier for CAR: [reg_no]

Figure 8.2 *A schema with non-lexical 1–m attributes*

Example 8.2   Consider the schema in Figure 8.2. The type PERSON is translated as in Example 8.1 above, and the type CAR gives rise to a new relation scheme, which we also call CAR. The attribute owner is represented by including a foreign key in CAR. This foreign key can correspond either to the key [ss_no] of PERSON or to the key [name, address]. In the first case, we obtain the following relational schema:

```
PERSON(SS no, Name, Address)
CAR(Reg no, Colour, Owner_ss_no)
CAR.Owner_ss_no << PERSON.SS_no
```

If we use the key [name, address] of PERSON, we obtain the following schema:

```
PERSON(SS no, Name, Address)
CAR(Reg no, Colour, Owner_name, Owner_address)
CAR.(Owner_name, Owner_address) << PERSON.(Name, Address)
```

In some cases, an attribute has to be represented by several columns that correspond to attributes from more than one type, as illustrated in the example below.

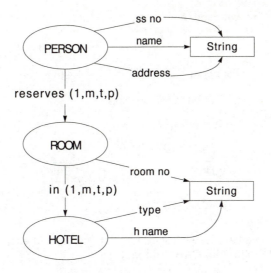

Identifiers for PERSON: [ss_no], [name, address]
Identifier for ROOM: [room_no, in]
Identifier for HOTEL: [h_name]

Figure 8.3 *A schema with a type whose identifier includes a non-lexical attribute*

Example 8.3 The schema in Figure 8.3 is translated into the following relational schema:

```
PERSON(SS no, Name, Address, Hotel, Room)
ROOM(Hotel, Room no)
HOTEL(H name, Type)
PERSON.(Hotel, Room) << ROOM.(Hotel, Room_no)
ROOM.Hotel << HOTEL.H_name
```

Note that the attribute `reserves` in the conceptual schema is represented by two columns (`Hotel`, `Room`) in the relation scheme `PERSON`.

In the above examples, attributes in the conceptual schema only give rise to additional columns in a relation scheme. For m–m attributes and m–1 lexical attributes, however, it is necessary to introduce extra relation schemes.

Example 8.4 In Figure 8.4, the attribute `owns` is m–m, and we translate it into an extra relation scheme:

```
PERSON(SS no, Name, Address)
CAR(Reg no, Colour)
OWNS(SS no, Reg no)
```

```
OWNS.SS_no << PERSON.SS_no
OWNS.Reg_no << CAR.Reg_no
```

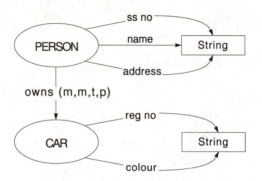

Identifiers for PERSON: [ss_no], [name, address]
Identifier for CAR: [reg_no]

Figure 8.4 *A schema with m–m attributes*

The primary key of the new relation scheme is a combination of the columns that constitute the primary keys of the relation schemes PERSON and CAR. In order to obtain a relation scheme in the first normal form, it is necessary to create a new relation scheme. If we had introduced an attribute owns in the relation scheme PERSON, it would no longer have fulfilled the requirements of the first normal form.

If a lexical attribute is m–1 it will give rise to an extra relation scheme, as illustrated in the following example.

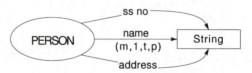

Identifier for PERSON: [ss_no]

Figure 8.5 *A schema with a lexical m–1 attribute*

Example 8.5   In Figure 8.5 the attribute name is m–1, which means that a person may have several names, but that two people cannot have the same name. We translate this schema into the following relational schema:

```
PERSON(SS no, Address)
NAME(SS no, Name)
NAME.SS_no << PERSON.SS_no
```

An ISA relation between two object types gives rise to a foreign key relationship between the corresponding relation schemes.

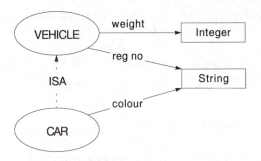

Identifiers for VEHICLE: [reg_no]
Identifier for CAR: [reg_no]

Figure 8.6 *A schema with ISA relations*

Example 8.6   The schema in Figure 8.6 translates into the following relational schema:

```
CAR(Reg no, Colour)
VEHICLE(Reg no, Weight)
CAR.Reg_no << VEHICLE.Reg_no
```

Note that a relation scheme corresponding to a subtype will contain columns corresponding to the identifiers of the supertypes.

8.3 An Algorithm for Schema Translation

In this section, we give a formal algorithm for translating a conceptual schema into a relational schema. In order for the translation process to work, we have to make certain assumptions concerning the form of the conceptual schema. First, we assume that for each non-lexical type an identifier is given that contains only 1–1 or 1–m attributes. Further, we define the *identifier graph* of a conceptual schema as the graph, the nodes of which are the non-lexical types of the schema, and the arcs of which are the attributes belonging to the identifiers of the types. We require an identifier graph to be acyclic, i.e. contain no cycles.

   The translation algorithm consists of three steps. In the first step, we identify and name the relation schemes that correspond to: the non-lexical types; the lexical m–1 attributes; and the m–m attributes. In the second step, we identify the columns of each scheme and its primary key. In the final step, we specify the foreign keys of the relational schema. A technical problem is to name columns so that they are unique within each relation scheme. The algorithm below achieves this by concatenating the names of the attributes. However, this approach often results in cumbersome and unnatural names, and it may therefore be worthwhile to simplify the names produced by the algorithm.

Before describing the algorithm, we introduce two functions used to name columns in a relation scheme that correspond to one or more attributes. We define an (infix) operator conc, which takes a string S and a list of strings L as parameters and constructs a list of strings such that each string in L is concatenated with S. A recursive definition of conc is

$$S \text{ conc } [\,] = [\,]$$
$$S \text{ conc } [H|T] = [\text{concatenate}(S, H) \mid S \text{ conc } T]$$

For example, a conc [b, c, d] = [a_b, a_c, a_d]. (The extra underscores are merely syntactic sugar.) The operator conc is useful in constructing unique names of columns.

We define a function λ that takes types in the conceptual schema and converts them into strings. Let T be a type. Suppose the identifier $(T) = [A_1, ..., A_n]$.

$\lambda(T) = \varepsilon$, if T is a lexical type (ε denotes the empty string)
$\lambda(T) = A_1 \text{ conc } \lambda(\text{range}(A_1)) + ... + A_n \text{ conc } \lambda(\text{range}(A_n))$, if T is a non-lexical type, and + denotes concatenation of lists.

The acyclicity of the identifier graph ensures that λ is well-defined. Loosely speaking, λ maps a given type onto an identifying set of lexical attributes, in which some of the attributes may be composed of other attributes. For example, $\lambda(\text{ROOM}) = [\text{room\_no}, \text{in\_hname}]$ in Example 8.3 above.

We are now ready to describe the algorithm for translating a conceptual schema into a relational schema. We follow the description with an example that illustrates how the algorithm can be applied.

1. The names of the relation schemes are $\mathbf{T} \cup \mathbf{MM} \cup \mathbf{M1}$, where $\mathbf{T}$ is the set of all non-lexical types in the conceptual schema, $\mathbf{MM}$ is the set of all m–m attributes, and $\mathbf{M1}$ is the set of all lexical m–1 attributes.

2. Next the columns of each relation scheme are specified. Let R be the name of a relation scheme. (Note that R is then also a type or an attribute in the conceptual schema.)

a) $R \in \mathbf{T}$. The columns of R are
$\cup_{A \in RD} (A \text{ conc } \lambda(\text{range}(A))) \cup$
$\cup_{A \in RR} (A \text{ conc } \lambda(\text{domain}(A))) \cup$
$\cup_{A \in RS} \lambda(A)$, where
RD is the set of all 1–1 or 1–m attributes the domain of which is R,
RR is the set of all m–1 attributes the range of which is R,
RS is the set of all supertypes of R.

The primary key of R is $\lambda(R)$.[1]

b) $R \in \mathbf{MM}$. The columns of R are
$\lambda(\text{domain}(R)) \cup A$ conc $\lambda(\text{range}(R))$
The primary key of R is the set of all columns in R.

c) $R \in \mathbf{M1}$. The columns of R are
$\lambda(\text{domain}(R)) \cup \{R\}$
The primary key of R is $\{R\}$. Note that in this case, the relation scheme will contain a column with the same name as the scheme, cf. Example 8.5 above. The domain of each column is derived from the range of the corresponding attribute.

3. The algorithm now produces the foreign keys of the relational schema.

a) If A is a non-lexical 1–1 or 1–m attribute and domain(A) = D and range(A) = R, then the following foreign key should be included in the relational schema:
$D.A$ conc $\lambda(R) \ll R.\lambda(R)$

b) If A is an m–1 non-lexical attribute and domain(A) = D and range(A) = R, then the following foreign key should be included:
$R.A$ conc $\lambda(D) \ll D.\lambda(D)$

c) If A is an m–1 lexical attribute and domain(A) = D, then the following foreign key should be included:
$A.\lambda(D) \ll D.\lambda(D)$

d) If A is an m–m attribute and domain(A) = D and range(A) = R, then the following foreign keys are to be included:
$A.\lambda(D) \ll D.\lambda(D)$
$A.A$ conc $\lambda(R) \ll R.\lambda(R)$, if R is a non-lexical type.

e) If A is a subtype of B, then the following foreign key should be included:
$A.\lambda(B) \ll B.\lambda(B)$

Example 8.7   We translate the conceptual schema of Figure 8.7 into a relational schema by applying the algorithm above. First we compute λ for each type of the conceptual schema:

$\lambda(\text{VEHICLE}) = $ [reg_no]
$\lambda(\text{CAR}) = $ [reg_no]
$\lambda(\text{PERSON}) = $ [ss_no]
$\lambda(\text{PURCHASE}) = $ [buyer_ss_no, object_reg_no]
$\lambda(\text{HOTEL}) = $ [hname]
$\lambda(\text{ROOM}) = $ [in_hname, room_no]

---

1) Here, the primary key is viewed as a list, rather than a set.

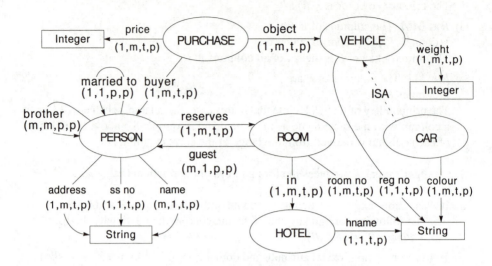

Identifier for PURCHASE: [buyer, object]
Identifier for ROOM: [room no, in]

Figure 8.7 *Example schema*

1. We find the names of all relation schemes.

T = {VEHICLE, CAR, PERSON, PURCHASE, ROOM, HOTEL}
MM = {BROTHER}
M1 = {NAME}

2. We find the columns of each relation scheme and specify the primary keys.

a) We give the columns for the relation schemes that correspond to non-lexical types in the conceptual schema:

For the type VEHICLE, RD = {reg_no, weight}, $RR = \emptyset$, $RS = \emptyset$.
VEHICLE(<u>Reg no</u>, Weight)

For the type CAR, RD = {colour}, $RR = \emptyset$, RS = {VEHICLE}.
CAR(<u>Reg no</u>, Colour)

For the type HOTEL, RD = {hname}, $RR = \emptyset$, $RS = \emptyset$.
HOTEL(<u>Hname</u>)

For the type ROOM, RD = {room_no, in}, $RR = \emptyset$, $RS = \emptyset$.
ROOM(<u>Room no, In hname</u>)

For the type PERSON, RD = {ss_no, address, married_to, reserves},
RR = {guest}, $RS = \emptyset$.
PERSON(<u>SS no</u>, Address, Married_to_ss_no, Reserves_room_no,
Reserves_in_hname, Guest_room_no, Guest_in_hname)

For the type PURCHASE, RD = {buyer, object, price}, $RR = \emptyset$, $RS = \emptyset$.

```
PURCHASE(Buyer ss no, Object reg no, Price)
```

b) We give the columns for the relation schemes that correspond to m–m attributes in the conceptual schema:

```
BROTHER(SS no, Brother ss no)
```

c) We give the columns for the relation schemes that correspond to lexical m–1 attributes in the conceptual schema:

```
NAME(Name, SS_no)
```

3. We now find the foreign keys of the relational schema.

a) Foreign keys due to non-lexical 1–1 or 1–m attributes:

```
PURCHASE.Buyer_ss_no << PERSON.SS_no
PURCHASE.Object_reg_no << CAR.Reg_no
PERSON.Married_to_ss_no << PERSON.SS_no
PERSON.(Reserves_room_no, Reserves_in_hname) <<
        ROOM.(Room_no, In_hname)
ROOM.In_hname << HOTEL.Hname
```

b) Foreign keys due to non-lexical m–1 attributes:

```
PERSON.(Guest_room_no, Guest_in_hname) <<
        ROOM.(Room_no, In_hname)
```

c) Foreign keys due to m–1 lexical attributes:

```
NAME.SS_no << PERSON.SS_no
```

d) Foreign keys due to m–m attributes:

```
BROTHER.SS_no << PERSON.SS_no
BROTHER.Brother_ss_no << PERSON.SS_no
```

e) Foreign keys due to ISA relations:

```
CAR.Reg_no << VEHICLE.Reg_no
```

8.4 Relational Database Management Systems

It is important to draw a distinction between the theoretical relational model and commercial database management systems. Most current relational systems do not support all the kinds of functional and inclusion dependencies of the relational model. On the other hand, almost all systems provide additional constructs that are not included in the relational model, like arithmetic and update operations. These differences between the theoretical relational model and commercial systems mean that the translation algorithm of the previous section needs to be complemented. In the definition of the algorithm, we have assumed that a relational schema contains a set of keys and foreign keys. However, as we just pointed out, many commercial relational database management systems support neither keys nor foreign keys. In certain systems, however, it is possible to maintain keys by means of cunning *ad hoc* solutions, such as defining a unique index for a set of attributes. A more general solution to maintaining keys and foreign keys is to ensure that the procedures that update the database are constructed in such a way that key and foreign key dependencies cannot be violated. In order to achieve this, all updates are performed by transactions, which check that no key or foreign key dependency is violated. The mechanism for doing this is similar to that of preconditions in event rules as described in Chapter 5.

A major limitation of the translation algorithm in Section 8.3 is that the only kinds of rules it takes into account are typing constraints and certain mapping constraints. Derivation rules, event rules, and many integrity constraints are not taken into consideration. Consequently, the relational schema produced by the algorithm contains less information than the conceptual schema from which it originated. The way in which derivation rules, event rules, and general integrity constraints are represented in a relational database management system depends very much on the specific features of that system. We can therefore only give a few general hints as to how to represent these types of rules. Event rules are typically implemented as transactions, which can be written in a language like embedded SQL together with some host language. Derivation rules can often be represented in relational systems by the "view" mechanism. Alternatively, derivation rules can be implemented by letting the transactions of the information system derive information and store it in the database. Certain integrity constraints can be maintained by mechanisms particular to the database management system. For instance, a column can be declared "NOT NULL" if the corresponding attribute is total. In general, however, integrity constraints must be maintained by including checking mechanisms in transactions, as described above.

The translation algorithm only produces a logical design of a relational schema as it does not take physical performance into account. It may therefore be necessary to make several modifications to a schema produced by the algorithm, in order to achieve acceptable performance. Adapting a logical design in this way is called *physical database design*. It lies outside the scope of this book to give a thorough treatment of physical database design, a topic on which there are several textbooks that the interested reader can pursue, e.g. [Fleming89]. We shall only provide an example, in which the algorithm above produces a schema which is clearly unsatisfactory from a performance point of view. The algorithm translates the schema depicted in Figure 8.8 into the following relational schema:

```
ANIMAL(Name, Weight)
MAMMAL(Name, Length)
DOG(Name, Tail_length)
ELEPHANT(Name, Trunk_length)
MAMMAL.Name << ANIMAL.Name
DOG.Name << MAMMAL.Name
ELEPHANT.Name << MAMMAL.Name
```

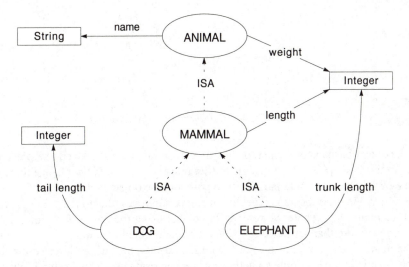

Figure 8.8 *Example schema*

A query put to this schema may obviously need to access several relation schemes, which may compromise performance. In order to improve performance, we might choose to collapse the relation schemes into a single one:

```
ANIMAL(Name, Weight, Length, Tail_length, Trunk_length, Mammal,
Dog, Elephant)
```

The domain of the columns `Mammal`, `Dog`, and `Elephant` is `Boolean`, and a value in one of these columns indicates whether a certain animal is a mammal, dog, or elephant, respectively. Note that any query now only has to access one relation.

8.5 Differences between the Relational Model and Conceptual Models

The fundamental difference between the relational model and the approach of conceptual modelling is that the former is *value-based* whereas the latter is *object-based*. The approach of conceptual modelling is called object-based because objects are the basic modelling construct around which all other modelling constructs are defined. In order to denote objects, conceptual modelling languages also provide special linguistic symbols, usually called object identifiers (see Section 3.1.1). The relational model, on the other hand, does not support the *object* concept, but prefers to use data values (see Section 3.1.3) as its basic building blocks. As an illustration of the difference between an object-based and a value-based approach to representing objects, consider Figure 8.9.

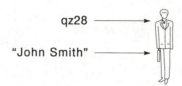

qz28 ⟶

"John Smith" ⟶

Figure 8.9 *Object identifiers and data values*

In the object-based approach, a specific object identifier is introduced to represent the object, in this case `qz28`. This object identifier must be stable and not change during the lifetime of the object. Its sole purpose is to point out the object and to act as a handle for it. The object identifier bears no specific meaning. Compare this to the value-based approach of Figure 8.9, where we refer to the object using the data value "John Smith". This string is more than an identifier, since it has additional meaning, such as implying that the man's parents were also called "Smith". Further, the string "John Smith" is not a stable identifier, since people sometimes change their names. This example illustrates a fundamental disadvantage of the value-based approach: a linguistic symbol is used simultaneously to identify an object and to describe some of the object's properties. Since most properties are changeable by nature, this approach makes it hard to find a stable identifier. It can also be difficult to find a set of properties the values of which are unique for each object. Continuing with our example above, it is clear that the name of a person may be insufficient to identify the person uniquely. It may therefore become necessary for the identifier to encompass additional attributes (address, telephone number, etc.) or to change to an altogether different identifying attribute, such as a social security number. The strength of the object-based approach is that it separates the concept of identity from that of property by introducing special symbols for identifying objects.

Another drawback with languages that reference objects through data values is that their expressions often become lengthy and clumsy in comparison with those of an object-based language. In the schema of Figure 8.10, we assume that the identifier of PER-SON is {p_name, is_born_at}, the identifier of STREET is {sname, lies_in}, and that of TOWN is {tname, belongs_to}. The corresponding relational schema is

```
COUNTRY(cname)
TOWN(tname, cname)
STREET(sname, tname, cname)
PERSON(p name, born street, born town, born country, lives_street,
lives_town, lives_country)
TOWN.cname << COUNTRY.cname
STREET.(tname, cname) << TOWN.(tname, cname)
PERSON.(born_street, born_town, born_country) <<
          STREET.(sname, tname, cname)
PERSON.(lives_street, lives_town, lives_country) <<
          STREET.(sname, tname, cname)
```

If we want to find all the people who have lived on the same street as John Smith, we could write the following query in Prolog:

```
?- p_name(J, 'John Smith'), is_born_at(J, S), lives_at(P, S).
```

Using SQL and the corresponding relational schema results in a much more complex query:

```
SELECT p_name, born_street, born_town, born_country
    FROM PERSON
    WHERE lives_street, lives_town, lives_country IN
        (SELECT born_street, born_town, born_country
        FROM PERSON
        WHERE p_name = 'John Smith')
```

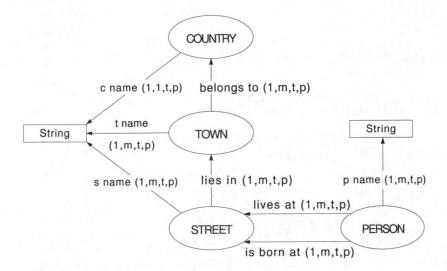

Figure 8.10 *Example schema*

Another advantage that the approach of conceptual modelling has over the relational model is that the former supports the concept of generalisation, which is an important structuring mechanism. As can be seen from the algorithm of Section 8.3, a subtype relation is represented in a relational schema by a foreign key. In the relational model, information about a single object may have to be spread out amongst several relations, as shown in the relational schema corresponding to Figure 8.8, where information about a particular dog is retained in three distinct tuples of DOG, MAMMAL, and ANIMAL.

8.6 Some Relevant Literature

There are many good textbooks on relational database theory and design, e.g. [Date90], [Ullman88], and [Abiteboul95]. The text [Fleming89] also covers physical database design. A more formal but excellent treatment is given in [Kanellakis90]. Comparisons between conceptual modelling approaches and traditional database models can be found in [Codd79], [Tsichritzis82], and [Teorey86].

8.7 Exercises

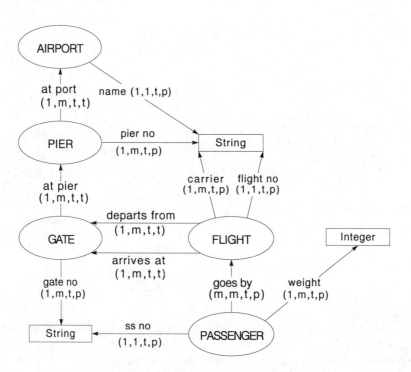

Identifier for GATE: [gate no, at pier]
Identifier for PIER: [pier no, at port]

8.1 Construct a relational schema that corresponds to the graphical representation of the conceptual schema above.

8.2 Construct a relational schema that corresponds to the graphical representation of the conceptual schema below.

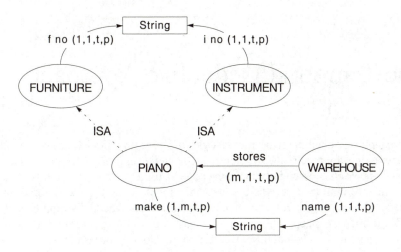

Identifier for PIANO: [i no]

8.3 Determine whether a relational schema produced by the algorithm of Section 8.3 will always be in the third normal form. Pay special attention to derived attributes.

8.4 Explain why the conceptual schema of Figure 8.5 above cannot be translated by including a column, Name, in the relation scheme PERSON of Example 8.5.

8.5 Try to construct a relational schema that corresponds to the graphical representation of the conceptual schema below. You will discover that you soon run into trouble. Explain the cause of the problem and suggest how the conceptual schema can be changed to make the translation possible.

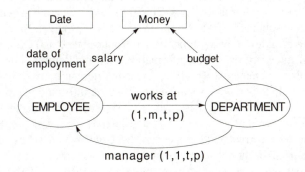

Identifier for EMPLOYEE: [works at, date of employment]

CHAPTER 9

The Temporal Deductive Approach

In this chapter we examine two extreme styles of conceptual modelling. We denote them "the operational approach" and the "temporal deductive approach", respectively. The operational approach is essentially the same style as used in Chapter 5 in this book. It assumes an information base where statements about some UoD are stored and then updated by transactions in response to events. The temporal deductive approach does not include the update concept. The information base for this modelling style contains stored information about events that have occurred in the UoD. Every event is associated with a time stamp, its intrinsic time. All other information about the UoD is represented as derived information. This chapter presents both these styles and discusses their advantages and drawbacks. Section 9.1 introduces the basic concepts, and Section 9.2 describes a simple inventory management case including a number of rules and constraints. Section 9.3 presents a solution of this case according to the operational approach, while Section 9.4 gives a solution using the temporal deductive approach. Section 9.5 compares the styles with respect to a number of quality criteria.

9.1 Characterisation of the Approaches

In Chapter 3, we introduced a framework for the relationship between a UoD and a conceptual schema and an information base. This framework is summarised in Figure 9.1, where a conceptual schema $CS(t)$ at a point in time t is an abstract, formal view of some UoD and defines all relevant entity types and attributes, static and dynamic constraints, derivation rules, and event rules. The information base at a point in time t, $IB(t)$, is a set of type and attribute statements. Recall that by using derivation rules of the conceptual schema, it is possible to derive new statements from the information base.

For instance, an information base can contain attribute statements of the type `quantity_on_hand(article, quantity)` and `price(article, money)`. The information base must be correct with respect to the UoD, which entails that it must be updated as soon as an event occurs; these updates are performed according to the event rules of the conceptual schema. An example of a type of derived statement is `value_of_inventory(article, money)`. It is assumed that the conceptual schema contains a derivation rule stating how to calculate this value from `quantity_on_hand` and `price` statements.

Figure 9.1 depicts how the information base changes from IB(t) to IB(t +1) as a response to changes in the UoD from the point in time t to t +1 owing to the occurrence of an external event at t +1. Using this framework, we will now characterise the operational and the deductive approaches. For both approaches, we assume that the conceptual schema does not change from t to t +1, i.e. CS(t) = CS(t +1). The schema is assumed to be unchanged during the entire life span of the information system.

In the *operational approach*, an event induces a transaction which replaces the information base IB(t) by IB(t +1). This is done by inserting, deleting, or modifying statements in IB(t) and thereby creating a new information base IB(t +1).

In the *temporal deductive approach*, all statements in the information base are associated with a point in time that states when the information is valid. Thus, all statements, base statements as well as derived statements, are represented as $p(a,b,...,t)$, which states that $p(a,b,...)$ holds at time t. We assume that time is represented by a standard time unit (second, hour, day, etc.), chosen small enough to avoid ambiguities, cf. the time model in Section 3.2.1. The deductive approach thus considers the information base to exist during the life span of the information system, $T = \{t_0,..., t_f\}$, where t_0 and t_f are the initial and final time points of the system. As all statements are associated with a time point, it is possible to write expressions which refer to all time points of a system's life cycle. For an information base to be valid at time t, IB(t) must not violate any static or dynamic constraint stated in the conceptual schema. While the deductive approach does not make a particular distinction between static and dynamic constraints, we can say that a constraint is static if it involves information of time point t only. If a constraint references information valid at different time points, it is dynamic.

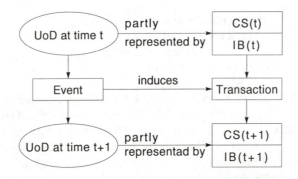

Figure 9.1 *Relationships between a UoD and a conceptual schema with its information base at different points in time*

The information representing an event is seen as a tuple $E(t) = p(a,b,...,t)$ which says that the information $p(a,b,...)$ holds at time t, cf. the notion of an event message in Chapter 3. In the deductive approach a transaction never deletes or modifies any statement of

IB(t); it only adds the event information to the information base. Thus, event information is simply added to the existing information base IB(t) giving the new information base at time point $t+1$, IB($t+1$) = IB(t) $\cup$ {$E(t+1)$}. Hence, all base statements in the deductive approach represent events.

In popular terms, the deductive approach assumes a set of base statements representing information about relevant events in the UoD. All other information is seen as derived from these base statements. This also implies that the size of the information base is continually growing as information about events is added to it. Consistency is defined by a set of global integrity constraints which may refer to information bases at different points in time.

The two characterisations above represent two extreme points of view. Time-stamped statements may be introduced in the operational approach permitting derivation and quantification over several states or time points for these types of statements. In the same way, preconditions may be introduced in the deductive approach, thereby guarding the information base from entering an inconsistent state. For the sake of illustration we will, however, consider in this chapter the extreme cases only.

9.2 The Inventory Case

The case chosen to study both these extreme approaches is a simple inventory case. The inventory contains various article types, called articles in this section. Every article belongs to an article group, called group. The conceptual model to be designed must meet the following information requirements:

1. The current quantity on hand of article a.
2. Last month's sales (in money) of article a.
3. Yesterday's sales (in money) of article group g.
4. The current number of articles in group g.

Assumptions to be considered about the UoD are as follows. New articles may be introduced at any time. Articles may also be deleted at any time. A deleted article may be introduced again at some later point in time. Thus articles may have several, non-contiguous periods of existence. The same holds also for article groups.

When an article is introduced, its group and initial values of quantity on hand and of its price are given. Later, prices may change at any time.

Obvious constraints which have to do with events are:

1. An existing article cannot be introduced.
2. An existing group cannot be introduced.
3. A non-existing article cannot be deleted.
4. A non-existing group cannot be deleted.

5. A sales event may not occur if the corresponding article does not exist.
6. A delivery event (from the supplier) cannot occur if the corresponding article does not exist.
7. A new price cannot be set if the corresponding article does not exist.

Additional constraints are:

8. A group cannot be deleted if it contains articles.
9. The price of an article cannot decrease.
10. The quantity on hand of an article must at all times be non-negative.
11. An article cannot be introduced if at that time its group does not exist.

Other, obvious constraints are that the attributes group membership, quantity on hand, price, the number of articles per group, etc., are total and single valued.

9.3 The Operational Approach

The conceptual schema for the inventory case contains the following entity types and attributes, see also Figure 9.2.

`article(A)`	A is an article
`group(G)`	G is an article group
`agroup(A,G)`	article A belongs to group G
`price(A,P)`	the price of article A is P
`qoh(A,Q)`	the quantity on hand of article A is Q
`aingroup(G,N)`	the number of articles in group G is N
`masales(A,M)`	last month's sales of article A is M dollars
`cmsales(A,CM)`	accumulated sales of article A during this month is CM
`ysales(G,Y)`	yesterday's sales of article group G is Y
`cdsales(G,CD)`	accumulated sales of article group G during this day is CD

Note that the attributes `qoh`, `msales`, `ysales`, and `aingroup` correspond to the information requirements 1 to 4. The attributes `cmsales` and `cdsales` are auxiliary attributes, required by the particular operational solution chosen (see the event rules below) in order to handle temporal information. The other attributes are needed to formulate the different rules and constraints.

All instances of the attributes above are maintained by the event rules given below. The attribute `aingroup` is a derived attribute, defined by the following derivation rule:

```
aingroup(G,N):- findall(A, agroup(A,G), Gbag), count(Gbag, N).
```

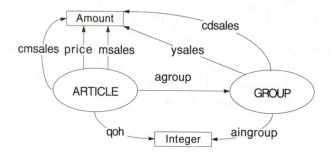

Figure 9.2 *The inventory case*

The next step is to specify a set of event rules. The following are needed:

`newart`	introduce a new article
`newgroup`	introduce a new group
`newprice`	set a new price
`delart`	delete an article
`delgroup`	delete a group
`sales`	sales transaction
`delivery`	delivery transaction (from supplier)

Below we present fragments of that solution. We first show the event rules `newart`, `newprice`, and `sales`. For instance, `newart` starts with checking conditions 1 (an existing article cannot be introduced) and 11 (the article's group must exist).

```
event(newart, [A, Q, P, G], ['Article', 'Quantity', 'Price',
'Group']):-
                precondition(not article(A), group(G)),
                insert(article(A)),
                insert(price(A,P)),
                insert(agroup(A,G)),
                insert(qoh(A,Q)),
                insert(msales(A,0)),
                insert(cmsales(A,0)).

event(newprice, [A, P], ['Article', 'Price']):-
                precondition(article(A), not (price(A,P1), P<P1)),
                insert(price(A,P)),
                delete(price(A,P1)).

event(sales, [A, S], ['Article', 'Sales']):-
                precondition(article(A), S>0, qoh(A,Q), S≤Q,
                agroup(A,G), price(A,P), cdsales(G,CD),
                cmsales(A,CM),
```

```
Q1 is Q-S, CD1 is CD+S*P, CM1 is CM+S*P),
insert(qoh(A,Q1)),
insert(cdsales(G,CD1)),
insert(cmsales(A,CM1)),
delete(qoh(A,Q)),
delete(cdsales(G,CD)),
delete(cmsales(A,CM)).
```

In a similar way preconditions are tested by `newprice` and `sales`. The preconditions of `newprice` check constraint 9, an article's price cannot decrease, as well as the obvious constraint that the article must exist. In `sales`, we test that the number of sold articles is greater than zero and that this number is less than or equal to the current quantity on hand, thus conforming to constraint 10.

There is, however, one more problem with the operational approach, namely the passing of time and the change of days and months. We need two more events that signal the end of the day and the end of the month respectively. At these time points, `cdsales` (accumulated daily sales of group) and `cmsales` (accumulated monthly sales of article) must replace `ysales` (yesterday's sales of group) and `msales` (last month's sales of article). This must be done for all articles and groups. The following event rule handles the daily updates for a given article group:

```
event(newday, G, ['Group']) :-
              precondition(cdsales(G,C)),
              replace(cdsales(G,0)),
              replace(ysales(G,C)).
```

Note that this solution has the nasty effect that information about yesterday's sales (`ysales`) of an article group deleted today is hereby lost. The same problem applies to the `msales` attribute, i.e. the deletion of an article during month *m* implies the loss of information about last month's sales of that article. How to solve this problem of not losing historical information in the framework of the operational approach is left as an exercise. We have not presented a solution to this problem as it was not explicitly stated in the requirements.

9.4 The Temporal Deductive Approach

In the temporal deductive approach, the base statements in the information base correspond to events that have occurred in the UoD. In the inventory case the external event types are as follows:

`newart(A,Q,P,G,T)`	a new article A is introduced at time T with quantity on hand Q, price P, and membership in group G
`newgroup(G,T)`	a new group G is introduced at time T
`delart(A,T)`	article A is deleted at time T
`delgroup(G,T)`	group G is deleted at time T

```
newprice(A,P,T)        group G is deleted at time T
sales(A,S,T)           a new price P is set for article A at time T
delivery(A,L,T)        L units of article A are delivered from the supplier at time T
```

An information base in the temporal deductive approach will, thus, differ from an operational information base as it contains facts about events that have occurred – it does not contain type and attribute statements. Some examples of facts in an information base are the following:

```
newart(sofa32, 5, 2500, furniture, t238).
newprice(sofa32, 2700, t419).
delart(sofa32, t726).
```

In addition to this there are, owing to the information requirements, a number of derived entity types and attributes, represented by the following Prolog predicates:

```
article(A,T)           article A exists at time T
group(G,T)             group G exists at time T
qoh(A,Q,T)             quantity on hand of article A at time T is Q
agroup(A,G,T)          article A belongs to group G at time T
price(A,P,T)           price of article A at time T is P
msales(A,S,M)          sales of article A during month M is S
dsales(G,S,D)          sales of group G during day D is S
aingroup(G,N,T)        the number of article types in group G at time T is N
```

Below we illustrate derivation rules in Prolog for the derived predicates `article`, `qoh`, and `msales`. For instance, the first derivation rule states that an article A exists at time T if there exists an event `newart(A,_,_,_,T1)` such that T1 is less than or equal to T, and that the article is not deleted between this event and the time point T.

```
article(A,T):-newart(A,_,_,_,T1), T1≤T,
              not (delart(A,T2), T2≥T1, T2<T).

qoh(A,Q,T):-  article(A,T),
              newart(A,Q0,_,_,T0), T0≤T,
              not (newart(A,_,_,_,T1), T1>T0, T1≤T),
              findall(S, (sales(A,S,TS), TS≥T0, TS≤T), SLIST),
              findall(L, (delivery(A,L,TL), TL>T0, TL<T), DLIST),
              sum(SLIST, SS),
              sum(DLIST, DS),
              Q is Q0 + DS + SS.

msales(A,M,MN):-findall(S*P, (sales(A,S,T), in(T,MN),
                price(A,P,T)), MSLIST), sum(MSLIST, M).
```

Note that the second and third lines of the `qoh` expression find the latest introduction of the corresponding article, assuming that an article can have several periods of existence. Furthermore, note the need to utilise the attribute `in`, as defined in the time model of Section 3.2.1. Here, `in(T, MN)` means that the time point T occurs in the time interval MN.

Note that no constraint checking is embedded in the derivation rules of this solution. Instead, we define a set of separate Prolog rules for the constraints 1 to 11; the syntax of these rules is analogous to the `inconsistent` rules. It is assumed that these constraints are checked when external events occur. Below we illustrate the specification of constraints 1, 5, 9, and 10. For instance, `incons(c1,A,T)` checks that the external event rule is not introducing an article that already exists.

```
incons(c1,A,T):- newart(A,_,_,_,T), article(A,T-1),
                 not delart(A,T-1).
incons(c5,A,T):- sales(A,_,T), not article(A,T).
incons(c9,A,T):- newprice(A,P,T), price(A,P2,T-1), P<P2.
incons(c10,a,t):- sales(A,_,T), qoh(A,Q,T), Q<0.
```

9.5 Discussion and Assessment

The basic methodological difference between the operational and the temporal deductive approaches, apart from the temporal dimension, is the following. In the operational approach, when specifying event rules, one has to perceive and know all fact types in the information base which might be affected by the event rules. In the temporal deductive approach, when specifying derivation rules, one has to perceive and know all external events which may potentially affect the derived fact types.

How can these two approaches be assessed? We make an attempt to make an assessment along the quality criteria that were introduced in Section 6.5.

9.5.1   Ease of Understanding

In the operational approach, the meaning of a base predicate, i.e. a predicate whose instances are stored in the information base, is understood by examining all event rules affecting it. However, nothing in the definition of a base predicate states which event rules do affect it. Therefore, in order to understand a base predicate, a sequential scan must be made through all event rules. In the temporal deductive approach, the meaning of a base predicate is that it represents an external event. The meaning of a derived predicate is explicitly stated in the derivation rule, which includes references to base predicates and possibly to other derived predicates. On the other hand, in the operational approach, it is for each event rule stated which facts the rule affects. No such explicit statement is present in the temporal deductive approach.

Our conclusion regarding understandability is that the operational approach favours understanding of event rules, whereas the temporal deductive approach favours understanding of states and behaviour of the UoD. Which of these kinds of understanding is more important is an open issue. When examining a conceptual model, both kinds of understanding may be needed in different analysis situations. It is, however, obvious that when examining a production system, in the temporal deductive approach a user can view each predicate in a historical – temporal perspective and study the changes of its instances over time. This is not possible in the operational approach, where the information base reflects only those time slices which were stated beforehand in the information requirements.

9.5.2   Completeness

A good conceptual schema should adhere to the 100 per cent principle, see Section 6.5.4. Therefore, modelling concepts and constructs used to build conceptual schemas should be powerful enough to be able to express everything that is needed to specify of a UoD. Furthermore, it should be possible to build a schema without cunning *ad hoc* solutions and too much effort from the analysts and designers.

In this respect, the operational approach lacks adequate constructs for dealing with temporally related information. References to historical information are in most conceptual schemas needed frequently. This may concern output requirements or the definition of different types of constraints, like "employees employed before and who stopped working less than six months ago should, when re-employed, have a salary equal or greater to what they had when they left the job". In these cases the designer is forced to include additional constructs in the schema in the form of new attributes and even entity types. Often these additions are not directly relevant to the problem at hand and may make understanding of the model more difficult.

Consider, for example, the predicate msales, denoting last month's sales of an article. It is included in the model owing to the second information requirement. The facts corresponding to this predicate cannot, however, be derived at the end of the month, because at that time information about sales during the month, price changes, etc., are not available in the information base. The designer has, therefore, to introduce a spurious (from the problem point of view) predicate cmsales (accumulated monthly sales), which is initialised with the value 0 at the beginning of a month, updated by each sales transaction during the month, and shifted to msales at the end of the month. In the temporal deductive approach, on the other hand, such spurious attributes are not needed to handle the information requirement above, since this approach assumes the availability of all historical information. Therefore, it needs no particular *ad hoc* solutions to represent such information.

9.5.3   Conceptual Focus

According to the conceptualisation principle, a conceptual schema should not include any implementation-dependent decisions. One reason for this is that a conceptual schema should not delimit the designer's freedom to develop the best implementation in a given hardware and software environment. However, implementation of conceptual schemas according to the operational approach is usually done assuming that the database content is identical to that of the information base. In this respect, no real design decisions are made in the implementation phase. The reason for this is that the close dependence between the information base and the event rules makes it difficult to develop design alternatives.

In contrast, the temporal deductive approach does not make any implementation decisions of a performance-affecting nature; it leaves an open end to improve the performance of a production system designed according to a specification. An obvious way to improve performance – at the cost of decreased usability and stability – is to restrict the production system's time perspective of some or all of its derived predicates. For instance, if there is no reference to the value of a derived predicate for other time than its current value, then an implementation solution may store only this current value. In conclusion, defining a conceptual schema according to the temporal deductive approach is like setting up the equations of some problem. The set of equations does not prescribe any particular way of solving them, whereas the operational approach does.

9.5.4 Stability

A conceptual schema is stable if small changes in the UoD and new information requirements give rise only to small changes of the schema, see Section 6.5.3. It turns out that schemas constructed according to the temporal deductive approach become much more stable than schemas constructed according to the operational approach. In order to explain why this is so, we consider a new information requirement for the inventory case:

> The company wants to be able to query the system at any time T and for any article A for how much (in money) the article has been sold during the interval from and including the year of an arbitrary time point T and until five years back.

This requirement implies considerable changes in the object structures of the operational approach as well as in its event rules. In this case we more or less need a table for each article listing its sales for a number of years back corresponding to the lifetime of the system. We need new event rules, or changes to existing event rules, in order to maintain and update the table. In the temporal deductive approach no changes in existing definitions are needed. What is needed are just a few new derivation rules. We need a derived predicate that calculates the sales (in money) for year Y of article A. And we need an expression that sums up the sales of A in the interval six consecutive years ending with the year of time point T.

The fact that the temporal deductive approach operates over all historical events makes it easy to query the information base for any kind of information which can be derived from the base predicates, the external events. Further, the temporal dimension and the declarative style make the conceptual schema according to the temporal deductive approach often much simpler to change and to accommodate new requirements.

9.6 Concluding Remarks

In this chapter we have presented two extreme styles of conceptual modelling, the operational and the temporal deductive approaches. We have evaluated both approaches with respect to a number of dimensions and found that the temporal deductive approach has a number of advantages, considered as a specification language. We believe that the temporal deductive approach has a number of interesting properties that may improve the work of specifying as well as of implementing and maintaining information systems. The temporal deductive approach contributes primarily to qualities such as system changeability, stability, and security. Another advantage of systems of this kind is the improved audibility.

One of the main arguments against the temporal deductive approach is the problem of achieving good performance in implemented systems according to the approach. Only a few research results on the problem of implementing a temporal and deductive model have been reported [Olivé89]. We have reason to believe that the performance of a system built according to the temporal deductive approach can be mastered in the future, for instance by storing instances of frequently updated, derived predicates. This will considerably reduce the search time for matching. The introduction of optical disks with inexpensive, non-destructive storage has further improved the "practicality" of the temporal deductive approach. There are a number of information system modelling approaches which are temporally oriented. Two notable ones are the ERAE [Dubois89] and the TEMPORA [Theodoulidis91] approaches. These approaches are, however, not deductive in the sense we have explained above. Instead they can be seen as operational approaches with extended possibilities to represent and deal with historical and temporally oriented information base states. For instance, in TEMPORA, every entity type or attribute is defined with or without a temporal dimension. If an entity is defined as having a temporal dimension, then we can reason about it and its existence in an extended time perspective.

Another issue worth commenting on is the multi-temporal aspects of information. By the multi-temporal aspect we mean that there are often different times when the information is valid, when the information is observed, and when it is received by an information system. The first time is often called the *valid time*, the second is called the information's *event time*, and the third the information's *transaction time*. For instance, the information that "Ericsson-A stock price on the Tokyo market at 11.15 hours February 12, 1996 (the valid time), dropped 3%", became known in Stockholm one minute later (the event time), and was fed into the computer system at Stockholm at 11.20 Tokyo time (the transaction time).

Furthermore, in most requirements analysis situations the information system is not a monolithic entity but rather a network composed of a number of more or less autonomous, but co-operating, systems, which may be geographically distributed (e.g. federated information systems). Time delays occur in their communications, and information collected by one system may be more or less out of date.

In a requirements specification, we need to express not only functional requirements, e.g. a conceptual schema of some relevant part of the environment, but also non-functional requirements. One class of non-functional requirements concerns the temporal qualities of information. We can, for instance, imagine situations where we would wish to express requirements on the age of information of different kinds, how the faithfulness of some information, or derivations of it, may depend on its age, or on the particular environment where the information was observed. Likewise, we may wish to express requirements on response times in human-computer interactions, requirements on query-processing times in a decentralised system, etc. The general case seems to be that all information, processed by a particular node in a network, reflects historical situations in different environments, i.e. nodes of the network. These situations may no longer be reliable or valid at the time of processing.

The discussion above shows that we are almost always operating with and using more or less obsolete, historical information. The possibility of our using information in an adequate way depends on our knowledge of the information's age (as well as of its source) and on our knowledge of its event time as well as its transaction time. If we know that the information is old, we may assign adequate significance to it or calculate the likelihood of its current validity. As the deductive approach easily permits multi-temporal time stamping of information, it opens up new possibilities of evaluating the validity of any kind of information. This kind of evaluation seems particularly relevant in environments where the validity of information is extremely time dependent, e.g. in international money markets, or in controlling space-craft. We can also conceive that the multi-temporal notion of information can be of value in data-mining applications.

9.7 Some Relevant Literature

The temporal deductive approach was first presented in [Bubenko77; Bubenko80]. A method based on this approach, CIAM, is described in [Gustafsson82]. Further work on the approach was carried out by Olivé's group in Barcelona (e.g. [Olivé86] ; [Olivé89]). This chapter is to a large extent based on [Olivé86] and [Bubenko87].

9.8 Exercises

9.1   The interest rate for savings accounts in a bank may vary from day to day. The balance of an account on a particular day is the balance on the previous day plus interest earned during that day. Construct an operational as well as a temporal deductive model for this situation, assuming that the information requirement is "What is the current balance of account X?" The owner of the account can deposit and withdraw money each day. Discuss the differences between both models.

9.2   Extend Exercise 9.1 in that the bank wishes to introduce a constraint "It is not permitted to withdraw more than 1,000 dollars in three consecutive days". In what way would you change the operational and the temporal deductive models above?

9.3   Exercise 9.2 is extended by the information requirement: "What is the balance of the account on any day in the interval one month back until the current day?" How would you respond to this requirement in both approaches?

9.4   Exercise 9.3 is extended by the additional requirement "How many transactions (deposits or withdrawals) has this account had in the last month?" Discuss the problems of change in both approaches.

9.5   How are mapping constraints maintained by both approaches in this chapter?

9.6   In the operational solution of the case of this chapter is the nasty effect that information about yesterday's sales (ysales) of an article group deleted today is lost if the group is deleted. The same problem applies to the msales predicate, i.e. the deletion of an article during month *m* implies the loss of information about last month's sales of that article. How would you change the operational solution in order to avoid this loss?

9.7   Specify the changes needed in both solutions in this chapter to define the concept of a "best-selling article", defined as an article that sells in a one month interval for more than 100 million dollars. Assume the information requirement is "What are our best-selling articles now?" Additionally, what changes are needed to accommodate the new requirement "What have been our best-selling articles for six months in a row?"

9.8   Take as a basis the club case of Appendix 2 and model it by the operational as well as the temporal deductive approach. What changes are needed in the operational solution in order to accommodate the following, additional information requirements: (a) What was the club's membership count N years back ($N < 6$)? (b) How much has the percentage of female members changed between years N and $N-1$ back? ($N < 6$), (c) How many honorary members are there now? (An honorary member is a person who has, without interruption, been a member for 25 years or more.)

9.9   Take as a basis the employee case of Appendix 3 and model it by the operational as well as the temporal deductive approach. What changes are needed in the operational solution in order to accommodate the following, additional information requirements: (a) How many, and which projects were there for a particular department at some historical time (expressed as a date)? (b) What persons have, historically, been assigned to more than one project? (c) What is the project salary at some historical time T of project P?

CHAPTER 10

Enterprise Modelling

Existing information modelling methods and techniques have mainly been concerned with promoting various representation formalisms for formally describing information systems, and discussing the expressive power of these. In this chapter, we take another track. Information systems and their formal descriptions are there for a reason. Entities, relationships, and rules are defined because there is a need and rationale behind it. The problem is to bridge the gap between ill-defined problems and application situations, and specification of the formal and precise definition of functional requirements of the information system. This gap is wide and spans different trains of thought and scientific enquiry, in the field of computing and information science. We outline an extended requirements and information modelling paradigm, based on *enterprise modelling*, i.e. the capture of, negotiations about, and specification of business objectives, concepts, processes, rules, and actors. This paradigm throws up a number of new problems and issues of scientific enquiry that augment the traditional approach, and bring it closer to problems experienced in real-life system development and maintenance projects.

The so-called *enterprise model (EM)* focuses on the *WHY?* aspect of conceptual modelling. The purpose is to document why certain business processes, concepts, and actors exist. We will explain its components, and discuss how they can be applied to practical situations. Section 10.2 explains the five submodels of an EM and Section 10.3 their interrelations. We use, as an illustration, the problem of developing an information system to support the enterprise modelling process itself. In Section 10.4 we comment on the work methodology when developing a requirements specification, and the EM in particular. In the concluding section, various research aspects are discussed.

10.1 Overview

The main objective of the EM and the enterprise modelling technique is to support stakeholder understanding of the business as well as to document the business, its objectives, problems, concepts, actors, and activities better and in a more structured way than by simply providing natural language descriptions. The EM is the structured description of application knowledge, assumptions, and requirements, required for the design and implementation of an information system. It has to answer the following questions:

1. Why was the system built; what is its justification?
2. What are the business processes, and which ones are to be supported by the system?
3. Who are the actors of the organisation performing the processes?
4. What concepts are they processing or talking about; what are their information needs?
5. What initial objectives and requirements can be stated regarding the information system to be developed?

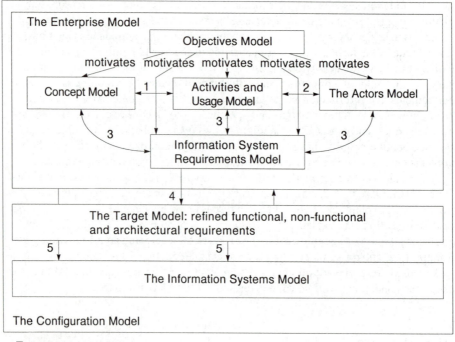

TYPES OF RELATIONSHIPS:

1 deals-with
2 performed-by
3 concerns
4 refined-by
5 implemented-by and supported-by

Figure 10.1 *The EM and its interrelated models*

Enterprise modelling and requirements specification are based on the notion that a requirements specification process, from a documentation point of view, implies populating (instantiating) a number of interrelated meta-models (see Figure 10.1). The EM includes the following interrelated submodels: an *objectives model* (*OM*), an *activities and usage model* (*AUM*), an *actor model* (*AM*), a *concept model* (*CM*), and an *information system requirements model* (*ISRM*). These submodels correspond to questions 1 to 5 above.

As can be understood from Figure 10.1, the OM is assumed to be *motivating*, or driving, the development of the other submodel instances of the EM. This is, however, not always the best path in practical situations. At times, some information system requirements are "already there" (correctly or erroneously) and can easily be stated. Elaboration of these is then done bottom up by asking the reason for their existence, the concepts that they concern, the activities they apply to, etc. At other times it may be helpful to start modelling with some essential concepts or objects of the enterprise. This is the case in situations where there is little understanding of what main concepts the business is about, i.e. when the conceptual framework is unclear. The EM is linked by *implemented_by* relationships to the *information system model* (*ISM*) component, and by *refined_by* relationships to more precisely defined requirements in the so-called *target model* (*TM*).

The concept of *enterprise* must be interpreted here in a very wide sense. It could mean the whole enterprise, or it could mean some small part of it. More often than not, in developing information systems, the concept of enterprise will in fact denote a limited area of activity of the enterprise with which we are concerned. As we will show later, a particular interpretation of the concept of enterprise could be *the process of capturing requirements and developing a requirements specification.* Depending on how familiar we are with the application domain, its conceptual structure, and the requirements for computer support, the need to perform an extensive and in-depth environment modelling may vary. For instance, in a limited technical situation, where the requirements and the conceptual model are well defined, the need for extensive enterprise modelling is limited.

How is enterprise modelling related to conceptual modelling as discussed in the other chapters of this book? Our view is as follows. Enterprise modelling *extends* the notion of a conceptual model by requiring the modelling of other aspects of a universe of discourse, such as objectives, processes, and actors, and by relating their components to components of the conceptual model. The CM, as discussed in this section, can very well be a model constructed as in Chapter 5. The model may not be as detailed as such a schema, but include only major types of concepts, objects, and relationships in order to establish a "vocabulary" for the domain. This vocabulary is used to define components of the other model types, e.g. goals, processes, information flows, etc.

In the following sections we describe in more detail the different submodels of the EM. We will exemplify them using fragments of the so-called F^3 *project case*. F^3 stands for "From Fuzzy to Formal", an ESPRIT project (No. 6612) in which a requirements modelling method and a tool-set, the information system for model building, group work, and communication, were developed.

10.2 The Enterprise Submodels

The EM framework includes a number of interrelated submodels, as shown in Figure 10.1. In the information system modelling and design phase, semantic links are established from these models to the information systems model, reflecting the rationale, or the motivation, for designing specific components. For instance, when selecting an object of the ISM, e.g. a data model component, it should be possible to trace its rationale and origin (such as why it has been introduced) back to the EM and TM components.

The submodels each contain a number of components, i.e. objects and relationships of different types, typical of that submodel. Relationships can be internal to a submodel (*intrarelationships*) or external, relating components of two or more submodels (*interrelationships*). Objects as well as relationships may have attributes. This makes it natural to think of the relationships as relationship types, as introduced in Section 3.5. Instances in the models and in their relationships are controlled by static and dynamic integrity constraints.

A few words about the F^3 case are in order. The project was in the process of developing a new method and a tool-set for requirements engineering. It was assumed that the method and tool-set would be useful in a large number of organisations and for a variety of systems. The enterprise here is the environment for using a new method and a supporting tool-set for the capture, refinement, and specification of requirements for the information system of an organisation. The environment may differ from one user to another, so we have to assume particular types of actors and working procedures. We also have to assume a set of objectives, problems, and requirements for a method and the supporting tool-set. In F^3, these assumptions are made on the basis of initial statements about the requirements for methods and tools made by the industrial partners in the project. Their statements, made in the initial stages, were neither consistent, nor complete.

This is how the requirements engineering process is assumed to start. The problems we are tackling are wicked. It seems that general principles, issues and problems of technology, planning, and design are equally applicable in determining requirements for information systems. There is no subjectively right or best system for a particular problem and environment. Furthermore, the environment is never static, and the problems it has to tackle change. The requirements for information systems are generated by people. They reflect what people currently think is important for the organisation, or for themselves. The examples shown below in connection with the different model types should be interpreted in this way – they are the current *beliefs* of people who were asked what properties they would find useful in a method and a tool for requirements engineering. The people, the so-called *design actors*, are the ones who decide what a good or satisfactory solution is.

10.2.1   The Objectives Model

The OM is intended for structurally describing and discussing the reason or motivation for the activities, actors, and concepts of the other submodels. It addresses the *WHY?*

perspective of the enterprise and information systems development. The concepts of this model are related to the enterprise itself and determined by the rationale of its members. The OM component types are typically: *enterprise goal*, *problem*, *cause*, *opportunity*, and *rule*, all informally described below. The relationship types used are *motivates* and *influences*. For instance, a goal may motivate a set of subgoals, and influence (positively or negatively) other kinds of goals.

Goal

A *goal* describes a desired set of states of the enterprise a design actor aspires the enterprise to be in. A goal can be operational (measurable) or non-operational. It may concern different strategic levels (strategic, tactical, operational), and concern different subject matter, e.g. business areas, processes, or products.

Problem

A *problem* describes a set of undesirable states that the design actor finds the enterprise in. Problems typically imply that the design agent is aware (or can be made aware) of a goal obstructed by the problem as formulated. Thus, every problem must eventually, in the modelling process, be related to a goal by a relationship of negative influence type.

Cause

A *cause* is a description of the reason for the existence of a problem.

Opportunity

An *opportunity* describes a situation that exists in or is available for the enterprise, and that can be taken advantage of in continued enterprise modelling work, e.g. to support some goal.

Rule

A *rule* describes something affecting the enterprise, which limits the actions that can be taken. It can be an internal constraint or an external rule, typically a legislative rule.

Relationships

The OM includes two types of relationships:

• *motivates:* A *motivates* relationship normally refines a higher level OM component into a set of more precise components. It can also be used for refining rules and for linking components of the OM to components of other types of submodels.

• *influences:* An *influences* relationship describes how one component of the OM may influence another (set of) components. The influential link has a direction, a sign, and a strength. The direction indicates the causality direction between the components, the sign indicates whether the influence is contributive or the opposite, the strength, if applied, indicates the degree of influence, i.e. strong, medium, or weak.

In Figure 10.2, a small fraction of the F^3 OM, at some development stage, is shown. A number of issues can be discussed here. First, we should note that the enterprise and its objectives is here the hypothetical organisation being a future user of the F^3 method and tool-set. The OM is, therefore, concerned with setting up the goals, problems, etc., for the method and its appropriation in the environment.

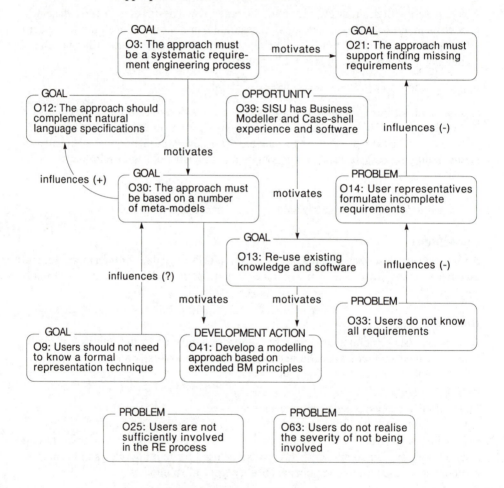

Figure 10.2 *An OM instance*

We can assume that this model has been developed in a number of group sessions, where participants have each announced a number of different goals, problems, opportunities, and causes. The problem now is to "sort things out" by eliminating, as much as possible, redundancies in the propositions. Moreover, one must relate propositions to each other by *motivates* and *influences* relationships, and refine components by introducing components of finer granularity, as well as generally agree on what has been proposed. The graph in Figure 10.2 reflects an early stage of the analysis at which there is not yet a common agreement, nor an understanding among the design actors. Some components are not connected to other components, e.g. O25 and O63. What goals do these problem statements reflect? Whether O9 influences O30 is also a point for further analysis, and the components could be reformulated. As previously noted, the details are neither (objectively) right, nor complete. But they reflect user and domain expert *opinions* at some development stage, and *they are explicitly stated*. Every proposition in this model can, therefore, be examined, discussed, and criticised, and its relationships to other components investigated. The basic reasons for designing a new information system are put on explicit trial here. Experience shows that in several cases, such objectives modelling has drastically changed the initially intended course of action in systems development projects.

10.2.2   The Activities and Usage Model

In the AUM, the organisational activities, i.e. the processes and tasks of the enterprise, are described and new ones are possibly designed for the future. External actors outside the scope of the organisational activity area have to be identified. Material and information flows, connecting the processes, as well as information needs for a process, are described. Instances of this submodel should be motivated by the enterprise goals and development actions suggested during OM development. Processes are carried out by components of the AM. Processes are performed on or with reference to components of the CM. Naturally, every kind of component of the AUM, e.g. processes, information, material, and external actors, can be decomposed into subcomponents.

In our F^3 example, Figure 10.3 reflects a small, incomplete fraction of an AUM dealing with the hypothetical case of developing information system requirements. As the approach is not linear, we have some difficulties presenting it in a top-down, so-called *waterfall*, fashion, by decomposing processes. The graph in Figure 10.3 illustrates a stage in the project that consists of thinking about how the approach could be imagined from a development process point of view. We may assume that the design here is *motivated* by some component or proposition of the OM. The graph also illustrates that we are thinking of the enterprise modelling process as a communication between a number of user processes. In this particular case, the user process is assumed to supply new OM components to the support system, and obtains in return a confirmation and possibly error messages. The work focus varies between different user processes. Some issues may drive users to enter the CM component acquisition process, then return to the OM component acquisition process, and then perhaps move to a kind of a process which is outside the EM sphere, such as specification reuse type of processes.

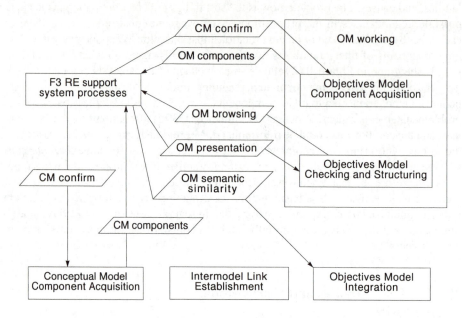

Figure 10.3 *An AUM instance*

Building the AUM for the F[3] case forces us to think about, and explicitly document, what the F[3] method being designed really is, in terms of processes, and how it will be applied by users and requirements engineers. It forms a part of developing the method, a part of developing the human–computer interaction, and it is a way of forming a basis for discussing how users will be involved in the method application process.

10.2.3   The Actor Model

The AM defines the types of actors involved in the enterprise activities. Actors can be organisational units, at different levels of the organisation, human individuals, or groups of individuals. Roles played by units or individuals can also be actors, as can non-human resources of different kinds, e.g. computing devices. Goals, concepts, actions (tasks), and information system requirements are defined by design actors. Activities (processes) are performed by actors running the business. We have here two specialisations of the actor concept, one related to the process of developing the requirements specification (the design actors), and one related to running the business at hand (the business actors).

Continuing our F[3] example, Figure 10.4 shows an instance of a part of the AM at some development stage of the project. A number of business actors, organisational units, and roles, and some relationships, have been identified. Their relationships are, however, not yet fully investigated and documented here. The graph in Figure 10.4 is a documented basis for further modelling and discussions, and for relating actors to components of other model instances.

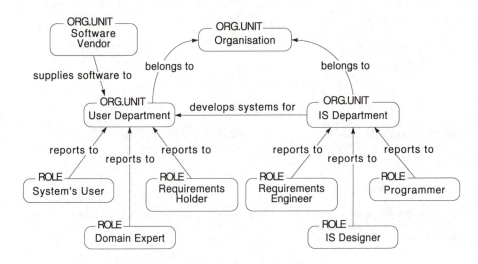

Figure 10.4 *An AM instance*

10.2.4 The Concept Model

The CM describes "what we are talking about", i.e. the set of concepts, object types, relationship types, and object or relationship properties of the application, and of the domain of interest, needed to understand better the requirements specification or to perform the business processes. Every application-oriented component of the information system's database is supposed to be an implementation of one or more kinds of CM components. A CM may, however, include components which are never implemented in the information system, but used either for improving understanding of the enterprise and its objectives, or for stating the particular information system requirements with respect to objects in the enterprise.

In developing the conceptual model, we may initially use logic programming for prototyping and by describing static and dynamic integrity constraints for the enterprise. Rules in the CM are usually seen as operational refinements *motivated* by higher level business goals and objectives, formally defined to a lesser extent in the OM.

The CM instance in Figure 10.5 shows a number of types of components that the F[3] approach is concerned with. A few of their relationships are also shown. What we see here is the top of the EM generic hierarchy (at some development stage), where the model component is specialised into submodel component types. Rules defined for this model are not shown graphically. Examples of rules are: "An OM is incomplete if it contains a problem which is not related to any of its goals", and "The priority of a goal motivated by another goal should not be higher than the motivating goal's priority". Rules included in the conceptual model can be more or less restricting and firm. When not satisfied, rules may often point to the need to reformulate and change the components of the conceptual model or of the other models.

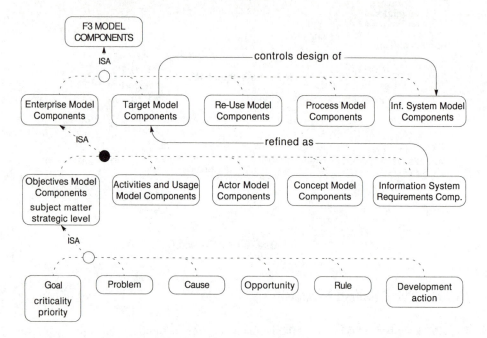

Figure 10.5 *A CM instance*

The CM is the *product model* of the requirements definition and design activity. The importance of such models for developer co-operation and communication is well established. The components developed by individual developers can, via this model, be conceptually well described, and the relations between them can be established.

10.2.5   The Information System Requirements Model

The ISRM describes the requirements, functional as well as non-functional, we have regarding the information system. They must conform to the enterprise objectives and support the processes of the enterprise. We include in the ISRM those goals, problems, and constraints, not only concerning the information system, but also concerning the development process itself. Initially these components are described informally. Many of them will also remain informally described, and will therefore resemble the types of components of the OM.

At a refined level, information system requirements can be described using two kinds of requirements: functional and non-functional. *Functional requirements* concern the target information system's functionality such as operations for searching, creating, modifying, and deleting database objects and relationships; for displaying, querying, and browsing objects and relationships; functionality for checking and analysing objects, etc. *Non-functional requirements* can be categorised in a number of different ways, e.g. as operating constraints, political constraints, economical constraints, constraints concerning accuracy of information, security aspects, etc.

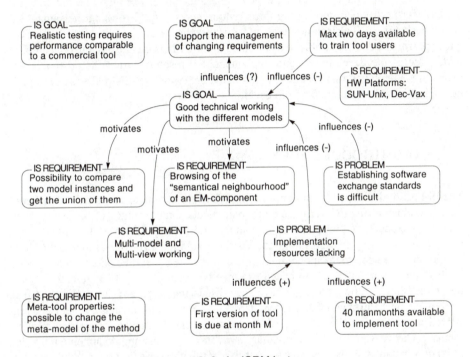

Figure 10.6 *An ISRM instance*

In the ISRM, we use the following set of component types.

- **IS GOAL**
  A proposition of an important and desirable characteristic of the information system or the development process.
- **IS PROBLEM**
  A statement of a situation which in some way obstructs the achievement of a better system or better design process.
- **IS REQUIREMENT**
  A statement of a concrete requirement regarding the system.

- **IS F REQUIREMENT**
  A statement of a functional and required characteristic of the information system, typically a refinement of an information system requirement.
- **IS NF REQUIREMENT**
  A statement of a non-functional and required characteristic of the information system, typically a refinement of an information system requirement.

The graph in Figure 10.6 illustrates a fraction of theISRM, as seen at some development stage of the F^3 approach. It shows the goal "Good technical working with the different models" further refined, motivating three requirements, e.g. "Browsing the semantical neighbourhood ...". It also shows goals to be further discussed, e.g. "Realistic testing requires performance comparable to a commercial tool". This goal is obviously in conflict with some of the development and implementation resources given as other requirements. It is interesting that a small fraction of a more complete ISRM already presents a number of issues which are far from trivial to decide upon.

10.3 Intermodel Links

The EM is not developed by first developing relatively complete submodels of different kinds, and then trying to interrelate their components. On the contrary, the development process is expected to change focus frequently, and the population of the submodels is done by short "visits" in each submodel. Visiting a submodel B from a submodel A often implies either a need to document a relationship between A and B, or a need to develop further components of B as motivated by some component of A. In Figure 10.7, some intermodel links of the models we have been discussing so far are shown. For instance, the posting of the problem O33 in OM "Users do not know all the requirements" is registered as motivating the IS GOAL "Support the management of changing requirements". The reason for this particular *motivates* relationship, documented by that *motivates* instance, is the assumption that the fact that "Users do not know all requirements" may lead to many changes and reworkings. Therefore the IS GOAL is formulated and a link from O33 is recorded. The model fraction of Figure 10.7 is, we assume, also used for discussing how different actors can be involved in the OM work. This model suggests, for instance, that OM checking and structuring is to be done by the requirements engineers, a decision that may later relax the requirements for human–computer interfaces to that part of the tool.

10.4 Work Methodology

We have presented a number of linked product models of the requirements specification. The question is – how are these developed, and in what sequence? The answer is that there is no fixed sequence that can be prescribed for all possible cases. The models can, instead, be populated and refined in many different ways. The current development situation at hand and its purpose, including the kind of people participating in the process, will determine how they will be developed and populated.

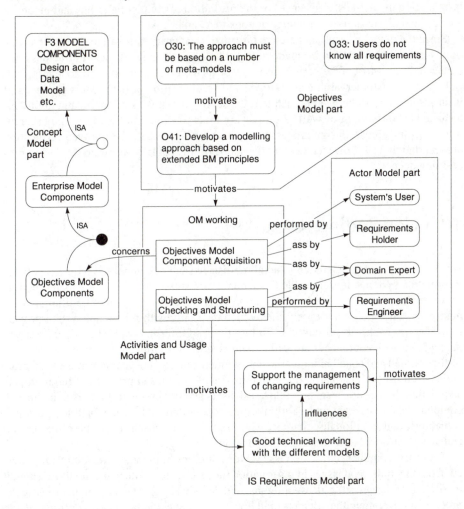

Figure 10.7 *EMs have links relating their component objects*

The EM activity primarily addresses the user–customer–developer co-operation part of the systems development process. This is assumed to be an early part of the process, where the needs of users and requirements should be formulated as close to the conceptual framework of the user as possible. However, this does not mean that the users and customers alone, without proper training and skills, can perform this activity. There is normally also a need for a user-oriented information systems architect, with skills in guiding and facilitating modelling and modelling processes, and with sufficient knowledge of the application domain to support users and customers in this process. The support typically implies the generation of driving questions in order to encourage users in instantiating the models, assistance for the resolution of conflicting issues and inconsistencies, and discussion of alternative actions that can be taken.

Since the models discussed here are informal, or at best semi-formal (but structured), only some verification can be made automatically, such as syntactical correctness and connectedness. Most of the verification, as well as the validation, must be done informally by a user–customer–architect dialogue and scrutinisation of the models produced. It is an assumption of the F^3 approach that the set of normative, structured, and highly interlinked set of models, as well as supporting tools (for presentation, browsing, searching, projecting, reuse, design process trace, etc.), will contribute to improved verification and validation. It is, however, beyond the scope of this book to penetrate the design process any deeper.

10.5 Concluding Remarks

We have presented an approach to acquire, discuss, and document the requirements for information systems. It is controlled by a number of submodels, none of which is new as such – the combination of them is. The approach is also an extension of traditional information systems modelling approaches which deal only with functional system properties. The approach was presented in an intuitive and informal way. This is partly due to the fact that such approaches are still in a process of development in which they must be further refined and tested in industrial environments during the years to come. The informality is, however, also partly due to the nature of the wicked problem of requirements acquisition. It does not seem possible to ask users and requirements holders to be formal, complete, and consistent when formulating propositions and ideas which are personal, subjective, and emotionally charged. The modelling approach must, therefore, permit and accept informal and imprecise propositions.

There are a number of research issues worth looking at in the future, which are different from the traditional issues in information modelling in that they also focus on explicit modelling of design actor ideas, opinions, and decisions. They also try to incorporate the process of developing the artefacts, and how work here could be better co-ordinated and managed by the use of information technology. Information systems modelling and design is extending its scope, in that organisational and social as well as cognitive aspects are given increased consideration.

A particularly interesting application of EM seems to be the area of *business process reengineering (BPR)* or *business process innovation*. In short, re-engineering means to restructure or redesign the organisation, including its business processes, concepts, actors, and their relationships, in order better to meet changed organisational objectives and constraints, caused by pressure from, and changes in, the environment. This can be illustrated as in Figure 10.8, in which two versions of EMs are shown, one at time T1 and one at time T2. For simplicity, we have described the EM here as consisting of an "intentional part", containing the goals, constraints, and rules of the organisation, and an "organisational part" consisting of concepts, processes, actors, and their relationships. At T1 we may also study the fit, or the lack of fit, between current organisational components and current intentions.

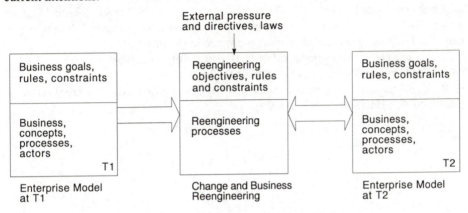

Figure 10.8 *Use of the EM framework to perform BPR*

The problem of re-engineering is to restructure, i.e. change the EM at T1 to a new EM at T2 (clearly several versions are possible at T2). In addition to misfits between the intentions of the organisation and its structure at T1, the re-engineering is also controlled by new external rules, regulations, and general "pressure". The classical BPR example is "the need to improve the current extremely long time to process customer orders". This shows a misfit between the current goal of the organisation of efficient customer order processing and its actual processes, actors, and their relationships (performing actor, responsible actor, etc.) in the realm of customer order processing. A re-engineering of this misfit may lead to a large number of changes, e.g. a modified responsibility structure, more streamlined processes, less checkpoints, as well as possibly new types of actors, concepts, or processes. The intriguing research topic is to examine the re-engineering area in order to see to what extent generic re-engineering rules and processes can be defined in order to be able systematically to collect experience for guiding future change processes.

10.6 Some Relevant Literature

This chapter is based on [Bubenko94a]. The first version of the EM technique was initially developed in mid-1980s at the Swedish Institute for Systems Development (SISU)

[Willars91]. It included the objectives model, the activities and usage model, and the concept model. This technique was extensively applied in a number of Swedish organisations. The EM technique was further developed in the ESPRIT Project F^3 (From Fuzzy to Formal), No. 6612. A short description of the rationale of F^3 as well as a demonstration of how information system requirements relate to the EM is given in [Loucopoulos94] and in [Bubenko94b]. A full description of the F^3 project, including the EM technique, as well as samples of its application are presented in [F395]. A tool for capturing EMs has been developed by [Song94]. The aspect of reusing components of a model is dealt with in [Bellinzona94]. A way to capture and to represent the process of developing an EM based requirements specification is presented in [Rolland93].

Some research publications related to enterprise modelling are [Bubenko94a; Gustas95; Kirikova94a; Kirikova94b; Nellborn94; Song95].

Readers interested in business process re-engineering or innovation are directed to [Davenport93; Hammer93; Hammer95].

Appendix 1—Schema Syntax

This appendix contains syntax diagrams for conceptual schemas specified according to the conventions in Chapter 5. The rounded boxes contain terminal symbols in the grammar, while the rectangular ones contain non-terminal symbols.

Syntax diagrams for Prolog

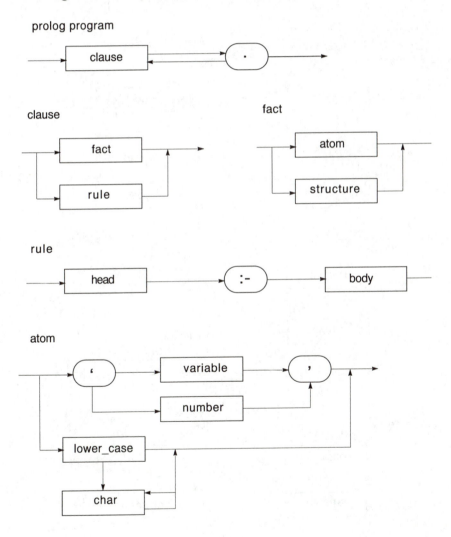

prolog program

clause

fact

rule

atom

structure

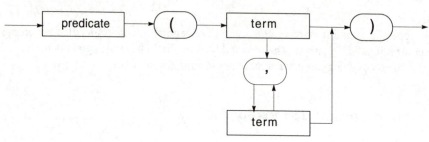

head

body

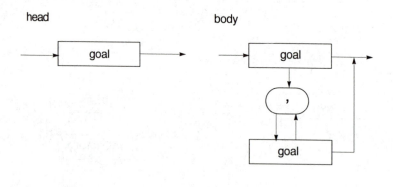

variable

number

predicate

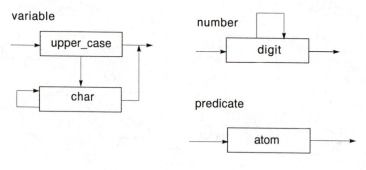

term

goal

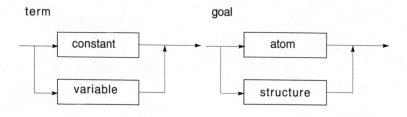

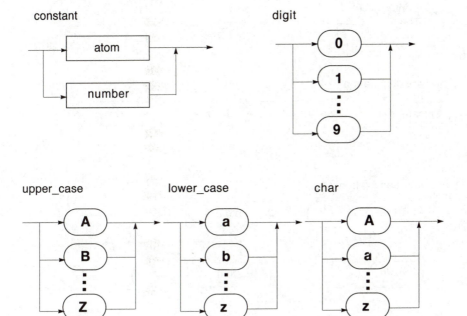

Syntax diagrams for conceptual schemas

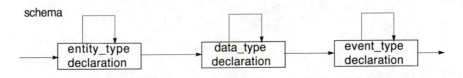

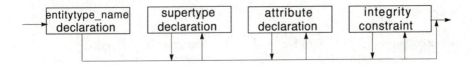

entitytype_name declaration

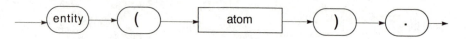

supertype declaration

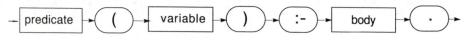

attribute declaration

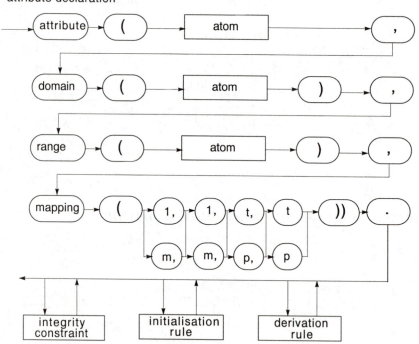

derivation rule

initialisation rule

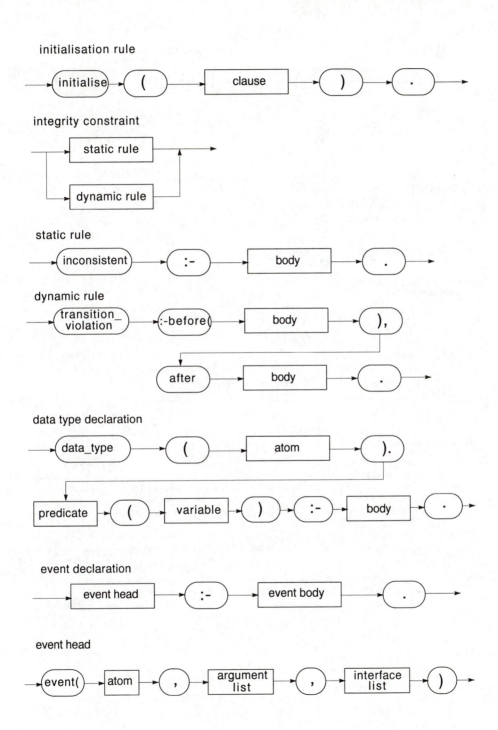

integrity constraint

static rule

dynamic rule

data type declaration

event declaration

event head

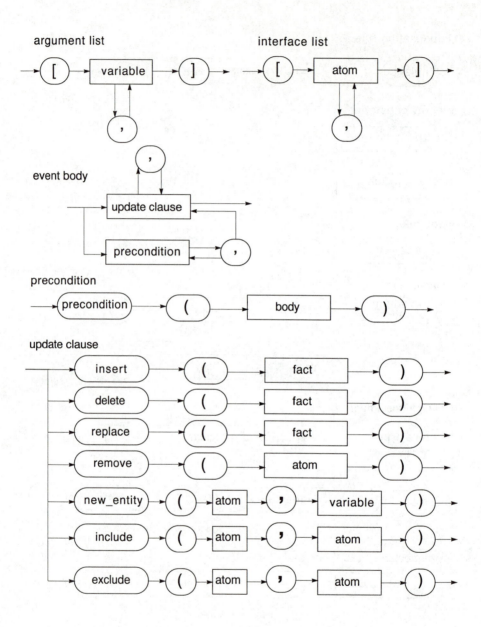

Appendix 2—The Club Case

```
*********************************************************** PERSON ***/

entity(person).

attribute(ssnum,
          domain(person),
          range(nr),
          mapping(1,1,t,p)).

attribute(full_name,
          domain(person),
          range(p_name),
          mapping(1,m,t,p)).

attribute(tel,
          domain(person),
          range(nr),
          mapping(1,m,t,p)).

attribute(salary,
          domain(person),
          range(money),
          mapping(1,m,t,p)).
          transition_violation :-
                    before(salary(Per,Before_sal)),
                    after((salary(Per,After_sal),
                    After_sal<Before_sal)).
          /* The salary of a person may not decrease */

attribute(tax,
          domain(person),
          range(money),
          mapping(1,m,t,p)).

attribute(net_income,
          domain(person),
          range(money),
          mapping(1,m,t,p)).
          net_income(Person,Net):- salary(Person,Sal),
                    tax(Person,Tax), Net is Sal - Tax.

attribute(club_cost,
          domain(person),
          range(money),
          mapping(1,m,t,p)).
          club_cost(Per,Cost):- findall(Fee,(membership(Memb),
                    fellow(Memb,Per),
                    in(Memb,Club),fee(Club,Fee)),Fees),
                    sum(Fees,Cost).
```

```
attribute(married_to,
            domain(person),
            range(person),
            mapping(1,m,t,p)).
            married_to(Man,Woman):- marriage(Mar),
                        husband(Mar,Man), wife(Mar,Woman).
            married_to(Woman,Man):- marriage(Mar),
                        husband(Mar,Man), wife(Mar,Woman).

identifier(person,[ssnum]).

inconsistent :- person(P), not(man(P)), not(woman(P)).

/* A person is either a man or a woman */

inconsistent :- man(P), woman(P).

/* A person cannot be both a man and a woman. */


/*************************************************** MAN ***/

entity(man).
person(X):- man(X).


/*************************************************** WOMAN ***/

entity(woman).
person(X):- woman(X).


/*********************************************** MARRIAGE ***/

entity(marriage).

attribute(husband,
            domain(marriage),
            range(man),
            mapping(1,m,t,p)).

attribute(wife,
            domain(marriage),
            range(woman),
            mapping(1,m,t,p)).

attribute(m_date,
            domain(marriage),
            range(date),
            mapping(1,m,t,p)).


/*************************************************** CLUB ***/

entity(club).
```

```
attribute(club_name,
             domain(club),
             range(text),
             mapping(1,1,t,p)).

attribute(address,
             domain(club),
             range(text),
             mapping(1,m,t,p)).

attribute(president,
             domain(club),
             range(person),
             mapping(1,m,t,p)).

attribute(treasurer,
             domain(club),
             range(person),
             mapping(1,m,t,p)).

attribute(nr_of_members,
             domain(club),
             range(numerical),
             mapping(1,m,t,p)).
             nr_of_members(Club,Num):- club(Club),
                         findall(Memb,(membership(Memb),
                         in(Memb,Club)),Memberships),
                         count(Memberships,Num).

attribute(fee,
             domain(club),
             range(money),
             mapping(1,m,t,p)).

inconsistent :- president(Club,Pres), treasurer(Club, Treas),
             married_to(Pres,Treas).
/* The president of a club must not be married to its treasurer */

inconsistent :- president(Club,Person), treasurer(Club,Person).
/* Nobody may be both the president and the treasurer of a club */

inconsistent :- president(Club,Pres),
             not((membership(Memb),in(Memb,Club),
             fellow(Memb,Pres))).
/* The president of a club must be a member of the club */


/*********************************************** MEMBERSHIP ***/

entity(membership).

attribute(in,
             domain(membership),
             range(club),
             mapping(1,m,t,p)).
```

```
attribute(fellow,
               domain(membership),
               range(person),
               mapping(l,m,t,p)).

attribute(entry_date,
               domain(membership),
               range(date),
               mapping(l,m,t,p)).


/********************************************** DATA TYPES ***/

data_type(salary).
salary(S):- number(S),S>0, S< 50000.

data_type(money).
money(M):- number(M),M>0.

data_type(numerical).
numerical(N):- number(N).

data_type(nr).
nr(N):- atom(N).               /* An integer is not an atom */

data_type(p_name).
p_name(P):- atom(P).

data_type(text).
text(D):- atom(D).

data_type(date).
date(D):- atom(D).


/************************************** EVENT CHANGE_SALARY ***/

event(change_salary,[Ss,Nsal],['Ssnum','New salary']):-
               precondition((ssnum(P,Ss),person(P))),
               precondition(money(Nsal)),
               replace(salary(P,Nsal)).


/************************************** EVENT ELECT_PRESIDENT ***/

event(elect_president,[Ss,Cname],['Ssnum','Club']):-
               precondition((ssnum(P,Ss),person(P))),
               precondition((club_name(Club,Cname),club(Club))),
               replace(president(Club,P)).


/************************************** EVENT ELECT_TREASURER ***/

event(elect_treasurer,[Ss,Cname],['Ssnum','Club']):-
               precondition((ssnum(P,Ss),person(P))),
               precondition((club_name(Club,Cname),club(Club))),
               replace(treasurer(Club,P)).
```

```
/***************************************** EVENT JOIN_CLUB ***/

event(join_club,[Ss,Cname,Date],['Ssnum','Club','Date']):-
            precondition((ssnum(P,Ss),person(P))),
            precondition((club_name(Club,Cname),club(Club))),
            precondition((not((membership(Mem),in(Mem,Club),
                          fellow(Mem,P))))),
            new_entity(membership,M),
            insert(in(M,Club)),
            insert(fellow(M,P)),
            insert(entry_date(M,Date)).


/***************************************** EVENT LEAVE_CLUB ***/

event(leave_club,[Ss,Cname],['Ssnum','Club']):-
            precondition((ssnum(P,Ss),person(P))),
            precondition((club_name(Club,Cname),club(Club))),
            precondition((membership(Mem),in(Mem,Club),
                          fellow(Mem,P))),
            remove(Mem).


/***************************************** EVENT MARRY ***/

event(marry,[SsHus,SsWife,Date],['Ssnum of husband','Ssnum of
wife','Date']):-
            precondition((ssnum(Man,SsHus),person(Man))),
            precondition((ssnum(Woman,SsWife),person(Woman))),
            precondition((not((marriage(Mar),husband(Mar,Man),
                          wife(Mar,Woman))))),
            new_entity(marriage,M),
            insert(husband(M,Man)),
            insert(wife(M,Woman)),
            insert(m_date(M,Date)).


/***************************************** EVENT DIVORCE ***/

event(divorce,[SsHus,SsWife],['Ssnum of husband','Ssnum of wife']):-
            precondition((ssnum(Man,SsHus),person(Man))),
            precondition((ssnum(Woman,SsWife),person(Woman))),
            precondition((marriage(Mar),husband(Mar,Man),
                          wife(Mar,Woman))),
            remove(Mar).


/*                                                  */
/*        Example of an information base            */

man(joe).
ssnum(joe,'2345_67').
full_name(joe,'Joe Smith').
```

```
tel(joe,'111111').
salary(joe,9000).
tax(joe,3000).

man(pete).
ssnum(pete,'3456_78').
full_name(pete,'Peter Roberts').
tel(pete,'222222').
salary(pete,9000).
tax(pete,3000).

woman(mary).
ssnum(mary,'4567_89').
full_name(mary,'Mary Roberts').
tel(mary,'222222').
salary(mary,12000).
tax(mary,4000).

woman(sally).
ssnum(sally,'5678_90').
full_name(sally,'Sally Jones').
tel(sally,'333333').
salary(sally,6000).
tax(sally,2000).

marriage(m1).
husband(m1,pete).
wife(m1,mary).
m_date(m1,'910804').

club(lion).
club_name(lion,'Lion').
address(lion,'22 Covent Garden').
fee(lion,200).
president(lion,pete).
treasurer(lion,sally).

club(rotary).
club_name(rotary,'Rotary').
address(rotary,'14 Trafalgar Square').
fee(rotary,300).
president(rotary,joe).
treasurer(rotary,sally).

membership(ms1).
fellow(ms1,joe).
in(ms1,rotary).
entry_date(ms1,'810801').

membership(ms2).
fellow(ms2,pete).
in(ms2,lion).
entry_date(ms2,'810801').
```

```
membership(ms3).
fellow(ms3,mary).
in(ms3,lion).
entry_date(ms3,'810801').

membership(ms4).
fellow(ms4,sally).
in(ms4,rotary).
entry_date(ms4,'810801').

membership(ms5).
fellow(ms5,sally).
in(ms5,lion).
entry_date(ms5,'840701').
```

Appendix 3—The Employee Case

```
/******************************************************* PERSON ***/

entity(person).

attribute(ssnum,
               domain(person),
               range(nr),
               mapping(1,1,t,p)).

attribute(full_name,
               domain(person),
               range(p_name),
               mapping(1,m,t,p)).

attribute(tel,
               domain(person),
               range(nr),
               mapping(1,m,t,p)).

identifier(person,[ssnum]).


/****************************************************** EMPLOYEE ***/

entity(employee).

person(X):- employee(X).

attribute(empnum,
               domain(employee),
               range(nr),
               mapping(1,1,t,p)).

attribute(date_of_employment,
               domain(employee),
               range(date),
               mapping(1,m,t,p)).

attribute(base_salary,
               domain(employee),
               range(salary),
               mapping(1,m,t,p)).
               initialize(base_salary(_,1000)).
               transition_violation :- before(base_salary(P,S)),
                           after((base_salary(P,T),T<S)).

attribute(tot_salary,
               domain(employee),
               range(salary),
               mapping(1,m,t,p)).
               tot_salary(P,Tot):- base_salary(P,Base),
```

```
                                    findall(A_sal,(empl(Ass,P),
                                    ass_salary(Ass,A_sal)),A_salaries),
                                    sum(A_salaries,Sum),Tot is Base + Sum.
                      inconsistent :-
                                    tot_salary(P,T),boss(P,B),
                                    tot_salary(B,Bt),Bt<T.

attribute(dept,
                domain(employee),
                range(department),
                mapping(1,m,t,t)).

attribute(boss,
                domain(employee),
                range(employee),
                mapping(1,m,t,p)).
                boss(P,B):- dept(P,D),manager(D,B).


/************************************************** DEPARTMENT ***/

entity(department).

attribute(deptname,
                domain(department),
                range(d_name),
                mapping(1,1,t,p)).

attribute(manager,
                domain(department),
                range(employee),
                mapping(1,1,t,p)).
                inconsistent :- manager(D,M), not(dept(M,D)).


/***************************************************** PROJECT ***/

entity(project).

attribute(projnum,
                domain(project),
                range(nr),
                mapping(1,1,t,p)).

attribute(belongs_to,
                domain(project),
                range(department),
                mapping(1,m,t,p)).

attribute(supervisor,
                domain(project),
                range(employee),
                mapping(1,m,t,p)).
                inconsistent :- supervisor(Proj,Emp),
                                belongs_to(Proj,Dept),
                                not(dept(Emp,Dept)).
```

```
attribute(nr_of_workers,
            domain(project),
            range(numerical),
            mapping(1,m,t,p)).
            nr_of_workers(Proj,Num):-
                        findall(Ass,proj(Ass,Proj),
                        Assignments),
                        count(Assignments,Num).

attribute(proj_salary,
            domain(project),
            range(money),
            mapping(1,m,t,p)).
            proj_salary(P,Sal):-
                        findall(A_sal,(proj(Ass,P),
                        ass_salary(Ass,A_sal)),A_salaries),
                        sum(A_salaries,Sal).


/*************************************************** ASSIGNMENT ***/

entity(assignment).

attribute(empl,
            domain(assignment),
            range(employee),
            mapping(1,m,t,p)).
            inconsistent :- empl(A,E), proj(A,P), boss(E,B),
                        not((empl(Ass,B), proj(Ass,P))).

attribute(proj,
            domain(assignment),
            range(project),
            mapping(1,m,t,p)).
            transition_violation :- before(proj(_,Project)),
                        after(not(proj(_,Project))).

attribute(ass_salary,
            domain(assignment),
            range(money),
            mapping(1,m,t,p)).


/*********************************************** DATA TYPES ***/

data_type(salary).
salary(S):- number(S),S>0, S< 50000.

data_type(money).
money(M):- number(M),M>0.

data_type(numerical).
numerical(N):- number(N).

data_type(nr).
nr(N):- atom(N).                /* An integer is not an atom */
```

```
data_type(p_name).
p_name(P):- atom(P).

data_type(d_name).
d_name(D):- atom(D).

data_type(date).
date(D):- atom(D).


/*************************************************** EVENT HIRE ***/

event(hire,[Ss,Name,Enum,Dept],[ssnum,name,empnum,department]):-
            precondition(nr(Ss)),
            precondition((deptname(D,Dept),department(D))),
            new_entity(employee,E),
            insert(ssnum(E,Ss)),
            insert(full_name(XX,Name)),
            insert(empnum(E,Enum)),
            insert(dept(E,D)).


/*************************************************** EVENT FIRE ***/

event(fire,[Ss],[ss]):-
            precondition((ssnum(P,Ss),employee(P))),
            remove(P).


/**************************************** EVENT CHANGE_SALARY ***/

event(change_salary,[Ss,Nsal],[ssnum,new_salary]):-
            precondition((ssnum(P,Ss),employee(P))),
            precondition(salary(Nsal)),
            replace(base_salary(P,Nsal)).


/**************************************** EVENT CHANGE_MANAGER ***/

event(change_manager,[Ss,Dept],[ssnum,depart]):-
            precondition((ssnum(P,Ss),employee(P))),
            precondition((deptname(D,Dept),department(D))),
            replace(manager(D,P)).


/*********************************************** EVENT NEW_DEP ***/

event(new_dep,[Dname,Man],[deptname,manager_ssnum]):-
            precondition(ssnum(Emp,Man),employee(Emp)),
            new_entity(department,D),
            insert(deptname(D,Dname)),
            replace(dept(Emp,D)),
            insert(manager(D,Emp)).
```

```
/****************************************** EVENT START_PROJECT ***/

event(start_project,[Pn,Dept],[projnum,department]):-
            precondition(nr(Pn)),
            precondition((deptname(D,Dept),department(D))),
            new_entity(project,P),
            insert(projnum(P,Pn)),
            insert(belongs_to(P,D)).


/********************************************** EVENT ASSIGN ***/

event(assign,[Ss,Pn,Sal],[ssnum,projnum,salary]):-
            precondition(ssnum(E,Ss),employee(E)),
            precondition(projnum(P,Pn),project(P)),
            new_entity(assignment,A),
            insert(empl(A,E)),
            insert(proj(A,P)),
            insert(ass_salary(A,Sal)).


/****************************************** EVENT LEAVE_PROJECT ***/

event(leave_proj,[Ssnum,Pn],[ssnum,projnum]):-
            precondition(ssnum(Emp,Ssnum),projnum(Proj,Pn)),
            precondition(empl(Ass,Emp),proj(Ass,Proj)),
            remove(Ass).


/*                                         */
/*         Example of an information base   */

employee(huey).
ssnum(huey,'2345_67').
full_name(huey,'Huey').
tel(huey,'111111').
empnum(huey,'25').
date_of_employment(huey,'860101').
base_salary(huey,1200).
dept(huey,pie).

employee(dewey).
ssnum(dewey,'3344_55').
full_name(dewey,'Dewey').
tel(dewey,'222222').
empnum(dewey,'34').
date_of_employment(dewey,'860101').
base_salary(dewey,1200).
dept(dewey,peanut).

employee(louie).
ssnum(louie,'4455_77').
full_name(louie,'Louie').
```

```
tel(louie,'333333').
empnum(louie,'38').
date_of_employment(louie,'860101').
base_salary(louie,1200).
dept(louie,pie).

employee(donald).
ssnum(donald,'4567_89').
full_name(donald,'Donald D.').
tel(donald,'444444').
empnum(donald,'232').
date_of_employment(donald,'860101').
base_salary(donald,3000).
dept(donald,peanut).

department(peanut).
deptname(peanut,'Peanut Marketing').
manager(peanut,donald).
department(pie).
deptname(pie,'Pie R&D').
manager(pie,huey).

project(p1).
projnum(p1,p1).
belongs_to(p1,peanut).
supervisor(p1,dewey).

project(p2).
projnum(p2,p2).
belongs_to(p2,peanut).
supervisor(p2,dewey).

assignment(hp1).
empl(hp1,huey).
proj(hp1,p1).
ass_salary(hp1,200).

assignment(dp1).
empl(dp1,donald).
proj(dp1,p1).
ass_salary(dp1,200).

assignment(dp2).
empl(dp2,donald).
proj(dp2,p2).
ass_salary(dp2,200).
```

Appendix 4—Set Theory

Listed below are some of the basic definitions, axioms, and laws of classical set theory, followed by examples illustrating their use. Further explanation can be sought for instance in [Halmos60], an excellent textbook.

The primitive concept of a *set* of objects can be seen as fundamental to all mathematics. A set X is a *subset* of a set Y, written $X \subseteq Y$, if all the elements of X are also elements of Y. If X and Y are known not to be identical, we use $X \subset Y$ to denote that X is a *proper subset* of Y. Conversely, Y is a (proper) *superset* of X. *The empty set*, denoted by $\emptyset$, is a proper subset of every other set.

An object z is either an element of a set X, written $z \in X$, or not, written $z \notin X$. Hence, $\emptyset$ is the unique set without elements; for every z, it holds that $z \notin \emptyset$. If there is a procedure for deciding whether $z \in X$ or not, for any z, then X is a *recursive set* and the procedure is a *decision procedure* for X. The problem of deciding whether $z \in X$ or not is then a *decidable problem*. Not all problems are decidable; there are sets for which the decision problem is only *semi-decidable*, or even *undecidable*. An example of the former is the set of logically valid formulae in FOL (cf. Chapter 4). This set is not recursive, but *semi-recursive*. A semi-recursive set is *recursively enumerable*. There are non-recursive sets which are not even recursively enumerable. An example is the complement of the set of logically valid formulae in FOL.

Given any set X, the elements of which belong to some universe U, the *complement* X' of X is the set of elements in U not in X. Given any sets X and Y, their *union* $X \cup Y$ is the set whose members belong to X or to Y (or both), and their *intersection* $X \cap Y$ is the set whose members belong to both X and Y. Finally, their *difference* $X - Y$ is the set of members of X which are not in Y. These operations may be combined. For instance, using the symbol $\hat{U}$ to denote the universe of all sets, X' is $\hat{U} - X$. We thus have the following definitions:

$$X' = \{x : x \notin X\}$$
$$X \cup Y = \{x : x \in X \vee x \in Y\}$$
$$X \cap Y = \{x : x \in X \wedge x \in Y\}$$
$$X - Y = \{x : x \in X \wedge x \notin Y\}$$

Example 10.1   Using the above definitions with the set $\mathbb{N}$ of natural numbers, let $X = \{0,1,2,3\}$ and let $Y = \{2,3,4,5\}$. It now holds that:

$$X \cup Y = \{0,1,2,3,4,5\};$$
$$X \cap Y = \{2,3\};$$
$$X - Y = \{0,1\}; Y - X = \{4,5\};$$
$$X' = \{n : n > 3\};$$
$$Y' = \{0,1\} \cup \{n : n > 5\};$$
$$(X \cup Y)' = X' \cap Y' = \{n : n > 5\}.$$

The following laws can easily be proven, e.g. by using Venn diagrams or some other graphical method of constructing sets.

Law of commutativity:
$$A \cup B = B \cup A$$

Laws of identity:
$$A \cup \varnothing = A$$
$$A \cup \hat{U} = \hat{U}$$
$$A \cap \varnothing = \varnothing$$
$$A \cap \hat{U} = A$$

Laws of idempotency:
$$A \cup A = A$$
$$A \cap A = A$$

Laws of associativity:
$$(A \cup B) \cup C = A \cup (B \cup C)$$
$$(A \cap B) \cap C = A \cap (B \cap C)$$

Laws of duality (de Morgan's laws):
$$(A \cup B)' = A' \cap B'$$
$$(A \cap B)' = A' \cup B'$$

Informally, the *cardinality* of a set $X = \{1,2,3,...,n\}$, written $|X|$, is n. Two sets with the same cardinality are said to be *equipotent*. If X has no elements, that is to say $X = \varnothing$, then $|X| = 0$. If $|X| = 1$, then X is called a *singleton set*. If $|X| = |\mathbb{N}|$, that is to say X is equipotent with the set of natural numbers, then X is *countably infinite* and has cardinality $\aleph_0$ ("alef zero"). This implies the existence of a bijection (a one-to-one correspondence) between X and $\mathbb{N}$. If $|X| = |\mathbb{R}|$, that is to say X is equipotent with the set of real numbers, then X is *uncountably infinite* and has cardinality $\mathbf{c}$ ("small c").

The *Cartesian product* $X \times Y$ of two sets X and Y is the set $\{\langle x,y \rangle : x \in X \wedge y \in Y\}$. If, for example, $X = \{1,2\}$ and $Y = \{0,2,4\}$, $X \times Y = \{\langle 1,0 \rangle, \langle 1,2 \rangle, \langle 1,4 \rangle, \langle 2,0 \rangle, \langle 2,2 \rangle, \langle 2,4 \rangle\}$. From the previous definitions, it immediately follows that $|X \times Y| = |X| \cdot |Y|$.

The power set $\mathbb{P}(X)$ of a set X is the set of all subsets of X, including $\varnothing$ and X itself. The name 2^X often used for a function returning the power set is explained by the fact that $|\mathbb{P}(X)| = 2^{|X|}$.

A *family C* of sets is denoted by $C = \{X_i : i \in I\}$, where I is a non-empty set called the *index set*, and a set X_i is associated with every $i \in I$.

A *partition P of a set X* is a family of non-empty subsets of X such that P is the union of all sets in the family, and such that the two sets in every pair of sets in the family are *disjoint*, i.e. have no element in common. For instance, a partition into recursive, semi-recursive (but not recursive), and non-recursive sets can often be defined for a set of sets.

From [Halmos60], we now cite the most important axioms of set theory. These are rarely used as axioms in computer science contexts, but by looking at their formulation one may learn something about the smallest linguistic units used for the language of arithmetic, for instance.

Axiom of extension:
Two sets are equal iff they have the same elements.

Axiom of specification:
To every set A and to every condition $S(x)$ there corresponds a set B whose elements are exactly those elements x of A for which $S(x)$ holds.

Axiom of pairing:
For any two sets there exists a set that they both belong to.

Axiom of unions:
For every collection of sets there exists a set that contains all the elements that belong to at least one set of the given collection.

Power set axiom:
For each set there exists a collection of sets that contains amongst its elements all the subsets of the given set.

Axiom of infinity:
There exists a set containing 0 and containing the successor of each of its elements.

Axiom of choice:
The Cartesian product of a non-empty family of non-empty sets is non-empty.

The axioms relate to the fundamental definitions in various ways. Suppose we wished to sharpen the power set axiom. As it stands, it does not supply the definition of power set given previously, but rather a superset of the power set. More formally, the axiom states that if X is a set, then a set P exists such that if $Y \subseteq X$, then $Y \in P$. However, P may contain elements other than subsets of X. We can remedy this by applying the axiom of specification in order to form the set $\{Y \in P : Y \subseteq X\}$. Rewritten as $\mathbb{P} = \{Y : Y \subseteq X\}$, this set yields the definition of the power set of X. The dependence of $\mathbb{P}$ on X is denoted by writing $\mathbb{P}(X)$ instead of just $\mathbb{P}$.

A technical comment on the axiom of infinity is appropriate here. The axiom is used for arithmetic, and hence it refers to 0 rather than $\varnothing$. The mapping (or, more formally, the bijection) is straightforward: $0 = \varnothing$; $1 = \{0\}$, $2 = \{0,1\}$, $3 = \{0,1,2\}$,....

Appendix 5—Prolog

Prolog is a programming language used to solve problems involving objects and relationships between objects. This appendix presents the basic elements of Prolog, covering facts, queries, variables, conjunctions, rules, lists, and negation. (This appendix is partly based on the text [Clocksin90].)

Many problems can be expressed by means of objects and their interrelationships. For example, when we say "John owns the car ABC123", we are declaring that ownership exists between the object John and the object ABC123. John is an instance of a person, ABC123 an instance of a car, and ownership is a relationship between them. Furthermore, the relationship has a specific order: John owns the car, but the car does not own John.

When describing relationships between objects, it is common to use rules. For example, the rule "Two people are sisters if they are both female and have the same parents" defines what it means to be sisters. The rule also provides a procedure for determining whether two people are sisters: simply check if they are both female and have the same parents.

Computer programming in Prolog consists of the following three different activities:

1. Declaring facts about objects and their interrelationships.
2. Defining rules about objects and their interrelationships.
3. Asking queries about objects and their interrelationships.

Facts

A typical example of a Prolog fact is the following:

```
has_father(mary, john).
```

This fact states that Mary's father is John. We note three important syntactic details concerning facts in Prolog:

1. The names of all relationships and objects must begin with a lower-case letter, for instance `mary`, `john`, and `has_father`.
2. The relationship is written first, and the names of the objects, separated by commas, are written inside a pair of parentheses.
3. A full stop "." must come at the end of each fact.

Example A5.1   Some Prolog facts and their possible interpretations:

```
woman(jane).                    Jane is a woman.
married_to(john, jane).         John is married to Jane.
has_father(jane, george).       Jane's father is George.
owns(john, abc123).             John owns the car abc123.
owns(john, def456).             John owns the car def456.
```

```
president(bush).                George Bush is a president.
borders_on(sweden,norway).      Sweden borders on Norway.
```

We now introduce some terminology for talking about facts and their constituents. The names of objects are called *atoms*, e.g. jane, john, and sweden in the example above are atoms. The first symbol in a fact is called a *predicate symbol*, for instance woman, married_to, and owns are predicate symbols. The atoms occurring in a fact are called *arguments*. So, the first argument of married_to(john, jane) is john and the second argument is jane. It is important to pay attention to the order in which the arguments are written. Even though the order is arbitrary, we must decide on some order and adhere to it. For example, the fact has_father(mary, john) states that Mary has John as father, and not the other way around.

It is good practice to choose verbs as predicate symbols in binary facts, i.e. facts with two arguments. The fact can then be read in the following way:
The first argument — The predicate symbol — The second argument.
For example, we read loves(peter, mary) as "Peter loves Mary".

A Prolog fact can contain an arbitrary number of arguments. Here are two examples of facts with three arguments, stating that two people are playing a game:

```
plays(john, mary, tennis).
plays(joe, jim, badminton).
```

Queries

Given a number of facts, we can ask queries about them. In Prolog, a query begins with a question mark and a hyphen and continues with a fact. The following query

```
?- married_to(john, jane).
```

is interpreted as "Is John married to Jane?" When a query is put to Prolog, the Prolog interpreter searches through all available facts and looks for a fact that matches the query. If such a fact is found, the interpreter responds "yes", otherwise "no".

Example A5.2   Continuing Example A5.1, we list a number of queries with the answers a Prolog interpreter might give them, supposing Prolog knew about the facts from this example.

```
?- married_to(john, jane).
yes
?- woman(jane).
yes
?- woman(john).
no
?- woman(lisa).
no
?- borders_on(sweden, norway).
yes
```

In order to find out to whom John is married, it would be very tedious to have to ask a large number of queries of the form "Is John married to Mary?", "Is John married to

Lisa?", and so forth. It would be preferable for a query to receive the form "Is John married to x?" and let the Prolog interpreter substitute x with an answer for x. In Prolog, not only can particular objects be named, but also they can be substituted with dummy names like x, as the interpreter sees fit. Names of the latter kind are called *variables*. Prolog distinguishes atoms from variables by interpreting any name beginning with a capital letter as a variable. Variables can also be used in queries. For example:

```
?- married_to(john, X).
```

This query prompts Prolog to search for a fact that matches the query. When one of the arguments in the query is a variable, Prolog allows it to match any argument with the corresponding position in a fact.

In this case Prolog would search for a fact where the predicate symbol was married_to, the first argument was john, and the second argument might be anything. When, and if, such a fact is found, Prolog would print the answer and wait for further instructions. Given the facts in Example A5.1, Prolog would find the matching fact married_to(john, jane), and write the answer

```
X = jane.
```

If you were now to press the RETURN key, Prolog would stop searching for more matching facts. If instead of RETURN, you were to type a semi-colon followed by RETURN, Prolog would search for more answers.

Prolog continues to search for, and print, more answers to the query either until the RETURN key is pressed, which returns the user to the ?-prompt, or until there are no more matching facts, upon which Prolog prints "no". When Prolog finds a fact that matches a query that uses a variable, we say that Prolog instantiates the variable in the query with the atom in the found fact, where the variable and the atom have the same position. In the example above, Prolog instantiates the variable x with jane.

Example A5.3   Given the facts from Example A5.1, Prolog provides the queries below with the answers shown. Note that these particular semi-colons are typed by the user.

```
?- owns(john, X).
X = abc123 ;
X = def456 ;
no

?- borders_on(X, norway).
X = sweden ;
no
```

Let us now consider more complicated queries. Suppose we have the following facts:

```
loves(john, mary).
loves(peter, mary).
loves(mary, john).
```

If we wanted to know whether John and Mary love each other, we could submit the following query:

```
?- loves(john, mary), loves(mary, john).
```

Prolog interprets commas as conjunction (and) and responds with a "yes".

Example A5.4   Given the facts from Example A5.1, if we wanted to find the father-in-law of John, we could present the following query:

```
?- married_to(john, W), has_father(W, F).
W = jane, F = george
```

In this case, Prolog identifies two matching facts: `married_to(john,   jane)`, `has_father(jane, george)`. So, the variable `W` will be instantiated with `jane`, and the variable `F` with `george`.

Rules

In Prolog, rules are used to express that one fact is dependent on a set of other facts. In English, the word "if" is often used in rules. For example:

X is a human if
X is a biped, and
X does not have feathers.

or

X is a sister of Y if
X is a female, and
X and Y have the same parents.

The following expression is an example of a rule in Prolog:

```
has_father_in_law(X, Y) :- married_to(X, M), has_father(M, Y).
```

The symbol ":-" is read as "if" and the comma is read as "and". So, we could paraphrase this example as

X has father-in-law Y if
X is married_to M, and
M has the father Y.

In predicate logic, the rule above would have the following form:

```
∀x∀m∀y(Married_to(x, m) ∧ Has_father(m, y) →
            Has_father_in_law(x, y))
```

A rule consists of two parts: the *head* and the *body*. The head is the part of the rule to the left of the ":-" symbol, and the body is the part to the right. In the example above, the head is `has_father_in_law(X,  Y)`, and the body consists of `married_to(X,  M)`, `has_father(M, Y)`.

To explain the semantics of rules in Prolog, we need to digress to the topic of substitutions. A substitution is a set of ordered pairs, where each pair consists of a variable and an atom. For instance, `{X/mary, Y/john, Z/george}`. To apply a substitution to a formula entails replacing each variable in the formula with an atom, as specified by the substitution.

Example A5.5   Consider the formula `loves(X, Y)`, `has_father(X, Z)`, and the substitution `{X/mary, Y/john, Z/george}`. If we apply the substitution to the formula, we acquire the following facts:

```
loves(mary, john), has_father(mary, george).
```

We now introduce a useful notation for substitutions. Let F be a formula and Θ a substitution. Then, F[Θ] denotes the formula obtained by applying Θ to F.

Let F = `married_to(X, Y), eye_colour(Y, W),`

Θ = `{X/peter, Y/lisa, W/blue}`, and

Δ = `{X/joe, Y/susan, W/brown}`.

Now,

F[Θ] = `married_to(peter, lisa), eye_colour(lisa, blue)`, and

F[Δ] = `married_to(joe, susan), eye_colour(susan, brown)`.

A *Prolog program* is a set of Prolog facts and Prolog rules. An *atomic formula* is an expression with the same form as a Prolog fact, except that its arguments may be either atoms or variables. A *ground* atomic formula is an atomic formula, the arguments of which are all atoms.

Example A5.6   The following is an example of a Prolog program:

```
woman(jane).                        woman(lisa).
woman(susan).                       man(peter).
man(john).                          man(george).
married_to(john, jane).             married_to(peter, lisa).
has_father(jane, george).           has_father(lisa, george).
has_mother(jane, susan).            has_mother(lisa, susan).
owns(john, abc123).                 owns(john, def456).

is_owned_by(Car, Person):- owns(Person, Car).
has_father_in_law(X, Y):- married_to(X, M), has_father(M, Y).
has_mother_in_law(X, Y):- married_to(X, M), has_mother(M, Y).
has_sister(P, S):- woman(S), has_mother(P, M), has_mother(S, M),
                   has_father(P, F), has_father(S, F).
```

In Example A5.6, we would regard the ground atomic formula `has_mother(jane, susan)` as true, since this formula appears as a fact in the program. We would also regard the formula `is_owned_by(abc123, john)` as true, based on the first rule in the program and the fact `owns(john, abc123)`. We now attempt to formalise these inferences.

Let P be a Prolog program. A ground atomic formula A is *true in P* if either

- A appears as a fact in P, or
- A rule R exists in P and a substitution Θ exists such that A = head(R)[Θ] and body(R)[Θ] is true in P, where head(R) denotes the head of R, and body(R) denotes the body of R.

We can now motivate why `is_owned_by(abc123, john)` is true in the program above. Consider the first rule in the program and the substitution `{Car/abc123, Person/john}`. If we apply this substitution to the head of the rule, we obtain `is_owned_by(abc123, john)`. If we apply the substitution to the body of the rule, we obtain `owns(john, abc123)`, which is a fact in the program.

Example A5.7   In Example A5.6, the atomic formula A = `mother_in_law(john, su-san)` is true. To explain this, let

R = `has_mother_in_law(X, Y):- married_to(X, M), has_mother(M, Y).`

and

Θ = {X/john, M/jane, Y/susan}.

Then

A = head(R)[Θ], and

body(R)[Θ] = `married_to(john, jane), has_mother(jane, susan)`, are true in the given program, since both facts appear in it.

Sometimes it is helpful to think in a more procedural way and consider how, with respect to a certain program, the Prolog interpreter determines whether a given ground formula is true or not. Consider the formula `has_father_in_law(john, george)`, together with the program of Example A5.6. If Prolog is required to determine the truth of this formula, it first checks whether the formula appears in the program as a fact. In the example, the formula is not a fact in the program, so Prolog continues to search for a rule, the head of which matches the given formula. The second rule of the program fulfils this criterion. When the formula matches the head of the rule, the interpreter instantiates variable X with `john`, and Y with `george`. Prolog then instantiates the variables in the body accordingly, resulting in the formula `married_to(john,M),has_father(M,george)`. Prolog then checks whether this formula is true. By instantiating M with `jane` the formula is shown to be true, since both `married_to(john, jane)` and `has_father(jane, george)` appear as facts in the program.

We now turn to the issue of queries in the presence of rules. Let P be a Prolog program. If we submit a query that is a ground atomic formula, Prolog will answer "yes" if the formula is true in P and "no" otherwise. If we submit a query containing variables, Prolog tries to find a substitution which, when applied, will result in a formula that is true in P. If such a substitution is found, Prolog responds by printing it on the screen. When more than one substitution is found, Prolog prints them all if the user types a semi-colon after each answer. If Prolog cannot find an appropriate substitution, it responds with a "no".

Example A5.8   The following examples of queries and answers use the program in Example A5.6.

```
?- woman(X).
X = jane ;
X = lisa ;
X = susan ;

?- has_father_in_law(john, george).
yes
```

```
?- has_sister(X, jane).
X = lisa ;
no
```

Sometimes it is necessary to write more than one rule in order to define a predicate symbol. Take the predicate "uncle" for example. There are two ways of being an uncle: you can be the brother of a child's father, or you can be the brother of a child's mother. In Prolog, two rules are required to express this:

```
has_uncle(Child, Uncle):- has_father(Child, Father),
              has_brother(Father, Uncle).
has_uncle(Child,Uncle):-has_mother(Child,Mother),
              has_brother(Mother, Uncle).
```

This is an example of how disjunction in rules is represented in Prolog by defining several bodies for the same head.

Prolog provides a special form of negation based on the Closed World Assumption. The idea is that if a given formula is not true with respect to a program, then its negation is true. More precisely, if P is a program and A is a formula that is not true in P, then `not(A)` is true in P. For example, consider the program of Example A5.6 and the formula `has_father(lisa, john)`. This formula is not true for that program, so the formula `not(has_father(lisa, john))` is true. Negation is often useful when defining rules. For example, here is a rule for defining bachelors:

```
bachelor(X):- man(X), not(married_to(X, Y)).
```

This rule can be paraphrased in natural language as

X is a bachelor if
X is a man, and
no Y exists to whom X is married.

Prolog provides a few built-in predicates to handle arithmetic. The infix operator `is` can be used for assignment as in the following examples:

```
?- X is 3 + 5.
X = 8
?- X is 3 + 5, Y is 4 * 3, X > Y.
no
```

Sets and Lists

A set is an unordered collection of objects without duplicates. A list is an ordered collection of objects where duplicates may occur. Prolog offers special mechanisms for handling lists, but not sets, which need to be simulated using lists. Such simulated sets are usually called *multi-sets*, or *bags*, since a set cannot have duplicates.

Recall that sets can be defined explicitly or implicitly. In Prolog, we use brackets to give explicit definitions of sets, i.e. lists. Here are some examples:

```
[3, 4, 5, 6, 7]
[john, lisa, susan, george]
[3, 4, 5, 3, 6, 7, 5]
```

The last example shows that duplicates may occur in Prolog lists. Implicit set definitions are constructed using Prolog's special-purpose, built-in predicate, `findall`, which takes three arguments. The first argument corresponds to the set variable, the second to the set condition, and the third holds an explicit representation of the defined set. The following set expression defines the set of all men in the program of Example A5.6:

```
{x : man(x)}
```

In Prolog, this would be expressed as

```
findall(X, man(X), Men)
```

We read the last expression as "Find all X where X is a man and put the result into the list variable representing the bag Men". If this expression were presented to Prolog as a query, the interpreter would answer by instantiating the variable Men with a list:

```
?- findall(X, man(X), Men)
Men = [john, peter, george]
```

Example A5.9   A Prolog program with queries:

```
owns(john, abc123).      owns(john, def456).      owns(peter, ghi789).
earns(john, 12000).      earns(peter, 15000).     earns(mary, 17000).
age(john, 22).           age(peter, 32).          age(mary, 42).
```

```
?- findall(X, owns(john, X),      % Find all cars owned by John
    Cars).
Cars = [abc123, def456]
```

```
?- findall(X, (earns(X, S),       % Find all persons earning more than
    S > 13000), Result).          13,000.
Result = [peter, mary]            % If the condition is a conjunction it must be
                                  % enclosed in parentheses.
```

```
?- findall(X, (earns(X, S),
    S >13000, age(X, A), A < 30),
    Result).
Result = [ ]
```

The binary predicate `member` checks whether a certain element belongs to a given set. The first argument of `member` is an element, the second a list. For instance:

```
?- member(a, [a, b, c]).
yes
```

```
?- member(d, [a, b, c]).
no
```

The binary predicate `unique` can remove duplicates from a list. The first argument of `unique` is a list, possibly containing duplicates, and the second argument is a list for which the duplicates in the first argument have been removed.

```
?- unique([a, b, c, c, a], X).
X = [a, b, c]

?- unique([a, b, c], X).
X = [a, b, c]
```

The binary predicate count counts the number of elements in a list. The first argument of count is instantiated with a list, the second holds the number of elements in that list.

```
?- count([a, b, c], N).
N = 3

?- count([ ], N).
N = 0
```

The binary predicate sum sums up all the values of a list of numbers. The first argument must be instantiated with a list of numbers, the second gives the sum of these numbers.

```
?- sum([1, 2, 3], S).
S = 6

?- sum([ ], S).
S = 0

?- sum([a, b, c], S).
**** Syntax error, cannot add atoms
```

Exercises

A5.1 Consider the following Prolog predicates:

```
lives_in(Person, City)      % Person lives in City
lies_in(City, Country)      % City lies in Country
age(Person, Age)            % Person is Age years old
earns(Person, S)            % Person earns salary S
works_at(X, Y)              % X works at company Y
```

Use the predicates above to express the following statements as Prolog facts:

a) Peter lives in Oslo
b) Peter is 25 years old
c) Peter works at IBM
d) Oslo lies in Norway
e) Peter earns 12,000

A5.2

```
F = p(X, Y, Z), q(Y, Y)
G = p(X, Z, X), r(Y, Y, Z)
Θ = {X/a, Y/b, Z/c}
Δ = {X/a, Y/b, Z/a}
```

Use the formulae and substitutions above to compute the following:

a) F[Θ]
b) F[Δ]
c) G[Θ]
d) G[Δ]

A5.3

```
p(a).          p(b).              p(c).
q(a).          q(b).              q(d).

r(X):- p(X).
s(X):- p(X), q(X).
t(X):- p(X), not(q(X)).
u(X):- p(X).
u(X):- q(X).
```

Use the Prolog program above to answer the following queries. Supply all possible answers, not just one.

a) ?- p(X).
b) ?- r(X).
c) ?- s(X).
d) ?- t(X).
e) ?- u(X).

A5.4 Write Prolog queries for the following questions using the predicates in Exercise A5.1.

a)   Where does Peter work?
b)   In which country does Paris lie?
c)   Does Peter earn more than John?
d)   Who works at IBM?
e)   Do Mary and John have the same age?
f)   Who works at the same company as Mary?
g)   How many people earn more than 20,000?
h)   How many people working at IBM earn more than 20,000?
i)   What is the average salary at IBM?
j)   Is there anyone who is older than 30 years and does not work at any company?
k)   Who is the oldest person working at IBM, and how old is he or she?
l)   Does IBM have more employees than SKF?
m)   Is the average salary of people in Stockholm larger than the average salary of people in Oslo?

A5.5 Use the predicates in Exercise A5.1 to complete the following Prolog rules:

a) `high_income_earner(X):- ...`
   X is a high income earner if he or she earns more than 20,000.

b) `norwegian(X):- ...`

  X is a Norwegian if he or she lives in a city in Norway.

c) `unemployed(X):- ...`

  X is unemployed if he or she does not work at any company.

d) `earns_more(X, Y):- ...`

  X earns more than Y if X's salary exceeds that of Y.

e) `compatriots(X, Y):- ...`

  X and Y are compatriots if they live in cities in the same country.

Bibliography

[Abiteboul95] S. Abiteboul, R. Hull, and V. Vianu, *Foundations of Databases,* Addison-Wesley, Reading, Massachusetts, 1995

[Batini86] C. Batini, M. Lenzerini, and S. Navathe, "A Comparative Analysis of Methodologies for Database Schema Integration", *ACM Computing Surveys,* vol.18, no.4, pp. 323–364, 1986

[Batini91] C. Batini, S. Ceri, and S. Navathe, *Conceptual Database Design,* Benjamin/Cummings, Redwood City, California, 1991

[Bellenzona94] R. Bellinzona, S. Castano, V. D. Antonellis, M. Fugini, and B. Pernici, "Requirements reuse in the F3 project", *Ingénierie des systèmes d´information* (AFCET/HERMES, Paris, France), vol.2, no.6, pp. 699–717, 1994

[Biskup86] J. Biskup and B. Convent, "A Formal View Integration Method", in *ACM-SIGMOD International Conference,* C. Zaniolo (Ed.), Washington, DC, 1986

[Booch91] G. Booch, *Object Oriented Design with Applications,* Benjamin/Cummings, Redwood City, California, 1991

[Bubenko77] J. A. Bubenko, Jr, "The Temporal Dimension in Information Modelling", *IFIP WG 2.6 Working Conference on Architecture and Models in Data Base Management Systems*, Nice, France, G. M. Nijssen (Ed.), North-Holland, Amsterdam, 1977

[Bubenko80] J. A. Bubenko, Jr, "Information Modeling in the Context of Systems Development", *IFIP Congress 80*, Tokyo and Melbourne, S. Lavington (Ed.), North-Holland, Amsterdam, 1980

[Bubenko84] J. A. Bubenko, Jr and E. Lindencrona, *Konceptuell modellering — Informationsanalys*, Studentlitteratur, Lund, in Swedish, 1984

[Bubenko94a] J. A. Bubenko, Jr and M. Kirikova, "'Worlds' in Requirements Acquisition and Modelling", *4th European–Japanese Seminar on Information Modelling and Knowledge Bases*, Kista, Sweden, H. Kangassalo and B. Wangler (Eds), IOS, The Netherlands, 1994

[Bubenko94b] J. A. Bubenko, Jr, C. Rolland, P. Loucopoulos, and V. DeAntonellis, "Facilitating 'Fuzzy to Formal' Requirements Modelling", *IEEE International Conference on Requirements Engineering,* Colorado Springs, Colorado, and Taipei, Taiwan, ROC, IEEE, 1994

[Carnap67] R. Carnap, *The Logical Structure of the World,* University of California Press, 1967

[Carroll1872] L. Carroll, *Through the Looking Glass,* The World Publ. Co., 1872

[Chang73] C.-L. Chang and R.C.-T. Lee, *Symbolic Logic and Mechanical Theorem Proving*, Academic Press, Orlando, Florida, 1973

[Chang90] C. C. Chang and H.J. Keisler, *Model Theory*, 3rd edn, North-Holland, Amsterdam, 1990

[Chellas80] B. F. Chellas, *Modal Logic*, Cambridge University Press, 1980

[Chen76] P. Chen, "The Entity-Relationship Model — Toward a Unified View of Data", *ACM Transactions on Database Systems*, vol.1, no.1, pp. 9–36, 1976

[Clocksin90] W. Clocksin and C. Mellish, *Programming in Prolog*, 3rd edn, Springer-Verlag, Heidelberg, 1990

[Codd79] E. Codd, "Extending the Relational Database Model to Capture More Meaning", *ACM Transactions on Database Systems*, vol.4, no.4, 1979

[Crystal88] D. Crystal, *The Cambridge Encyclopedia of Language,* Cambridge University Press, 1988

[Date90] C. J. Date, *An Introduction to Database Systems*, 5th edn, Addison-Wesley, Reading, Massachusetts, 1990

[Davenport93] T. H. Davenport, *Process Innovation: Reengineering Work Through Information Technology*, Harvard Business School Press, Boston, Massachusetts, 1993

[Devitt87] M. Devitt and K. Sterelny, *Language and Reality,* Basil Blackwell, Oxford, 1987

[Dubois89] E. Dubois, J. Hagelstein, and A. Rifaut, *Formal Requirements Engineering with ERAE*, Revised version of *Philips Journal of Research*, vol.43, no.3/4, pp. 393–414, 1989

[ElMasri85] R. ElMasri, J. Weeldryer, and A. Hevner, "The Category Concept: An Extension to the Entity-Relationship Model", *Data and Knowledge Engineering*, vol.1, no.1, 1985

[F395] F3 Consortium, *The F3 Requirements Engineering Handbook*, SISU, Electrum 212, S-16440, Kista, Sweden, 1995

[Fleming89] C. Fleming and E. von Halle, *Handbook of Relational Database Design,* Addison-Wesley, Reading, Massachusetts, 1989

[Fromkin83] V. Fromkin and R. Rodman, *An Introduction to Language*, Holt-Saunders, New York, 1983

[Furtado88] A. L. Furtado, M. A. Casanova, and L. Tucherman, "The CHRIS Consultant", in *Proc. Entity-Relationship Approach*, S. T. March (Ed.), Elsevier Science Publishers, New York, 1988

[Gabbay84] *Handbook of Philosophical Logic,* vols I - IV, D. Gabbay and F. Guenthner (Eds), Kluwer, Dordrecht, 1984

[Gallaire78] *Logic and Data Bases,* H. Gallaire and J. Minker (Eds), Plenum Press, New York, 1978

[Gallaire84] H. Gallaire, J. Minker, and J. M. Nicholas, "Logic and Databases: A Deductive Approach", *ACM Computing Surveys*, vol.16, no.2, 1984

[Gallier87] J. H. Gallier, *Logic for Computer Science*, John Wiley & Sons, New York, 1987

[Gamut91] L. T. F. Gamut, *Logic, Language, and Meaning* (Two volumes), The University of Chicago Press, 1991

[Gogolla91] M. Gogolla and U. Hohenstein, "Towards a Semantic View of an Extended Entity-Relationship Model", *ACM Transactions on Database Systems,* vol.16, no.3, pp. 369–416, 1991

[Greenspan86] S. J. Greenspan, A. Borgida, and J. Mylopoulos, "A Requirements Modelling Language and its Logic", *Information Systems,* vol.11, no.1, pp. 9-23, 1986

[Gries81] D. Gries, *The Science of Programming*, Springer Verlag, Berlin, 1981

[Gustafsson82] M. R. Gustafsson, T. Karlsson and J. A. Bubenko, Jr, "A Declarative Approach to Conceptual Information Modeling", *Information Systems Design Methodologies: A Comparative Review*, Noordwijkerhout, The Netherlands, T. W. Olle, H. G. Sol, and A. A. Verrijn-Stewart (Eds), North-Holland, Amsterdam, 1982

[Gustas95] R. Gustas, J. A. Bubenko, Jr, and B. Wangler, "Goal Driven Enterprise Modelling: Bridging Pragmatic and Semantic Descriptions of Information Systems", *5th European–Japanese Seminar on Information Modelling and Knowledge Bases*, Sapporo, Japan, 1995

[Haack78] S. Haack, *Philosophy of Logics*, Cambridge University Press, 1978

[Hagelstein88] J. Hagelstein, "Declarative Approach to Information Systems Requirements", *Knowledge Based Systems*, vol.1, no.1, pp. 211–220, 1988

[Halmos60] P. R. Halmos, *Naive Set Theory*, van Nostrand, Princeton, New Jersey, 1960

[Hamilton78] A. G. Hamilton, *Logic for Mathematicians*, Cambridge University Press, 1978

[Hammer81] M. Hammer and D. McLeod, "Database Description with SDM: A Semantic Database Model", *ACM Transactions on Database Systems*, vol.6, no.3, pp. 351–386, 1981

[Hammer93] M. Hammer and J. A. Champy, *Reengineering the Corporation: a Manifesto for Business Revolution*, Harper Collins, New York, 1993

[Hammer95] M. Hammer and S. A. Stanton, *The Reengineering Revolution: The Handbook*, Harper Collins, Hammersmith, London, 1995

[Hanfling81] O. Hanfling (Ed.), *Essential Readings in Logical Positivism*, Basil Blackwell, Oxford, 1981

[vanHeijenoort67] Jean van Heijenoort (Ed.), *From Frege to Gödel*, Harvard University Press, 1967

[Hillier72] B. Hillier, J. Mushgrove and P. O' Sullivan, "Knowledge and Design", in *Environmental Design: Research and Practice*, W. Mitchell (Ed.), University of California Press, Los Angeles, California, 1972

[Hull87] R. Hull and R. King, "Semantic Database Modeling: Survey, Applications and Research Issues", *ACM Computing Surveys*, vol.19, no.3, pp. 201–260, 1987

[ISO82] *ISO — Concepts and Terminology for the Conceptual Schema and the Information Base*, J. J. v. Griethuysen (Ed.), ISO/TC97/SC5/WG3 - N 695, 1982

[Johannesson90] P. Johannesson, "MOLOC: Using Prolog for Conceptual Modelling", in *9th International Conference on Entity-Relationship Approach*, H. Kangassalo (Ed.), pp. 289–302, North-Holland, Lausanne, 1990

[Johannesson93] P. Johannesson, "A Logical Basis for Schema Integration", in *3rd International Workshop on Research Issues in Data Engineering — Interoperability in Multidatabase Systems,* Wien, IEEE Press, New York, 1993

[Kanellakis90] P. C. Kanellakis, "Elements of Relational Database Theory", in *Handbook of Theoretical Computer Science*, J. van Leeuwen (Ed.), Elsevier Science, Amsterdam, 1990

[Kirikova94a] M. Kirikova and J. A. Bubenko, Jr, "Enterprise Modelling: Improving the Quality of Requirements Specification", *Information Systems Research Seminar in Scandinavia*, IRIS-17, Oulu, Finland, 1994

[Kirikova94b] M. Kirikova and J. A. Bubenko, Jr, "Software Requirements Acquisition through Enterprise Modelling", *Software Engineering and Knowledge Engineering - SEKE'94,* Jurmala, Latvia, 1994

[Kung83] C. H. Kung, "An Analysis of Three Conceptual Models with Time Perspective", in *Information Systems Design Methodologies: A Feature Analysis*, T. W. Olle, H. G. Sol, and C. J. Tully (Eds), North-Holland, Amsterdam, 1989

[Kung88] C. H. Kung, "Conceptual Modeling in the Context of Software Development", *IEEE Transactions on Software Engineering,* vol.15, no.10, pp. 1176 ff., 1988

[Kurzweil90] R. Kurzweil, *The Age of Intelligent Machines*, MIT Press, 1990

[Lalement93] R. Lalement, *Computation as Logic*, Prentice Hall, Hemel Hempstead, 1993

[Langefors67] B. Langefors, *Theoretical Analysis of Information Systems,* Studentlitteratur, Lund, Sweden, 1967

[Lemmon87] E. J. Lemmon, *Beginning Logic*, 2nd edn, Chapman & Hall, London. First edition published in 1965.

[Lewis81] H. R. Lewis and C. H. Papadimitriou, *Elements of the Theory of Computation*, Prentice Hall, Englewood Cliffs, New Jersey, 1981

[Linsky70] L. Linsky, *Semantics and the Philosophy of Language,* University of Illinois Press, Urbana, 1970

[Lloyd87] J. W. Lloyd, *Foundations of Logic Programming,* 2nd edn., Springer-Verlag, Berlin, 1987

[Loucopoulos94] P. Loucopoulos, "The F3 (from fuzzy to formal) view on requirements engineering", *Ingénierie des systèmes d'information* (AFCET/HERMES, Paris, France), vol.2, no.6, pp. 639–655, 1994

[Lukaszewicz90] W. Lukaszewicz, *Non-Monotonic Reasoning*, Ellis Horwood, Chichester, 1990

[Miller 94] R. Miller, Y. Ioannidis, and R. Ramakrishnan, "Schema Equivalence in Heterogeneous Systems: Bridging Theory and Practice", in *Information Systems*, vol.19, no.1, 1994

[Minker88] J. Minker (Ed.), *Foundations of Deductive Databases and Logic Programming*, Morgan Kaufmann, Los Altos, California, 1988

[Naqvi89] S. Naqvi and S. Tsur, *A Logical Language for Data and Knowledge Bases*, Computer Science Press, Rockville, Maryland, 1989

[Nellborn94] C. Nellborn and P. Holm, "Capturing Information Systems Requirements Through Enterprise and Speech Act Modeling", *6th International Conference on Advanced Information Systems Engineering*, CAiSE'94, Utrecht, The Netherlands, G. Wijers, S. Brinkkemper, and T. Wasserman (Eds), Springer-Verlag, Berlin, 1994

[Nijssen77] G. M. Nijssen, "On the Gross Architecture for the Next Generation Database Management Systems", *Information Processing 77*, B. Gilchrist (Ed.), North-Holland, Amsterdam, 1977

[Nijssen89] G. M. Nijssen and T. Halpin, *Conceptual Schema and Relational Database Design*, Prentice Hall, Upper Saddle River, New Jersey, 1989

[Olivé86] A. Olivé, "A Comparison of the Operational and Deductive Approaches to Information Systems Modeling", *INFORMATION PROCESSING 86*, Dublin, Ireland, H.-J. Kugler (Ed.), Elsevier Science (North-Holland), Amsterdam, 1986

[Olivé89] A. Olivé, "On the Design and Implementation of Information Systems from Deductive Conceptual Models", *15th International Conference on Very Large Data Bases*, Amsterdam, P. M. G. Apers and G. Wiederhold (Eds), Morgan Kaufmann, San Mateo, California, 1989

[Peckham88] J. Peckham and F. Maryanski, "Semantic Data Models", *ACM Computing Surveys*, vol.20, no.3, pp. 153–190, 1988

[Pinker94] Steven Pinker, *The Language Instinct*, William Morrow, New York, 1994

[Quine66] W. V. Quine, *The Ways of Paradox and Other Essays,* Random House, New York, 1966

[Rittel84] H. W. J. Rittel and M. M. Webber, "Planning Problems are Wicked Problems", in *Developments in Design Methodology*, N. Cross (Ed.), John Wiley & Sons, Chichester, 1984

[Rolland93] C. Rolland, "Modeling the Requirements Engineering Process", *3rd European–Japanese Seminar on Information Modelling and Knowledge Bases*, Budapest, H. Kangassalo and H. Jaakkola (Eds), IOS, The Netherlands, 1993

[Rowe88] N. C. Rowe, *Artificial Intelligence Through Prolog*, Prentice Hall, Englewood Cliffs, New Jersey, 1988

[Rumbaugh92] J. Rumbaugh, M. Blaha, W. Premerlani, F. Eddy, and W. Lorensen, *Object-Oriented Modelling and Design*, Prentice Hall, New Jersey, 1992

[Russell95] S. Russell and P. Norvig, *Artificial Intelligence*, Prentice Hall, Upper Saddle River, New Jersey, 1995

[Sainsbury91] M. Sainsbury, *Logical Forms,* Basil Blackwell, Oxford, 1991

[Senko73] M. E. Senko, E. B. Altman, M. M. Astrahan, and P. L. Fehder, "Data Structures and Accessing in Database Systems", *IBM Systems Journal*, vol.12, no.1, 1973

[Shipman81] D. Shipman, "The Functional Data Model and the Data Language DAPLEX", *ACM Transactions on Database Systems*, vol.6, no.1, 1981

[Simon84] H. Simon, "The Structure of Ill-Structured Problems", in *Developments in Design Methodology*, N. Cross (Ed.), John Wiley & Sons, Chichester, 1984

[Song94] W. W. Song and M. R. Gustafsson, *Enterprise Model Capture Tool: User Guide*, F3 Project Deliverable, 94-06-17, SISU, Electrum 212, S-16440, Kista, Sweden, 1994

[Song95] W. W. Song, "OFEM: A Structural Representation to Support Objectives Modelling Integration", *CE'95*, Washington, 1995

[Speake79] J. Speake (Ed.), *A Dictionary of Philosophy*, Pan Books, London, 1979

[Sterling87] L. Sterling and E. Shapiro, *The Art of Prolog*, The MIT Press, 1987

[Tansel93] A. Tansel *et al.*, *Temporal Databases, Theory, Design, and Implementation*, Benjamin/Cummings, Redwood City, California, 1993

[Tarski93] Alfred Tarski, *Introduction to Logic and to the Methodology of Deductive Sciences*, Oxford University Press, 1993.

[Teorey86] T. Teorey, J. Yang, and J. Fry, "A Logical Design Methodology for Relational Databases Using the Extended Entity Relationship Model", *ACM Computing Surveys*, vol.18, no.2, pp. 197–222, 1986

[Teorey90] T. Teorey, *Database Modelling and Design*, Morgan Kaufmann, Los Altos, California, 1990

[Theodoulidis91] C. Theodoulidis, P. Loucopoulos, and B. Wangler, "A Conceptual Modelling Formalism for Temporal Database Applications", *Information Systems*, vol.16, no.4, pp. 401–416, 1991

[Tsichritzis82] D. Tsichritzis and F. Lochovsky, *Data Models,* Prentice Hall, Englewood Cliffs, New Jersey, 1982

[Ullman88] J. Ullman, *Principles of Database and Knowledge-Base Systems,* vols 1–2, Computer Science Press, Rockville, Maryland, 1988

[vonWright51] G. H. von Wright, *An Essay in Modal Logic*, North-Holland, Amsterdam, 1951

[Willars91] H. Willars, "Amplification of Business Cognition through Modelling Techniques", *11th IEA Congress*, Paris, 1991

[Winograd87] Terry Winograd and Fernando Flores, *Understanding Computers and Cognition*, Addison-Wesley, Reading, Massachusetts, 1987

[Wittgenstein61] L. Wittgenstein, *Tractatus Logico-Philosophicus,* (original German edition published in 1921), translation in English: Routledge and Kegan Paul, London, 1961

[Young58] J. W. Young and H. K. Kent, "Abstract Formulation of Data Processing Problems", *Journal of Industrial Engineering* (Nov.–Dec.), pp. 471–479, 1958

Answers to Selected Exercises

2.1 Centaur and unicorn.

2.2 Old Rowley believes that the word "pig" has an intrinsic connection to dirt and uncleanliness.

2.3 The prohibition "You should not eat this fruit" has the illocutionary effect of telling people that they are not allowed to eat certain fruit. However, the perlocutionary effect this prohibition has on people is the opposite, causing people to become even more interested in eating the fruit.

2.4 c), f), and i) are declaratives.

2.5 Only a) is extensional. To understand why c) is not extensional, suppose that Long John also has the name "John Smith".

2.6
  a) Syntactically incorrect.
  b) Pragmatically incorrect.
  c) Semantically incorrect.

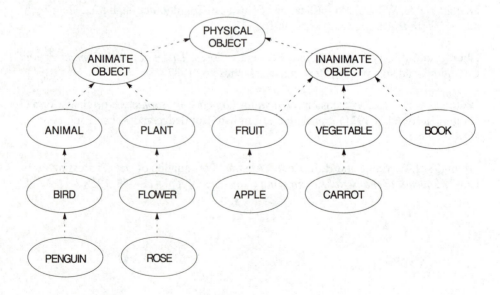

2.7 Suppose that the language L contains n words. Construct a directed graph G where each vertex corresponds to a word in L, and there is an edge from a vertex A to another vertex B if the word corresponding to A is defined using the word corresponding to B. We can construct a path, $C_1, \ldots, C_n$, in G with $n+1$ members in the following way. Let C_1 be an arbitrary word in L and let C_{i+1}, $i = 1, \ldots, n$ be a word which is used to define C_i. So, G contains a path of length $n+1$, and since G only has n vertices, this path must contain a cycle.

2.8 See the graph on the previous page.

2.9 Yes, a sentence that is semantically unambiguous will enforce one particular meaning upon any words that are ambiguous. Usually it is the compatibility of meanings that determines which meaning is intended. "They whitewashed the market." Whitewashed can mean paint white or conceal. Market can mean a bazaar or business affairs. There are two compatible ways to combine these meanings. However, if one of the two ambiguous words is changed so that only one interpretation of the rest of the sentence makes sense, we have an unambiguous sentence containing an ambiguous word.

2.10
   a) There is a particular woman whom every man loves. For every man, there is some woman whom he loves, but different men may love different women.
   b) Time passes by faster than our senses can appreciate. An insect, called the 'time fly', appreciates the appeal of an arrow (rather far fetched).
   c) Don Camino was the only person in the world who knew where Don Camino was. No man on Earth knew where they (themselves) were, except Don Camino. No man on Earth knew where some unnamed person 'he' was, but Don Camino knew.

2.12 The headmaster is making a prediction, whereas the terrorists are making a threat. What the terrorists mean by "is going to get killed" is "we shall murder", whereas the headmaster means "will get run over by a lorry in a fatal accident". To understand this difference, linguistic knowledge is not enough. Knowledge about the domain of the context is also necessary, in this case headmasters and terrorists.

2.13 The grammar below uses a set $\{V, Q, F^0, F^1, P^1, P^2, T, A, W\}$ of help symbols, so-called *non-terminals*, with the obvious mnemonic names (cf. Figure 2.9). All other symbols belong to the object language and are called *terminals*. Recall than 0-ary functions are constants and that, for example, the predicate R^1 is distinct from R^2, in view of their different arities.

$$
\begin{aligned}
V &\to x \mid y \mid z \\
F^0 &\to f^0 \mid g^0 \mid h^0 \\
F^1 &\to f^1 \mid g^1 \mid h^1 \\
P^1 &\to R^1 \mid S^1 \mid U^1 \\
P^2 &\to R^2 \mid S^2 \mid U^2
\end{aligned}
$$

```
Q  →  ∃ | ∀
T  →  V            ("something is a term if it is a variable...")
T  →  F⁰           ("...or a constant...")
T  →  F¹(T)        ("...or a term enclosed in parentheses and preceded
                    by a unary function")
A  →  P¹(T)        ("something is an atomic formula if it is a term
                    enclosed in parentheses and preceded by a unary
                    predicate...")
A  →  P¹(T,T)      ("...or a binary predicate; then the term has
                    another term next to it within the parentheses, with
                    a comma used for separation")
W  →  A            ("something is a well-formed formula (wff) if it is
                    an atomic formula...")
W  →  ¬A           (...which could be preceded by a negation
                    connective..."
W  →  (A→A)        (...or another wff followed by an implication
                    connective, all enclosed in parentheses...)
W  →  ∃VW          (...or an existential quantifier followed by a
                    variable...")
W  →  ∀VW          (...or a universal quantifier followed by a
                    variable")
```

2.14 The maximal compression of representations is not everything. It quickly becomes impossible to read longer propositions. Try to convert $(A \lor B \lor C) \land (A \to D)$, for instance. For this reason, the existence of systems with only one connective is of theoretical interest only.

3.1

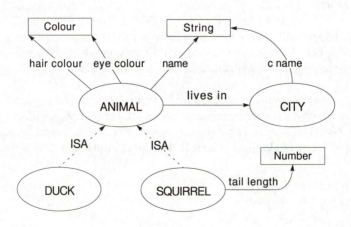

3.3

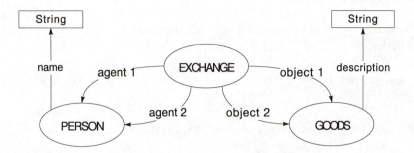

The idea is that agent1 exchanges his object1 for agent2's object2.

```
person(p1).                    name(p1,'Peter').
person(p2).                    name(p2,'Lisa').
goods(g1).                     description(g1,'Apple').
goods(g2).                     description(g2,'Orange').
exchange(e1).
agent1(e1,p1).                 agent2(e1,p2).
object1(e1,g1).                object2(e2,g2).
```

3.4

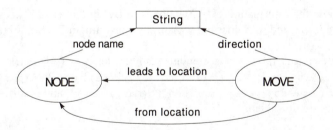

3.5 It is true that any schema containing generalisation relationships can be transformed into an equivalent schema without them, according to the approach sketched in the argument. However, a schema with generalisation relationships is often easier to comprehend, since it provides a more natural classification of the objects occurring in the UoD. A schema without generalisation relationships contains types that are often too general, and it is unable to show types that are more specialised.

3.6 It is true that derived attributes only paraphrase information that is already present in other parts of the conceptual schema. However, the purpose of conceptual modelling is not just to construct a language that makes it possible to reason about an object system. It is also important that the constructed language is convenient to use and that it provides a terminology that is familiar to the users of the information system. Derived attributes are often very helpful in providing convenient terminology, for instance through different kinds of aggregated information.

3.8 The following mapping constraints are only suggestions.

```
works_in            (m,m,p,t)
plays_in            (1,m,p,t)
supports            (1,m,p,p)
has_played_in       (m,m,p,p)
is_located_in       (m,m,t,p)
lives_in            (m,m,p,t)
```

3.9 E = MARRIED_PERSON, B = has_spouse, C = is_the_father_of.

3.10 (1,1,p,t)

3.11
a) Dynamic, deontic integrity constraint.
b) Static deontic integrity constraint.
c) Static derivation rule.
d) Static deontic integrity constraint.
e) Dynamic deontic integrity constraint.
f) Static necessary integrity constraint.
g) Static derivation rule.

3.13 b) Suppose the information base X belongs to B2. In that case X does not violate any constraint in C2, and so X does not violate any constraint in C1. So, X belongs to B1.

3.14 The statement is false. For a counter example, let A = {person(mary), person(john), person(pete), married_to(mary,pete)}, let B = {person(mary), person(john), person(pete), married_to(mary,john)}, and finally suppose that married_to is single valued.

3.15 The relation < is transitive, but non-symmetric, non-anti-symmetric, and not total.

3.16 A suitable example is as follows. A schema depicts club memberships. Even though it is true that member_who_owns_a_dog is a subtype of the entity type member, this relationship will not be represented in the schema (unless of course the club is a dog breeder's association). Perhaps a more illustrative example is the entity type androgen, which is typically ignored in applications that classify people according to their gender.

3.17

```
login_name (1,1,t,p)          written_by (1,m,t,p)
used_by (m,m,p,p)             written_in (1,m,t,p)
calls(m,m,p,p)                affects (m,m,p,p)
version_number (1,1,t,p)      of (1,m,t,t)
created_at (1,m,t,p)          d_name (1,1,t,p)
prim_key (m,1,t,p)            r_name (1,1,t,p)
```

```
belongs_to (1,m,t,p)          a_name (1,1,t,p)
in (1,m,t,t)
```

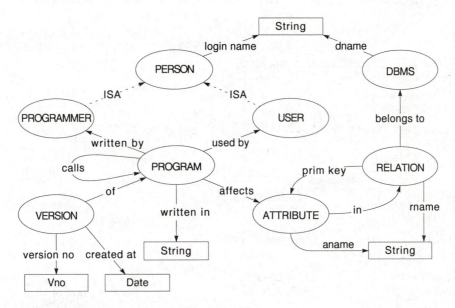

3.18 a) No, IB1 can be empty and hence (trivially) consistent.

b) No, suppose that the conceptual schema contains an integrity constraint stating that the attribute ss_no is total, and that the domain of ss_no is person. Let IB1 =

```
person(joe).
ss_no(joe, 123456).
```

Let IB2 =

```
cat(joe).
ss_no(joe, 123456).
```

Then the difference IB1 − IB2 is inconsistent, since it is

```
person(joe).
```

c) No, suppose that the constraints in b) are to hold, and let IB1 =

```
person(joe).
ss_no(joe, 123456).
```

and let IB2 =

```
person(joe).
```

Then the difference IB2 − IB1 is consistent, since it is empty.

d) No, IB1 can be empty and IB2 was inconsistent.

e) No, the intersection can be empty and hence (trivially) consistent.

f) No, suppose that IB2 ⊂ IB1. Then IB1 ∩ IB2 = IB2, and IB2 was inconsistent.

g) No, consider the example in c).

h) No, suppose that IB1 ⊆ IB2. Then IB1 ∪ IB2 = IB2, and IB2 was inconsistent.

3.19

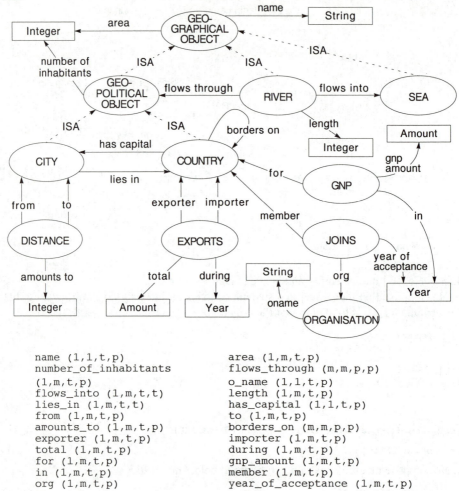

```
name (1,1,t,p)                    area (1,m,t,p)
number_of_inhabitants             flows_through (m,m,p,p)
(1,m,t,p)                         o_name (1,1,t,p)
flows_into (1,m,t,t)              length (1,m,t,p)
lies_in (1,m,t,t)                 has_capital (1,1,t,p)
from (1,m,t,p)                    to (1,m,t,p)
amounts_to (1,m,t,p)              borders_on (m,m,p,p)
exporter (1,m,t,p)                importer (1,m,t,p)
total (1,m,t,p)                   during (1,m,t,p)
for (1,m,t,p)                     gnp_amount (1,m,t,p)
in (1,m,t,p)                      member (1,m,t,p)
org (1,m,t,p)                     year_of_acceptance (1,m,t,p)
```

Examples of integrity constraints:

- The capital of a country must lie in that country.
- If *A* borders on *B*, then *B* must border on *A*.
- The population of a country must be equal to or larger than the population of its capital.
- The total cost for the import of goods and services may not exceed the GNP of any country in any year.

Examples of derivation rules:

- The number of rural inhabitants in a country equals the number of people in the country not living in any city in that country.
- The largest city in a country is that city which has the most inhabitants.

3.20 There can be another explanation. Suppose, for instance, that John is a bachelor, but the information base contains the erroneous data that John is married to Lisa. John now marries Mary and this event is reported to the information system. Since the information base has data that implies that John is already married, the necessary constraint (and there are some good arguments for this being a necessary constraint, given some assumptions about the relation "married to") that a person can have only one spouse will be violated. But the marriage described in the event message has indeed taken place.

4.1 a) No, let IB1 be

```
p.
q :- not(p),not(r).
```

and let IB2 be

```
r.
q :- not(p),not(r).
```

Now, q is derivable from neither, since the goal not(p) fails in IB1 and not(r) fails in IB2. The intersection IB1 ∩ IB2, on the other hand, is

```
q :- not(p),not(r).
```

and here q is derivable.

b) No, let IB1 be

```
p.
q :- not(p).
```

and let IB2 be

```
p.
q :- r.
```

Now, q is derivable from neither, since the goal not(p) fails in IB1 and r fails in IB2. The difference IB1 – IB2, on the other hand, is

```
q :- not(p).
```

and here q is derivable.

4.2 a) No, let IB1 be

```
p.
q :- p.
```

and let IB2 be

```
r.
q :- r.
```

Now, q is derivable from both information bases taken separately, but not from their intersection, since IB1 ∩ IB2 = ∅, and no atomic fact is derivable from an empty information base.

b) No, let IB1 be

```
p.
q :- p.
```

and let IB2 be the same information base

```
p.
q :- p.
```

Now, q is derivable from both information bases taken separately, but not from their difference, since IB1 − IB2 = ∅.

4.3 Sentence 7 cannot be expressed in Prolog. The naively intuitive

```
married_to(adam,X).
```

states that Adam is married to everyone.

Sentence 8 cannot be expressed in Prolog either. It is negated and thus subject to the same problems as sentence 6 in the question text.

Sentences 9 and 11 cannot be expressed in Prolog. What is meant by "many" and "most"? This weakness of Prolog was inherited from FOL (cf. Section 4.5.1).

The symmetry of sentence 11 can in fact be represented in Prolog, for instance, as

```
married_to(X,Y) :- married_to(Y,X).
```

but here one has to be very careful with the operational semantics of Prolog, since under certain circumstances the above rule will loop.

The very complicated (cf. Appendix 4) sentence 12 cannot even be represented in second-order logic. One (possibly controversial) way of explaining why it cannot be represented in Prolog is that the expressive power of Prolog (represented, for example, as the extension of every well-formedformula, i.e. clause of the language) is strictly included in the expressive power of second order logic.

Sentence 13 is easily expressible in Prolog, as

```
likes(X,X).
```

5.2 We give rules based on the schema in Exercise 5.1. To specify that emp_no is single-valued, we write:

inconsistent :- emp_no(E,N1), emp_no(E,N2), not(N1 = N2).

emp_no is injective:

inconsistent :- emp_no(E1,N), emp_no(E2,N), not(E1 = E2).

emp_no is total:

inconsistent :- employee(E), not(emp_no(E,N)).

dept is surjective:

inconsistent :- department(D), not(dept(E,D)).

To express that the domain of manager is DEPARTMENT, we write:

inconsistent :- manager(X,Y), not(department(Y)).
The range of manager is EMPLOYEE:
inconsistent :- manager(X,Y), not(employee(Y)).
How extension constraints can be expressed was shown in Section 5.3.1.

5.6

```
inconsistent :- has_capital(Country,City), not (lies_in(City,Coun-
try)).

inconsistent :- borders_on(A,B), not(borders_on(B,A)).

inconsistent :- has_capital(Country,City),
                number_of_inhabitants(City,X),
                number_of_inhabitants(Country,Y), X > Y.

inconsistent :- gnp(G),
                              for(G,Country),
                              gnp_amount(G,GnpAmount),
                              in(G,Year),
                              findall(Imp,
                              (exports(E),
                              importer(E,Country),
                              total(E,Imp),
                              during(E,Year)),
                              ImpBag),
                              sum(ImpBag,ImpTotal),
                              ImpTotal > GnpAmount.

number_of_rural_inhabitants(Country,Rurals):-
                number_of_inhabitants(Country,Tot),
                findall(I,
                (city(City),
                lies_in(City,Country),
                number_of_inhabitants(City,I)),
                Ibag),
                sum(Ibag,CityInh),
                Rurals is Tot - CityInh.

largest_city(Country,Largest):-
                lies_in(Largest,Country),
                number_of_inhabitants(Largest,Ln),
                not((city(X), number_of_inhabitants(X,Xn), Xn >
                Ln)).
```

5.7 a) For example, the grinch g2 macks more than 1,500, i.e. `grinch(g2)` and `mack(g2,2000)` are included in the information base.

b) No. Informal argument: every grinch must hatch a yertle, and if a grinch hatches a yertle, it must mack more than the yertle. But this can never be satisfied, since grinches may not mack more than 1,500 and yertles must mack more than 2,000.

5.8

a)

```
cabbit(c1).
cabbit(c2).
cabbit(c3).
name(c1,'Peter').
name(c2,'John').
name(c3,'Steve').
parry(c1,'XYZ').
parry(c2,'XYZ').
parry(c2,'QWERTY').
parry(c3,'XYZ').
lollie(c1,c2).
lollie(c2,c3).
```

b) No updates are performed, since adding `lollie(c1,c3)` would violate the single-valued property of `lollie`.

c) No updates are performed, since there is no cabbit named "Robert". The precondition cannot be satisfied.

d)

```
cabbit(c1).
cabbit(c2).
cabbit(c3).
name(c1,'Peter').
name(c2,'John').
name(c3,'Steve').
parry(c1,'XYZ').
parry(c2,'QWERTY').
parry(c3,'XYZ').
lollie(c1,c2).
```

e) No updates are performed since removing `parry(c1,'XYZ')` would violate the totality of `parry`.

5.9

```
non-lexical_object_type(membership).
non-lexical_object_type(club).
non-lexical_object_type(person).
lexical_object_type(string).
attribute(member).              domain(member,membership).
range(member,person).
mapping_constraints(member,'1mtp').
attribute(in).                  domain(in,membership).
range(in,club).                 mapping_constraints(in,'1mtt').
attribute(entry_date).          domain(entry_date,membership).
range(entry_date,string).
mapping_constraints(entry_date,'1mtp').
```

5.10

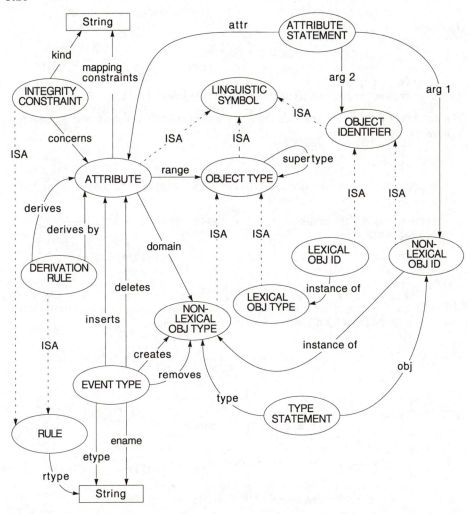

The attribute `kind` specifies whether a constraint is necessary or deontic.
The attribute `rtype` specifies whether a rule is static or dynamic.
The attribute `etype` specifies whether an event is external or internal.

5.11 a) Yes, ⟨change_wock, [`123456`, 250]⟩.
b) No, since (iii) violates the functionality of the `wock` attribute. Besides, we only have the possibility to update values, not to insert values.

5.12 The mapping constraint is (m, 1, p, t), the intuition being that one "switches the properties around". Because a is a function, b is injective, and since a is total, b is surjective. Because a is not surjective, b is not total. Finally, since a is not injective, b is not a function.

5.13 a)

```
insert_set(Type, []).
insert_set(Type, [H|T]):- new_entity(Type, H), insert_set(T).
```

(The notation `[H|T]` means that H is the first element (Head) of the list and T is the rest (Tail) of the list.)
b)

```
event(set_tax, [Ss_no], ['Ss number']):-
            precondition((person(P), ss_no(P,Ss_no)),
            update_tax(P).
```

update_tax(P):- earns(P,S), S < 20000, T is S * 0.2, replace(tax(P,T)).

update_tax(P):- earns(P,S), S >= 20000, T is S * 0.5, replace(tax(P,T)).

5.14 a) Either `married(jim, jane)` or `married(james, jane)` is added to the information base. In fact, MOLOC will choose the first alternative.

6.1

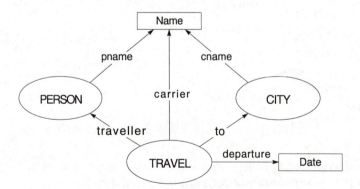

The attribute `travels_to` is reified into a new type.

6.2 Introduce two subtypes of SHIP, say MOTOR_SHIP and SAILING_SHIP.

6.4 Add a new attribute `previous_salary` to the type PERSON. The constraint now becomes

```
inconsistent :- earns(P, S), previous_salary(P, Old), Old > S.
```

8.1

```
AIRPORT(Name)

PIER(Pier_no,At_port_name)

GATE(Gate_no,At_pier_pier_no,At_pier_at_port_name)
```

In the next relation scheme, we simplify the column names:

```
FLIGHT(Flight_no,Carri-
er,Departure_gate_no,Departure_pier_no,Departure_airport,Arrival_
gate_no,Arrival_pier_no,Arrival_airport)

PASSENGER(SS_no,Weight)

GOES_BY(SS_no,Goes_by_flight_no)

PIER.At_port_name << AIRPORT.Name

GATE.(At_pier_pier_no,At_pier_at_port_name)<<
PIER(Pier_no,At_port_name)

FLIGHT(Departure_gate_no,Departure_pier_no,Departure_airport)<<

        GATE.(Gate_no,At_pier_pier_no,At_pier_at_port_name)

FLIGHT(Arrival_gate_no,Arrival_pier_no,Arrival_airport)<<

        GATE.(Gate_no,At_pier_pier_no,At_pier_at_port_name)

GOES_BY.SS_no << PASSENGER.SS_no

GOES_BY.Goes_by_flight_no << FLIGHT.Flight_no
```

8.2

```
INSTRUMENT(I_no)

FURNITURE(F_no)

PIANO(I_no,F_no,Make,Stores_name)

WAREHOUSE(Name)

PIANO.Stores_name << WAREHOUSE.Name

PIANO.I_no << INSTRUMENT.I_no

PIANO.F_no << FURNITURE.F_no
```

8.3 The algorithm does not always produce a relational schema in the third normal form. If an attribute is derivable from other attributes, there will be a functional dependency between the corresponding columns.

8.4 Including NAME would not result in a relational schema in the first normal form, since a person can have several names.

8.5 The root of the problem is that the identifier graph is not acyclic. A solution is to add an identifying attribute to EMPLOYEE or DEPARTMENT.

A5.1

```
lives_in(peter,oslo).     age(peter,25).
works_at(peter,ibm).      lies_in(oslo,norway).
earns(peter,12000).
```

A5.2

a) `p(a,b,c), q(b,b)`
b) `p(a,b,a), q(b,b)`
c) `p(a,c,a), r(b,b,c)`
d) `p(a,a,a), r(b,b,a)`

A5.3

a) X = a, X = b, X = c
b) X = a, X = b, X = c
c) X = a, X = b
d) X = c
e) X = a, X = b, X = c, X = d

A5.4

a) `?- works_at(peter,X).`
b) `?- lies_in(paris,X).`
c) `?- earns(peter,PS), earns(john,JS), PS > JS.`
d) `?- works_at(X,ibm).`
e) `?- age(mary,A), age(john,A).`
f) `?- works_at(mary,Company), works_at(X,Company).`
g) `?- findall(P, (earns(P,S), S > 20000), Persons), count(Persons,X).`
h) `?- findall(P, (works_at(P,ibm), earns(P,S), S > 20000), Persons),`
   `count(Persons,X).`
i) `?- findall(P, works_at(P,ibm), Persons), count(Persons,Nr_of_emp),`
   `findall(S, (works_at(P,ibm), earns(P,S)), Salaries),`
   `sum(Salaries,Totsal), Avg_salary is Totsal/Nr_of_emp.`
j) `?- age(X,A), A > 30, not(works_at(X,C)).`
k) `?- works_at(Oldest,ibm), age(Oldest, OA),`
   `not((works_at(Someone_else,ibm),`
   `age(Someone_else,SA), SA > OA)).`
l) `?- findall(P, works_at(P,ibm), IBMers), count(IBMers,IBMtot),`
   `findall(Q, works_at(Q,skf), SKFers), count(SKFers,SKFtot),`
   `IBMtot > SKFtot.`

A5.5

a) `high_income_earner(X):- earns(X,S), S > 20000.`

b) `norwegian(X):- lives_in(X,City), lies_in(City,norway).`

c) `unemployed(X):- not(works_at(X,Company)).`

d) `earns_more(X,Y):- earns(X,XS), earns(Y,YS), XS > YS.`

e) `compatriots(X,Y):- lives_in(X,City1), lives_in(Y,City2),`
`            lies_in(City1,Country), lies_in(City2,Country).`

Index